SOFTWARE, INFRASTRUCTURE, LABOR

Infrastructure makes worlds. Software coordinates labor. Logistics governs movement. These pillars of contemporary capitalism correspond with the materiality of digital communication systems on a planetary scale. Ned Rossiter theorizes the force of logistical media to discern how subjectivity and labor, economy, and society are tied to the logistical imaginary of seamless interoperability. Contingency haunts logistical power. Technologies of capture are prone to infrastructural breakdown, sabotage, and failure. Strategies of evasion, anonymity, and disruption unsettle regimes of calculation and containment.

We live in a computational age where media, again, disappear into the background as infrastructure. *Software, Infrastructure, Labor* intercuts transdisciplinary theoretical reflection with empirical encounters ranging from the Cold War legacy of cybernetics, shipping ports in China and Greece, the territoriality of data centers, video game design, and scrap metal economies in the e-waste industry. Rossiter argues that infrastructural ruins serve as resources for the collective design of blueprints and prototypes demanded of radical politics today.

Ned Rossiter is Professor of Communication with a joint appointment in the Institute for Culture and Society and the School of Humanities and Communication Arts at Western Sydney University. He is the author of *Organized Networks: Media Theory, Creative Labour, New Institutions* (2006).

SOFTWARE, INFRASTRUCTURE, LABOR

A Media Theory of Logistical Nightmares

Ned Rossiter

NEW YORK AND LONDON

First published 2017
by Routledge
711 Third Avenue, New York, NY 10017

and by Routledge
2 Park Square, Milton Park, Abingdon, Oxon OX14 4RN

Routledge is an imprint of the Taylor & Francis Group, an informa business

© 2017 Taylor & Francis

The right of Ned Rossiter to be identified as author of this work has been
asserted by him in accordance with sections 77 and 78 of the Copyright,
Designs and Patents Act 1988.

All rights reserved. No part of this book may be reprinted or reproduced or
utilised in any form or by any electronic, mechanical, or other means, now
known or hereafter invented, including photocopying and recording, or in any
information storage or retrieval system, without permission in writing from
the publishers.

Trademark notice: Product or corporate names may be trademarks or registered
trademarks, and are used only for identification and explanation without
intent to infringe.

Library of Congress Cataloging-in-Publication Data
Rossiter, Ned, author.
Software, infrastructure, labor : a media theory of logistical nightmares/
    Ned Rossiter.
New York : Routledge, 2016. | Includes index.
LCCN 2016005688
LCSH: Information society. | Mass media and culture. | Communications
    software. | Telecommunication. | Logistics.
LCC HM851 .R6785 2016 | DDC 303.48/33—dc23
https://lccn.loc.gov/2016005688

ISBN: 978-0-415-84304-1 (hbk)
ISBN: 978-0-415-84305-8 (pbk)
ISBN: 978-0-203-75811-3 (ebk)

Typeset in Bembo
by Apex CoVantage, LLC

Cover design by Kernow Craig
Concept by Ned Rossiter

CONTENTS

List of Figures		*vii*
Acknowledgments		*ix*
Preface		*xiii*

1	Introduction—Logistical Media Theory	1
2	Logistical Worlds	26
3	Into the Cloud	51
4	Economies of Waste	77
5	New Regimes of Knowledge Production	96
6	Coded Vanilla	119
7	Imperial Infrastructures	138
8	Sovereign Media and the Ruins of a Logistical Future	184

Index	*197*

FIGURES

1.1	Connecting bridge between waterside and dockside ports, Ningbo, China, 2009	2
2.1	Rajarhat "New Town," Kolkata, 2011	38
2.2	*Cargonauts* demo game, 2014	43
2.3	Site for Thriassion freight center and rail line to Piraeus port, 2013	45
3.1	Port Botany wharf data visualization, 2012	67
3.2	Port Botany road data visualization, 2012	70
4.1	Scales in small-waste business, Ningbo, 2009	83
7.1	Number of significant international submarine systems completed, 1851–1911	155
7.2	Combined comparative table of estimated cable systems landings per selected country/region	157
7.3	Estimated international submarine cable landings, 1845–1911	158
8.1	X-ray imaging system shows human passengers hidden in a truck	193

ACKNOWLEDGMENTS

This book stems from writings developed across three continental settings in the company of close friends, colleagues, and collaborators. My move back to Australia in 2011 to the University of Western Sydney (now Western Sydney University) was not something initially in the cards. But life has its twists. And so do jobs. The strong collegial atmosphere at WSU is a rare thing in universities these days, and I am thankful for that. In particular Lynette Sheridan Burns and Peter Hutchings in the School of Humanities and Communication Arts have been supportive of my work from the start. The Institute for Culture and Society has provided extraordinary research conditions with colleagues deeply committed to collaborative work. Ien Ang has long supported my work over the years and, more recently, Paul James has brought a refreshing energy and direction to the Institute.

Around 2004 or 2005 my friend and collaborator of many years, Geert Lovink, first put me on to the topic of global logistics. We were marveling at how our stuff had arrived in Europe from Australia and were checking out live tracking of ships online. It wasn't until I moved to China in 2007/2008 that the analytical potential and political significance of logistics started to crystalize as a research inquiry. Throughout this book Geert has passed on material on logistics that I would never have found otherwise. Some of the core concepts in this book have occurred in parallel to texts written with Geert and Soenke Zehle. The writings with Soenke in particular recast various concepts that are also present in much of this book. I am indebted to Soenke for his prolific feed of references, comments, and suggested phrasings over the years this book has been written. This book has been sustained by a long-term friendship, intellectual exchange, and, in more recent years, close institutional working relationship with Brett Neilson. Many of the ideas in this book have been tested with Brett and refined thanks to his feedback.

x Acknowledgments

Much of the research in the book occurred in the context of two Australian Research Council Discovery Project grants awarded since 2008 (DP0988547 and DP130103720, with Ien Ang joining me and Brett as a Chief Investigator on the first of these projects). Both of these grants made possible a still ongoing research collaboration with colleagues and friends across select research sites in China, India, Australia, Greece, and Chile. Sandro Mezzadra and Ranabir Samaddar have been core intellectual interlocutors throughout this time. Ranabir's Mahanirban Calcutta Research Group demonstrated with flair how to combine empirical research with historical flair and theoretical reflection. My thanks to Ishita Dey, Suhit Sen, and Mithilesh Kumar in particular for sharing their insights in Kolkata. Funding from the Asia-Europe Foundation also brought researchers together in Shanghai in 2010, and discussions from that meeting at the Goethe Institute and across the city have informed this book.

The following Partner Investigators have joined us in these projects and enriched the collective research experience and findings enormously: Wang Hui, Ursula Huws, Nelli Kambouri, William Walters, and Hernán Cuevas. Working with Nelli and our friends in Athens—Pavlos Hatzopoulos, Anna Lascari, Ilias Marmaras, Dimitris Parsanoglou, and Carolin Phillip—was especially important in terms of developing analytical insights into the intersection between software, infrastructure, labor, and politics both in Greece and on a transcontinental scale. With Ilias and Anna, Brett and I were able to develop the concept and demo of the *Cargonauts* video game.

A number of this book's chapters had earlier incarnations as journal articles and chapters in edited collections. The editors and reviewers of those publications contributed to the refinement of ideas, arguments, and expression of what are now reworked chapters in this book. My thanks, then, to Esther Milne, Anthony McCusker, Gerard Goggin, Rowan Wilken, Katherine Bode, Paul Arthur, Mark Coté, Alan Liu, Gillian Fuller, and David Bissell.

Translating concepts into a design language is the forte of Kernow Craig, and I thank him for all his work on our Transit Labour and Logistical Worlds websites, pamphlets, visualizations, and the cover of this book. Thanks to Anja Kanngieser, Katie Hepworth, and Mat Wal-Smith for their research on these projects and for their contributions to the thought within this book. I have also benefited from working with Liam Magee and Tanya Notley and thank them for their editorial and intellectual contributions to this book.

For discussions, suggestions, email exchanges, and support along the way, I thank Jon Solomon, Paolo Do, Allen Chun, Justin O'Connor, Wang Xioming, Rada Ivekovic, Ghislaine Glasson Deschaumes, Bert de Muynck, Mónica Carriço, Anna Greenspan, Paul Gladston, Andy White, Filippo Gilardi, Chen Hangfeng, Mauricio Corbalan, Manuela Zechner, Wilfried Eckstein, Giorgio Grappi, Stefano Harney, Armin Beverungen, Timon Beyes, Goetz Bachmann, Florian Sprenger, Martin Warnke, Claus Pias, Mercedes Bunz, Michael Dieter, Christoph Engemann, Christine Scherrer, Martina Leeker, Irina Kaldrack, Yuk Hui, David Berry, Orit Halpern (especially for her insightful comments and suggestions for chapters 7 and 8), Jussi Parikka, Tom Apperley, Andrew Murphie, Chris Gibson, Giulia Dal Maso, Shveta Sarda, Giovanna Zapperi, Richard Maxwell, Toby Miller, Melissa Gregg, Rutvica Andrijasevic, Brian Shoesmith, Hart Cohen, Juan Francisco Salazar, Kate Richards, Donald McNeill, Bob Hodge, Tony Bennett, Jack Parkin, Anna Reading, Tomás Ariztía, Elisabeth Simbürger, Kristoffer Gansing, Daphne Dragona, Geoff Cox, Christian Ulrik Andersen, Julian Kücklich, Manuela Bojadzijev, Brian Holmes, Daniel Hassan, and Akseli Virtanen.

Working versions of these chapters were presented at various seminars, conferences, and workshops. I am thankful to the organizers of these events held at the Centre for Contemporary Cultural Studies, Shanghai University; City University of Hong Kong; Centre for Digital Cultures (CDC) and Medienkulturen der Computersimulation (MECS), Leuphana University Lüneburg; University of Siegen; Darmstadt University of Technology; Monash University; Swinburne University of Technology; Australian National University; Collège International de Philosophie; Lingnan University, Hong Kong; Istituto Italiano per l'Africa e l'Oriente, Shanghai; Tokyo University of Foreign Studies; Chiao Tung University, Taiwan; School of Arts and Media, University of New South Wales; Department of Media and Film, University of Sussex; Australian Centre for Environmental Research (AUSCCER), University of Wollongong; School of Communication and the Arts, Victoria University, Melbourne; Calcutta Research Group, Kolkata; Department of Gender and Cultural Studies, University of Sydney; RMIT University; Universidad Diego Portales; Universidad de Valparaíso; and Transmediale, Berlin.

I thank Erica Wetter at Routledge for her early interest in this book, and her patience throughout its extended gestation. Thanks also to Simon Jacobs and Mia Moran for their input along the way.

My special thanks to Maren and Willem for their love and endurance.

The first six chapters in this book incorporate and rework material previously published in various journals and books, which I acknowledge here and thank the editors and reviewers for their contributions to the texts:

> "Coded Vanilla: Logistical Media and the Determination of Action," *South Atlantic Quarterly* 114, no. 1 (2015): 135–52.
> "Locative Media as Logistical Media: Situating Infrastructure and the Governance of Labor in Supply-Chain Capitalism," in Gerard Goggin and Rowan Wilken, eds., *Locative Media* (New York: Routledge, 2015), 208–23.
> "Logistical Worlds," *Cultural Studies Review* 20, no. 1 (2014): 53–76.
> "Materialities of Software: Logistics, Labour, Infrastructure," in Paul Arthur and Katherine Bode, eds., *Advancing Digital Humanities: Research, Theory, Methods* (Basingstoke: Palgrave Macmillan, 2014), 221–40.
> "Dirt Research," in Carolin Wiedemann and Soenke Zehle, eds., *Depletion Design: A Glossary of Network Ecologies* (Amsterdam: XMLab and the Institute for Network Cultures, 2012), 41–45.

xii Acknowledgments

"Logistics, Labour and New Regimes of Knowledge Production," *Transeuro-péenes: International Journal of Critical Thought*, August 8, 2011, http://www.transeuropeennes.org/en/76/new_knowledge_new_epistemologies.

"The Informational University, the Uneven Distribution of Expertise and the Racialisation of Labour," *Edu-Factory Journal* Zero Issue (January, 2010), http://www.edu-factory.org/edu15/webjournal/n0/Rossiter.pdf.

Republished in *darkmatter: in the ruins of imperial culture* (March, 2010), http://www.darkmatter101.org.

Republished in *ReFeng Xueshu* (2010), 18–29. (trans. Chinese)

"Translating the Indifference of Communication: Electronic Waste, Migrant Labour and the Informational Sovereignty of Logistics in China," *International Review of Information Ethics* 11 (2009), http://www.i-r-i-e.net/issue11.htm.

PREFACE

Logistical media determine our situation. While the missing flight MH370 is yet to be found, for the rest of us there is nowhere left to hide. The management dream of cybernetic extension into the vicissitudes of daily life is now well and truly a reality. CCTV cameras, motion capture technologies, RFID chips, smart phones and locational media, GPS devices, biometric monitoring of people and ecological systems—these are just some of the more familiar technologies that generate data and modulate movement and consumption within the logistical city, or what Friedrich Kittler terms "the city as medium."[1]

The logistical city marks a departure from both the global city of finance capital and the industrial city of factories. The logistical city is elastic; its borders are flexible and determined by the ever-changing coordinates of supply chain capitalism. Populated by warehouses, ports, intermodal terminals, container yards, and data centers, the logistical city is spatially defined by zones, corridors, and concessions. It is a city that subtracts the time of dreams to maintain the demands of 24/7 capitalism.[2]

For many, the model has become the world. Our tastes are calibrated and relayed back to us based on the aggregation of personal history coupled with the distribution of desire across sampled populations. Decision is all too frequently an unwitting acceptance of command. The biopolitical production of labor and life has just about reached its zenith in terms of extracting value, efficiency, and submission from the economy of algorithmic action.[3] Nowhere is this more clear than in the "sentient city," where the topography of spatial scales and borders gives way to the topology of ubiquitous computing and predictive analytics in which the digital is integrated with the motion of experience.[4] In the sentient city data becomes a living entity, measuring the pulse of urban settings and determining the mobilization of response to an increasingly vast range of urban conditions: traffic movements, air quality, chemical composition of soils, social flash points. The horror of urban life is just beginning. Florian Cramer phrased this nicely in a posting in 2014 to the nettime.org mailing list:

> This is likely the beginning of a social class and status symbol reversal for electronic technology and digital devices. It's foreseeable that affordable healthcare, transport, insurance policies, pension plans, will only be available to those who subscribe to behavioral tracking and control via mobile sensor devices, and have themselves monitored for compliant lifestyles. And whatever will be left of welfare cheques and unemployment severance pay, will only be paid on the condition of behavioral tracking as well . . . freedom of electronic devices will be a privilege of the wealthy. In the near future, to be upper class will no longer mean that you carry the latest electronic gadget, but that you can afford the luxury surcharge for a life without tracking devices.[5]

When loyalty cards proliferate in our virtual wallets, when coupon systems and location-based services are coupled with payment apps that track our patterns of consumption, we begin to get a sense of how shopping experiences are designed around economies of capture. To refuse is to perhaps miss out on that sweet feel of the discount, but at least we get a fleeting sense of having preserved our anonymity. Indeed, anonymity becomes a key algorithmic gesture, conceptual figure, and technical mechanism through which we might begin to design a black-box politics within the horizon of logistical media.[6] For to be anonymous renders the black box inoperable.

There is an element to the profiling of what I would term "post-populations" that is external to logistical media of coordination, capture, and control. I am thinking here of the peasants dispossessed of land on the urban fringes of Kolkata who commit willful acts of sabotage on infrastructure in the new IT towns, and of the proletariat and unemployed around the world who are not governed or managed in the name of political economy but unleashed as a necessary surplus to capital that requires relative stability for infrastructures of investment to withstand assault that arises from social chaos. Yet post-populations, who to some extent can be understood as ensembles of non-governable subjects, all too often become vital sources of technical invention awaiting expropriation that is absorbed into systems of production. Take, for instance, *shanzhai* culture, and the wild modification of mobile-phone features in China. The parameters of capital accumulation can only be replenished when elements of contingency are programmed into the operational requirements of the logistical city, and this is why post-populations are set free and indeed may never register within apparatuses of control. But this also assumes that capital is the primary agent, when the pressures of subsumption may be lower and more pervasive across the social body.

The problem with the post-digital settings of today is that we are unable to think within the box. We can speak of a politics of parameters, but ultimately this is still knowledge specific to engineers who design the architectures within which we conjure our imagination. We can no longer harness our imagination, only click on predetermined options. What, therefore, might it mean to design a program of research and cultural practice that exploits the geography of data infrastructure as we know it? The politics of infrastructure invites a critique of the quantified self, where self-tracking bodies are regulated as data-managed socialities as they move within the logistical city. In the society of compliance, normative measures and standards are set by the corporate-state seeking to expropriate value from labor through regimes of fear, insecurity, and self-obsession.

The dystopia of the present leaves little room for responses other than despair and depression. All too often resistance to the distribution of power and the penetration of financial capitalism is, as Max Haiven argues, not only futile but quite often reinforcing that which it claims to oppose.[7] Resistance is not interventionist so much as affirmative: "finance as we now have it, as a system that 'reads' the world by calculating the 'risk' of 'resistance' to 'liquidity' and allocating resources accordingly, already incorporates 'resistance' into its 'systemic imagination.'"[8] In this slaughterous world, the nihilistic option is to find joy in the pleasure of immediacy, consumption, and aesthetic gestures of critical self-affirmation.[9]

No matter the foibles of human life, predictive analytics and algorithmic modeling deploy the currency of data to measure labor against variables such as productivity, risk, compliance, and contingency. What, then, for labor and life outside the extractive machine of algorithmic capitalism? Can sociality reside in the space and time of relative invisibility afforded by the vulnerable status of post-populations? Can living labor assert itself beyond the calculations of enterprise planning software and the subjugation of life to debt by instruments of finance capital? These are disturbing, complicated questions that require collective analysis if we are to design a life without determination. Because of the difficulty of envisioning alternative futures from within the horizon of affirmative resistance, we need to step into the box even further and revisit the notion of being-determined on a much more fundamental level.

If infrastructure makes worlds, then software coordinates them. Logistics infrastructure manifests as roads, railways, shipping ports, intermodal terminals, airports, and communications facilities and technologies. Logistics infrastructure enables the movement of labor, commodities, and data across global supply chains. Increasingly, logistics infrastructure is managed through computational systems of code and software. As such, algorithms play a vital role in arranging the material properties and organizational capacities of infrastructure. Algorithms thus register a form of infrastructural power.

A media theory of logistics provides one index for reconstituting a political knowledge of what might be termed logistics in the age of algorithmic capitalism.

In addition to storage, processing, and transmission systems, the study of logistical media also includes attention to how the aesthetic qualities peculiar to the banality of spreadsheets, enterprise resource planning (ERP) systems, and software applications have arisen from particular histories in military theaters, cybernetics, infrastructural design, transport, and communications. Logistical media theory is interested in how logistical infrastructure is made soft through ERP systems designed to govern logistical operations. Gamification techniques further extend the power of logistical media as technologies that govern knowledge production. The subsumption of gaming and, more fundamentally, play itself under the operative logics of incentivization accelerates the dynamics of affirmative resistance. Questions of securitization, control, coordination, algorithmic architectures, protocols, and parameters are among those relevant to a theory of logistical media, and are ones explored throughout this book.

Much of the writing for this book has been done in the context of collective research over many years. Together with my students in international communications at the University of Nottingham Ningbo, we investigated port operations, electronic waste industries, and the relation between real estate development and the creative industries.[10] These topics were among others studied over a more extended period with friends, colleagues, and collaborators in transcontinental settings. Informed by a previous collective research project I coordinated in Beijing in 2007 that sought to identify the constitutive outside of creative industries in that city, the Transit Labour project (2009–2012) investigated circuits of labor and logistical operations in Shanghai, Kolkata, and Sydney.[11]

Transit Labour traced the informality of e-waste industries and the political economy of standards in printed circuit board manufacturing in China. An extensive period of fieldwork, site visits, and archival research made clear how the rise of "New Towns" supporting the IT sector in Kolkata was made possible by land zoning policies that resulted in the seizure of land from peasants, which we understood as a process of primitive accumulation. In Sydney our research focused on labor regimes of governance related to shipping-container loading and unloading times, transport routes, warehousing, and intermodal terminals. We saw how these primary components of a logistical city present a model of space, time, labor, and economy whose dynamics register in ways distinct from the global city of finance capital and the industrial city of factories. Peripheries become primary spaces of coordination and control. Global infrastructural and software standards stitch spaces, labor, and operational procedures together across diverse geographical scales and modalities of time.

Following our Transit Labour project, Brett Neilson, myself, and our friends and collaborators are working through a second program of research funded by the Australian Research Council that extends our interest in logistical operations along global lines of influence and connection marked by Chinese infrastructural expansion. Dubbed Logistical Worlds: Infrastructure, Software, Labour (2013–2015), this project moves between Athens, Kolkata, and Valparáiso, investigating regimes of circulation and containment that connect China's manufacturing industries to different corners of the world.[12]

Our interest is in how infrastructure and software combine as technologies of governance that coordinate and control logistical operations and labor practices situated in select sites along the China-centered trade network known as the New Silk Road. Recalling the historical Silk Road of trade and cultural transmission that connected Asia to Europe, the geostrategic concept of the New Silk Road has emerged to register the logistical measures already being put in place by commercial entities and policy makers to meet the expected changes as Asia overtakes Europe as the world's largest trading region. At stake is the forging of new trade corridors that connect East Asia to Latin America and extend across the Indian subcontinent to southern Europe, where China's state-owned shipping company, Cosco, has undertaken a major infrastructural investment in the Athens's port of Piraeus.

Against this backdrop, the writings in this book have arisen from interventions, propositions, and more sustained elaborations of how to think media theory through the core components of global logistics stretched over a planetary system and ecology in ruins. In devising a theory of logistical media, I turn the chapters of this book around various combinations of software and infrastructure, discerning how and where they hold a determining force in the production of subjectivity and labor. Not wishing to entirely submerge into an aesthetic of despair, the book also seeks out occasions and situations in which labor and life demonstrate a capacity for action beyond the actionable. If, as Paolo Virno proposes in his reading of Hannah Arendt, the once partitioned borders between labor and political action have today become indistinct, then we may attribute this turn in no small way to the power of logistical media to render flat the ontological qualities and unforeseen events that hitherto produce a world of variation, struggle, conflict, and contingency. The logistical imaginary disavows the political. Let us be sure, this world has not gone away but rather persists as the constitutive outside to the logistical fantasy of seamless interoperability.

"The sphere of politics," writes Virno, "follows closely the procedures and stylistic elements which define the current state of labor."[13] To retrieve a capacity for political action, as distinct from politics, requires inventing political practices and conceptual universes not easily subsumed into the logistical horizon of the actionable. Within logistics, the actionable is a task that can be executed with maximum efficiency. Anonymity offers one possible strategy of withdrawal from logistical regimes of calculation and control. But after the Snowden revelations of the penetrative power of the NSA machine, the scope for absolute anonymity might best be approached through the tactic of overexposure and a multiplication of noise. As much as algorithmic architectures of logistical media extract data and

xviii Preface

manage labor whose value is exploited through transactions as finance capital, there is also a freedom to be found in the indifference logistics has to subjectivity when difference is subsumed into data made actionable. To address these and other systems of control, we need to devise a theory of logistical media.

Notes

1. Friedrich A. Kittler, "The City Is a Medium," trans. Mathew Griffin, *New Literary History* 27, no. 4 (1996): 717–29.
2. See Jonathan Crary, *24/7: Late Capitalism and the Ends of Sleep* (London and New York: Verso, 2013).
3. See Ned Rossiter and Soenke Zehle, "Experience Machines," *Sociologia del Lavoro* 133 (2014): 111–32.
4. See Mark Shepard, ed., *Sentient City: Ubiquitous Computing, Architecture, and the Future of Urban Space* (Cambridge, MA: MIT Press, 2011). See also Saskia Sassen, "Unsettling Topographic Representation," in Shepard, *Sentient City*, 182–9.
5. Florian Cramer, "Re: <nettime> Will your insurance company subsidize your quantified self?," posting to Nettime mailing list, April 15, 2014, http://nettime.org.
6. See Ned Rossiter and Soenke Zehle, "Privacy Is Theft: On Anonymous Experiences, Infrastructural Politics and Accidental Encounters," in Martin Fredriksson and James Arvanitakis, eds., *Piracy: Leakages from Modernity* (Sacramento: Litwin Press, 2014), 343–53. See also Ned Rossiter and Soenke Zehle, "Toward a Politics of Anonymity: Algorithmic Actors in the Constitution of Collective Agency and the Implications for Global Economic Justice Movements," in Martin Parker, George Cheney, Valérie Fournier, and Chris Land, eds., *Routledge Companion to Alternative Organization* (London and New York: Routledge, 2014), 151–62.
7. Max Haiven, "Finance Depends on Resistance, Finance Is Resistance, and Anyway, Resistance Is Futile," *Mediations* 26, nos. 1–2 (Fall, 2012–Spring, 2013): 85–106, http://www.mediationsjournal.org/articles/finance-depends-on-resistance.
8. Ibid., 99.
9. Phrase lifted from Michael Wood, "At the Movies," *London Review of Books* 36, no. 8 (April, 2014), http://www.lrb.co.uk/v36/n08/michael-wood/at-the-movies.
10. See Urban-Media Networks: Anthropologies of Urban Transformation, 2009–2010, http://orgnets.cn/.
11. See Organized Networks—Mobile Research Labs, Beijing 2007 + 2008, http://orgnets.net/ and Transit Labour: Circuits, Regions, Borders, http://transitlabour.asia/.
12. Logistical Worlds: Infrastructure, Software, Labour, http://logisticalworlds.org/.
13. Paolo Virno, *A Grammar of the Multitude*, trans. James Cascaito, Isabella Bertoletti, and Andrea Casson (New York: Semiotext(e), 2004), 51.

1

INTRODUCTION—LOGISTICAL MEDIA THEORY

Driving past stacks of containers organized in long rows arranged in grid-fashion, the impression of lonely canyons of buildings in a city's finance district is distinct. Yet this is no business precinct in some anonymous city, but Beilun port, one of China's largest shipping hubs near the city of Ningbo, which is located a few hours south of Shanghai—the nearest competing deep-water port. We arrive at one of four loading docks (Figure 1.1). A few massive ships are lined up alongside container cranes. What's striking is the seeming absence of workers. For one of the biggest ports in the world, there was little of the activity one expects—not a lot of movement of containers, very few workers, and not many ships about. But perhaps this shouldn't be such a surprise—financial news in 2008–2009 reported on the savaging of the shipping industry in the first six months of the global economic crisis. Shipping companies were collecting 75–80 percent less on the cost of transporting containers; charter rates plunged to levels that no longer return profits, reproducing the falls in freight rates; smaller shipyards across China were abandoned, with half-finished ships never to be built; inventories of iron ore, electronics, textiles, and sports shoes were among the many commodities piling up in the ports across China, with no market destination.[1] Clearly, if you ever wanted to move goods across the oceans, this was the time to do it with prices so low.

In April 2009 the *Times* noted that "about 10 per cent of the world's 10,650 in-service container ships and bulk carriers are currently sitting empty and at anchor waiting for cargoes that are simply not emerging."[2] This figure varied according to region of trade and the type of goods transported. Around 25 percent of ships transporting "raw materials in the Pacific are now idle," claimed one report.[3] Many of these "parked" ships were in waters off Malaysia, Indonesia, and the Philippines,[4] presumably because of cheap oceanic real estate and less securitized waters than neighboring China, Taiwan, South Korea, and Japan. The environmental waste connected to "mothballed" ships was another disaster in the making, with toxic metals, fuel, and cargo corroding into the ocean's ecosystem. China has the world's largest ship-breaking industry, and along with the high rates of death among workers caused by accidents and the inhalation of toxic fumes, further damage to the environment is highly likely.[5] At the time, it was hard not to be alarmed at the prospect of toxic metals from Europe piling up in the parking lots of Asia's harbors with the collapse in electronic waste industries. Like any economy in woe at the time, the business press attributed the primary causes of this rapid decline in the shipping industry to the banks, of course, which in their "mistrust and nervousness" were refusing to pass on finance to an industry that depends on lines of credit in order to turn around deals and invest in infrastructure.[6] As many commentators were noting, liquidity in finance markets had fled the scene.

Things haven't gotten a whole lot better in the intervening years. As I write in the closing weeks of 2015, one of the world's largest shipbrokers issued this dire prognosis: "This market is looking like a disaster and the rates are a reflection of that."[7] The Baltic Dry Freight Index has collapsed to record lows, with the Shanghai Containerized Freight Index following a similar pattern. Reuters tell a similar story, reporting that "spot freight rates for transporting containers, carrying anything from flat-screen TVs to sportswear from Asia to Northern Europe, has fallen

FIGURE 1.1 Connecting bridge between waterside and dockside ports, Ningbo, China. Photograph by Ned Rossiter, 2009.

Introduction—Logistical Media Theory **3**

70 percent in three weeks." It now costs just USD $295 to transport a 200-foot container (TEU) from ports in Asia to Northern Europe. As noted by the multi-faceted Tyler Durden, this sort of drop in spot rates mirrors that of 2008 before the last crash. While some put this down to "mal-investment" in shipping construction resulting in an oversupply of ships brought about by market signals of recovery, global trade figures indicate an extended period of slow growth. When falling prices in commodities and resources coupled with weak manufacturing sectors and soft consumer spending are factored in, the horizon of the global economic future is looking pretty bleak, to put it mildly.

Amid the complexity and, for the most part, illegibility of global finance, the infrastructure and economy of logistics serve as diagnostic devices. The conjunction of financial crisis with global logistical industries was manifest within the urban economy and social life as I experienced it while living in China for a few years from 2007 to 2011. I distinctly recall scores of men, for the most part, wandering about often alone and without purpose through the streets of Shanghai and Ningbo. Many resembled images I had seen of shell-shocked war veterans. But these were not casualties returning from the front line of war, but rather the hollowed out faces of workers recently laid off from the scores of factories operating in southern China. It didn't take long for authorities to move these aimless souls off the streets of wealthy cities spread along the eastern seaboard. As clichéd as this may sound, China gave me a sense of the scale of logistical operations and the rule of the state in authorizing massive infrastructural developments in rail, road transport, housing, and ports. Indeed, China seemed to literally embody the idea of a logistical state at work—a sovereign entity in the business of managing people, finance, and things, incorporating contingencies as they arise to consolidate political interests and further support the accumulation of capital. In marked contrast to the bumbling efforts of the Bush administration's response to the social, ecological, and urban wreckage following Hurricane Katrina in 2005, the devastation wrought by the earthquakes in Sichuan in 2008 was met with government personnel, relief agencies and rescue teams, diagnostic experts, military support crews, and overseas aid and infrastructural support mobilized in a relatively swift fashion.

A study of the political handling of crisis events was not my focus in China, but such upheavals did confirm a broader sense of a country whose intense transformation was supported and indeed made possible to a large extent by highly sophisticated logistical systems coupled with surplus labor that made the world operational. China, then, spawned my interest in logistics as it bears upon the governance of labor, urban development, and the management of global supply chains. It was hard not to have a sense of awe in experiencing the speed of economy and society remade within a system of authoritarian capitalism, with entire streets, housing blocks, and roads often enough torn down and reconstructed in the course of a day. To be at the center of world-historical transformation was dramatically different from my experience of growing up in Perth, the most isolated city in the world on sand plains of the west coast of Australia. At that time,

4 Introduction—Logistical Media Theory

in a life under the harsh blue light of southern skies, the previous epochal change in world history was something one read about at school or viewed in picture books and paintings of the European Renaissance and Industrial Revolution a few hundred years earlier and many thousands of miles away. World history was a series of events and inventions in which the abstraction of the imaginary takes command, whereas China's compression of industrial modernity with a synthetic world conjured within the parameters of computer-aided design and drafting software made one marvel at the power of authoritarian capitalism to produce subjectivity and space, economy and time in ways that seemed to surpass history's precedents to remake a world in its own image. The flip side of the great Chinese spectacle was a foreboding sense of the future-present in which human labor and all forms of life were expendable and available for exploitation.

The globalizing power of China, then and now, indexes a world calibrated to extract value wherever and whenever the logic of capital accumulation intersects with the force of sovereign expansion. Within this nightmare on the brain of the living it is hard not to recoil in fear from the social and ecological damage wrought by the juggernaut of the logistical state as it spans the territory of China and beyond. If logistical operations are central to the emergence of new forms of sovereign power, then a media theory of logistics lends analytical traction to the collective work required to diagnose and critique contemporary regimes of rule.

This book investigates the material and design dimensions of software systems operative within global logistics industries. It identifies how software-driven systems generate protocols and standards that shape social, economic, and cross-institutional relations within and beyond the global logistics industries. Such operations result in the production of new regimes of knowledge and associated modes of "soft control" within organizational paradigms. The emergent "algorithmic architectures" are computational systems of governance that hold a variable relation between the mathematical execution of code and an "external" environment defined through arrangements of data.[8] The capacity of algorithmic architectures to organize and analyze data on labor productivity in real-time, for instance, means that they operate as key technologies for governing labor within logistical industries. My claim is that this has implications for the scope of research on logistical media.

Logistical Media Theory

Consisting of locational devices such as Voice Picking technology, GPS tracking, RFID (radio frequency identification) tags, radars, and biometric monitoring technologies, logistical media calibrate labor and life, objects and atmospheres. The spatial and temporal properties of these information and communication technologies are a determinate force in the production of subjectivity and economy. Their primary function is to extract value by optimizing the efficiency of living labor and supply chain operations. Logistical media—as technologies, infrastructure,

Introduction—Logistical Media Theory **5**

and software—coordinate, capture, and control the movement of people, finance, and things. Infrastructure makes worlds. Logistics governs them.

Anticipated in the work on "logistical modernities" by urban theorist and military historian Paul Virilio, and elaborated to some extent in the study on gameplay and war simulations by media philosopher Patrick Crogan, the term "logistical media" is named as such by communication historian and social theorist John Durham Peters.[9] For Peters, the concept of logistical media "stresses the infrastructural role of media."[10] Garnering no more than a passing mention in Peters's earlier writings and interviews, the concept of logistical media is fleshed out in more detail in his recently published *The Marvelous Clouds: Toward a Philosophy of Elemental Media.*[11] In this fascinating and remarkable book, Peters acknowledges the pioneering research of one of his former PhD students and now academic, Judd Ammon Case, who proposes the logistical media of radar, in particular, be considered as "media of orientation."[12] Peters suggests that a study of infrastructure provides a point of entry into "understanding the work of media as fundamentally logistical."[13]

Infrastructure provides an underlying system of elements, categories, standards, protocols, and operations that, as many note, are only revealed in its moment of failure and breakdown. Logistical media stitch these various components into a relation that makes the world operational. Peters: "The job of logistical media is to organize and orient, to arrange people and property, often into grids."[14] The politics of infrastructure intersects with the experience and condition of logistical labor and life within urban settings. But where, exactly, is the infrastructure that makes these planetary-scale economies, biopolitical regimes, and social lives possible? We see or become aware of infrastructure only when it no longer works. At that moment, the coordinating capacity of logistical media runs up against what the industry terms the "fault tolerance" of the infrastructural system. At this point the cybernetic dimension of logistical operations kicks in, rerouting supply chains, patching code, enlisting nonunionized workers—whatever is required to get the machine up and running again. This default of auto-correction is the power of logistical media: It sets "the terms in which everyone must operate."[15] And every thing. But this is an operational principle, not a foregone conclusion or fact. A system may correct itself, but that doesn't mean those in charge of its oversight are necessarily aware of a kind of operational autonomy. At this point media become sovereign. Consider, for example, developments such as General Electric's Industrial Internet coalition and their vision of predictive analytics and maintenance, which instantiates logistics in a relation of priority vis-à-vis infrastructure.[16] The sovereignty of logistical media resides in part in its capacity to extract value in novel ways.

The combinatory force of logistical media has a substantive effect on the composition of labor and production of subjectivity. The formation of logistical media theory therefore requires an analysis of how labor is organized and governed through software interfaces and media technologies that manage what anthropologist Anna

6 Introduction—Logistical Media Theory

Tsing identifies as "supply chain capitalism."[17] The flexibility of global supply chains and just-in-time modes of production shape who gets employed, where they work, and what sort of work they do. Logistical systems, in other words, govern labor. Logistical labor emerges at the interface between infrastructure, software protocols, and design. Labor time is real-time. Logistical labor is more than a unit to be measured according to key performance indicators (or KPIs). It is the lifeblood of economy and design, exploitation and consumption. Logistical labor underpins the traffic of infrastructure and circuits of capital.

In terms of labor management, the optimum state of governance arises at the moment in which the execution of a task, or standard operating procedure (SOP), is registered in the real-time computation of KPIs. As Katie Hepworth writes, "KPIs and the real-time measurement of labour imply a constant acceleration described in terms of improved productivity."[18] Yet logistics is not bound to the pursuit of speed. The temporal horizon of maritime industries, for example, may just as often require a slowing down of movement, or even periods of stasis.[19] The capacity to calibrate time according to multiple and frequently conflicting economic interests constitutes a form of "transactional impedance [that] relates to the power-geometries within supply chains."[20] As Hepworth explains, "It describes how diverse stakeholders and individuals are placed in quite distinct relations to commodity flows and it sets out the interconnections between global sites, as well as the ways in which these relations are manipulated for the benefit of particular actors within those networks."[21] Logistical software, ERP systems, and technologies of location play a central role in the mediation of such economies of transaction and data extraction.

In developing a media theory of logistics this book began, as many now do, with a not so indirect allusion to Friedrich Kittler's infamous dictum, "Media determine our situation."[22] In his critical appraisal of the scene of Kittler, Stefan Heidenreich writes the following: "If media really is the message, then in the moment a new medium arrives all that can be said must already be present. In other words, the situation is defined instantly."[23] The arrival of logistical media defines our situation instantly in real-time. Calculations of movement, productivity, efficiency, performance. These are the regimes that govern logistical labor and life as they intersect with the software and infrastructure that comprise logistical media. Let me start, then, with an overview of the theoretical, social, economic, historical, and technical coordinates for this intervention on a media theory of logistical nightmares.

Materialities of Communication

With its attention to flexibility, contingency, control, and coordination, logistical media critique opens the relation between economies of data and the remodeling of labor and life. In terms of disciplinary orientation, however, logistical media theory does not yet exist. It is a theory whose status has yet to coalesce into a sustained analytical and methodological body of research and knowledge. For the purpose of sketching some contours of influence, a disciplinary set of relations for logistical media theory can be drawn across the fields of network cultures, software studies, critical organization studies, Canadian communications research, and German media theory in addition to anthropological and historical research on infrastructure.

The history of materialist approaches to the study of communication is one obvious point of departure for a media theory of logistical systems of communication, coordination, and control.[24] A focus on the material properties special to transport and communications infrastructure can be analytically complemented with attention to how the algorithmic architectures of communication and transport infrastructure impact on the experience and conditions of labor operating within those industries. Drawing on the work of medium theorists such as Innis, McLuhan, and Ong, communication historian and cultural critic James Carey noted that the advent of telegraphy in the nineteenth century "freed communication from the constraints of geography."[25] This meant that the concepts and practices of communication could be understood beyond the dominant "transmission view" of communication in which the mobility of people, goods, and information involved equivalent operations (using railway networks, for example). For Carey, symbolic and ritualistic views of communication were able to develop.

But as a number of media and communication scholars working in the tradition of Carey and medium theorists have recently observed, the history of mobile technologies demonstrates an ongoing linkage with transportation technologies.[26] As Mimi Sheller explains, "the advent of mobile communication technologies and software-supported transportation networks also fundamentally changes how communication is thought about, but in this case by re-embedding it into transportation infrastructures and spaces of transit, which are also spaces of transmission."[27] Lisa Parks notes that the term "infrastructure" emphasizes the materiality and distribution of communication.[28] It also reminds us of the territoriality and geography of communication and transport, of questions of power, and of the challenge to devise new techniques and modes of visualizing these interrelations.[29]

The analysis of data is one key line of critique for logistical media theory. Forms of pattern recognition beyond the basic data hold relevance for how the emergent fields of digital humanities and software studies analyze the massive volume of big data generated by digital transactions and user-consumer practices online. Big data analysis of habits of consumption is interesting for commercial entities, but not particularly exciting for social and political analysis of network ecologies. How to ascertain a relation between data, materiality, and subjectivity is a problem little addressed by either digital humanities or software studies. Some notable exceptions include Matthew Kirschenbaum's research on "forensic materiality," Anne Balsamo's pedagogical experiments and design research on "technological imagination," N. Katherine Hayles's study of "technogenesis," and Jussi Parikka's "materialities of technical media culture."[30] Yet despite the materiality of much logistical media,

8 Introduction—Logistical Media Theory

a theory of logistical media can present itself as elusive. A key reason for this has to do with the proprietary control of the high-end software systems, making a study of logistical software difficult to undertake. Even if one had the resources at hand to analyze code, the algorithmic architectures and troves of data remain beyond reach for media theory.

Software studies, as it has emerged from the study of network cultures and critical studies of digital media, is another key field for developing a theory of logistical media. Although much more attuned to the work of critique and an often high technical knowledge of digital media, there is a tendency in software studies to focus on open source software and investigate questions of materiality in terms of design and "cultural analytics," "protocological control," "media ecologies," "memory and storage," and "media archaeology."[31] Combining empirical study with concept development constitutes an intervention within the emergent field of software studies by shifting the analytical gaze from open source software cultures and "cultural analytics" to the vaporware–meets–hard edge of consultancy culture and global infrastructures.[32] The closed, proprietary systems of software that manage global supply chains have a substantive impact on modes and practices of work. As such, they require our attention.

Locative media are media of logistics. Yet at the conceptual and empirical levels, research on locative media has next to nothing to say about logistical media and supply chain operations whose spatial-temporal operations are frequently enough overseen by locative media—GPS, RFID, Voice Picking technology, ERP systems, social media software, and the like. The deployment of these technologies across logistical supply chains produces what Anja Kanngieser calls "microtechnologies of surveillance" designed "to track and trace workers by constantly tying them to territorial and temporal location[s]."[33] From the embedding of RFID microchips under the skin of employees to the automated instructions on picking lists for workers in warehouses and distribution centers, the use of locational devices within logistical industries results in the extraction and relay of data that holds high commercial value.[34]

While geodata may be used in positive ways in the case of managing delivery fleets aimed at fuel efficiency and "ecorouting," locative media also generate data that affects how workers are monitored in workplace settings. Along with privacy issues that arise with the tracking of consignments in transport industries via GPS and cell phones that make visible in real-time the location of workers, there is also concern by unions over how the software parameters of Voice Picking technologies and the generation of data by RFID can result in the profiling and categorization of workers along lines of race and class that may have deleterious effects on employment conditions and prospects in industries that are frequently characterized by insecure modes of work.

Logistical media are also very different from location-based media characterized by the capacity of users to "control and personalize" the borders between public and private spaces.[35] The agency afforded to users of locative media is much less

Introduction—Logistical Media Theory **9**

clear in the case of logistical media, which as an instrumentalization of location-aware mobile technologies are designed to exert control over the mobility of labor, data, and commodities as they traverse urban, rural, atmospheric, and oceanic spaces and traffic through the circuits of databases, mobile devices, and algorithmic architectures. A further distinction between locative and logistical media is marked by the tendency of users of locative media to search urban spaces for services related to consumption, while logistical media provide the very conditions for urban settings to function in such a way.

The global logistics industry is an emergent regime of what Alexander Galloway terms "protocological control" that already shapes the conditions of labor and life for many, and increasingly affects how knowledge production is governed and undertaken now and in future.[36] With military origins, logistics emerged as a business concept in the 1950s concerned with the management of global supply chains. Enterprise resource planning software is often used to govern such movement. Yet for the most part ERP software remains a black box for those not directly using these systems as a matter of routine in their daily work across a range of industries, which include but are not limited to logistical industries. The healthcare, medical insurance, education, mining, and energy industries, along with retail and service sectors, also adopt ERP systems to manage organizational activities. One key reason for the scarce critical attention to ERP systems is related to the prohibitive price of obtaining proprietary software, which often costs millions of dollars for companies to implement. The aesthetics of ERP software are also notoriously unattractive, and the design is frequently not conducive to ease or pleasure of use.

The result for fields such as software studies and the digital humanities is that ERP software analysis is largely overlooked and undertaken—for good reasons—by those working in IT services and programmers associated with the shipping, warehousing, aviation, rail and road transport industries, and procurement, human resources, inventory, and supply chain management.[37] As such, logistical software may seem to hold little relevance as an object of study for software studies and digital humanities researchers. However, I argue in this book that logistics has a broad social reach and impact in terms of how people undertake work. Logistical software functions as a technology of governance and control, measuring the productivity of labor using real-time KPIs. Central to logistics is the production of new subjectivities of labor. More than any other aspect of logistical industries, this characteristic of logistics software makes it relevant to researchers in digital humanities. Why? Because such techniques of management are finding their way into academic workplace settings, which are undergoing a transformation into what I term in chapter 5 the logistical university. The recent rise of MOOCs (massive open online courses) is a logistical operation that will result in the offshoring and outsourcing of knowledge production. But that's only if MOOCs continue, and one is inclined to say that it won't, at least in its current form. Even the "M" in MOOCs is changing to denote "mentored" rather than "massive" as the earlier

10 Introduction—Logistical Media Theory

model of taped lectures is modified to "incorporate the human touch" in the teaching of courses.[38] In any case, the offshoring and outsourcing of knowledge production is a standard practice in many organizations and economies. As neo-liberal capitalism diversifies its modes of accumulation from the debt economy of housing to the extraction of wealth from student debt and global education markets, logistical critique becomes ever more pressing as a political, social, and intellectual undertaking.[39] A focus on logistical media is one line of entry into the development of such a critique.

Logistics, the Cold War, Fordism

To date the study of logistics has largely been undertaken by researchers working in the fields of business and management studies,[40] military history,[41] and economic geography.[42] With military origins, logistics emerged during the Napoleonic wars (1803–1815) as a forecasting technology in the art of warfare, complementing the limits of strategy and tactics.[43] Earlier, in the seventeenth and eighteenth centuries, logistical oversight of supply lines enabled military planners to overcome the practices of pillage and plunder, which kept troops constantly on the move, always in search of food, water, and animal fodder. Logistical operations transformed this nomadic condition, allowing battle to become entrenched around the infrastructure of fortified towns and more sedentary as provisions, troops, and munitions were transported to the front lines of conflict.[44] From its outset, then, "logistical rationality" approached the management of labor through systems of command and control. However, this book's point of departure is not focused on the military-industrial complex so much as the interface between infrastructure, software protocols and design, and labor situated across global supply chains (shipping, rail and road transport, procurement, warehousing, IT R&D).

Understood broadly as a geopolitical, ideological confrontation between Western nations and the Soviet Union, the Cold War traded heavily in the cultivation of fear among populations over the imminent threat of nuclear catastrophe and planetary annihilation. Situated alongside the Cold War, Fordism served as a geo-industrially circumscribed architecture of relief, providing a rhythm of regularity and sense of security to the borders of labor and life, and thus offsetting and containing the ever present specter of contingency, threat, and total destruction embodied in the political imaginary of the Cold War. Alexander Klose considers logistics as the "methodological child" of modern systems of rationalization.[45] Logistics, as it emerged in the period of the so-called Second Cold War (1979–1985),[46] operates as a kind of third force or articulating device that, on the one hand, negotiates the economic and structural demand for secure national and increasingly global supply chains, while, on the other hand, serves as an adjunct to the arms race by advancing new organizational systems aimed at efficiently managing labor, mobility, and the accountability of things. Logistics was later consolidated as a business management practice as the Cold War began to thaw in the

1980s, and Western economic interests penetrated the new markets and, more particularly, harnessed the surplus labor of ex-Soviet states.[47] For Brian Holmes, "The 1980s were the inaugural decade of neoliberalism, which brought new forms of financialized wealth-creation and motivational management into play, alongside the militaristic technologies of surveillance and control that had been inherited from the Cold War."[48]

Sociologists Edna Bonacich and Jake Wilson date what they call the "logistics revolution" from the 1970s, with a particular emphasis on the Reagan and Thatcher eras of market and institutional deregulation along with neoliberal international free trade agreements.[49] They characterize this organizational revolution in terms of the rise of retailer power over producers and manufacturers in conjunction with changes in production (flexibility and outsourcing), logistics ("intermodalisation" and freight distribution), and labor (intensification of contingency, weakening of unions, racialization of labor, lower labor standards).[50] Contemporary logistics aims to minimize inventory buildups, or over-accumulation, which leads to overproduction by manufacturers and retail overstocking (or understocking, as the case may be).[51] In both instances, manufacturers and retailers strive for rationalization and efficiency in communications in order to minimize overinvestment in stocks that decline in economic value over time. But there is an important prehistory to the so-called logistics revolution to be found in cybernetics and the Fordist era following World War II. Nigel Thrift provides the following overview of logistics that resulted in major changes to the "geography of calculation":

> As a formal field of study rather than a military "art," logistics dates back to the 1940s and application of various operational research models to problems of inventory (storage) and distribution (flow), most especially in the context of the demands made by the Second World War. In the 1960s logistics became bound up with systems engineering and an associated array of technologies like life-flow charts, life-cycle analysis, network analysis, including scheduling approaches like PERT (program evaluation and review technique) and CPM (critical path method), and so on. More recently, logistics has expanded again to become seen as an integral element of what production is, rather than as something subsequent to it (as "distribution"). In turn, this has led to new means of production like distributive manufacturing. The third impulse is new means of countability which have provided new possibilities of calculation.[52]

Deborah Cowen explains how RAND Corporation's development of "total cost analysis" inherited from war-time operations research into aircraft maintenance brought logistics and systems engineering together, resulting in value-adding distribution systems once the market and military became "entangled" in the science of business logistics.[53] Before returning to RAND, I wish to focus some more on the role of cybernetics in the development of logistical systems. In his fascinating

12 Introduction—Logistical Media Theory

book on cybernetic warfare, Antoine Bousquet analyzes the "closed world" discourse that informed the cybernetic understanding and computerized management of Cold War scenarios of nuclear attack. He notes how the abstract formalism of systems analysis, gaming, simulation, communication, and information were privileged over "experiential and situated knowledge."[54] Part of this circumscribed adoption of cybernetics by military strategists was due to the technological limits of computers at the time, whose slow processing speeds and storage capacities could not handle large volumes of data, or the feedback of contingency into the system.[55] Here, cybernetics assumes a world that can be made visible, knowable, and controlled. Within the military-industrial complex of the Cold War, cybernetics did not share the interest in contingency that defined the lively and non-consensual debates and writings of the diverse range of scholars working on the topic in the 1960s such as anthropologists Gregory Bateson and Margaret Mead and architect Buckminster Fuller, along with luminaries in the fields of mathematics, game theory, computer science, neuropsychology, molecular biology, and biophysics, such as Wiener, Bertanfly, McCulloch and von Neumann, and later Maturana and Varela.[56] Logistics is more closely connected to the subfields of organizational, management, and entrepreneurial cybernetics, which are interested in new systems of governance.

In his great synoptic essay on experimental cartographies of ethico-aesthetic invention, Brian Holmes assembles writer-activist Félix Guattari, psychotherapist Mony Elkaïm, and scientists such as Ilya Prigogine and Isabelle Stengers as standout figures in the contest against "the reductionism of the post-war cybernetic paradigm."[57] Holmes makes the connection between the collective experiments in the anti-psychiatry movements in Europe in the late 1950s–1970s, in which meta-models around institutional analysis and subjective transformation were developed that sought to overthrow the repressive and authoritarian tendencies in society, and the advent of neoliberal capitalism, whose "aim is to extract surplus value not only from our labor but also from our inherent sociability, our desires to love, play, flourish and therefore to produce and consume."[58] In revisiting in this book the question of technological determination with the rise of logistical media, the analytical terrain of anti-psychiatry provides one point of reference for examining how logistics probes life as a system from which value is extracted. Testing whether techniques of affirmative resistance can be devised within the milieu of logistics and its infrastructures is a core task for politics today.

Cybernetic Power

The cybernetic mediation of perception, labor, and life as constitutive components of economic and social systems finds a pre-war precursor in the work of Edward Bernays—the nephew of Freud and pioneer of modern public relations.[59] In his book with the entirely unambiguous title, *Propaganda* (1928), Bernays sets out "to explain the structure of the mechanism which controls the public mind."[60]

Perceiving a landscape of economic and social turbulence, rapidly expanding and independent media systems, and potentially ungovernable populations, Bernays sees the public mind and its proliferation of opinions as chaotic and in need of control: "[There is a] multitude of cleavages which exist in our society, and along which flow information and opinion carrying authority to the individual groups." Bernays's model of perception management—and thus governance of populations—is decidedly top-down and changed little following World War II, which served to clarify and consolidate his views on the need for public consent to be *engineered* by leaders across government, community organizations, education, and, in particular, communications media. Bernays: "This invisible, intertwining structure of groupings and associations is the mechanism by which democracy has organized its group mind and simplified its mass thinking. To deplore the existence of such a mechanism is to ask for a society such as never was and never will be."[61] Advertisers and public relations professionals take up a special role in making visible these invisible relations, formalizing the organic motion of democracy into a science modulating the opinions and desires of populations. In this respect, the public relations models of Bernays shares the military desire for cybernetic systems of command and control. As Holmes puts it, the political-economic "organizational paradigm" of cybernetics:

> . . . uses feedback information to coordinate vast logistical supply lines of industrial production and distribution, it organizes people into a functional hierarchy, and it always seeks to home in on a predetermined target (production, sales, efficiency, etc.). These were the major issues of the Fordist economies of scale in the 1930s-60s, which gradually caught up to the global scale of simultaneous multi-theater operations attained by the military in WWII. Clearly, the kinds of logistical control at a distance provided by first-generation cybernetic systems were key to this expansion of industry and trade.[62]

Michel Foucault's lectures on biopolitics provide an account of the German and American schools of economists that founded the political rationality of "neoliberalism" in the aftermath of World War II. Both identified as their central problem the question of the state and its relation to the market. Market freedom, security, state legitimacy, juridical arbitration, the "individualization of social policy," and the exercise of political power "modeled on principles of a market economy" comprise the constellation of problems for German ordoliberalism and its "renewal of the liberal art of government."[63] As Foucault tells us, the diffusion of the German model of neoliberalism to France and the United States (via the likes of emigrants such as Hayek) moved around a shared need to address the economic crises of the 1930s that held its own specificities and institutional-political mechanisms of response at the national scale.[64] To the German model and its preoccupation with the question of the state (a key difference between ordoliberal and

14   Introduction—Logistical Media Theory

neoliberal thought), the American neoliberals add the subject of labor and the individual's allotment of scarce resources—both of which belong to the "qualitative modulations" and "strategic rationality" of human activity or capital.[65] Such terminology overlaps with that of cybernetics and game theory as it emerged after the Second World War and shares something, I would suggest, with the interest in human psychology and behavior as seen in the work on public relations by Edward Bernays.

Paranoia with RAND

The shady advisory role to U.S. administrations of RAND Corporation is one of many examples of organizations that devised a strategy of institutional consolidation and financial extension by building on the enhanced environment of "risk" that followed in the aftermath of the September 11 attacks in 2001. In a report on security recommendations for containerized shipping and global supply chains, Henry Willis and David Ortiz set out a logistics framework of "three independent and interacting networks":

> A physical logistics system for transporting goods; a transaction-based system that procures and distributes goods and that is driven primarily by information flows; and an oversight system that implements and enforces rules of behavior within and among the subsystems through standards, fines, and duties. Network components are *nodes*, such as factories and ports, and *edges*, such as roads and information links.[66]

These RAND authors are clear on the centrality of security for global supply chains, which they envisage as a network of interconnected layers, nodes, and edges.[67] The aim of the report is to assess the proliferation of securitization methods for managing the risk of threat and potential attack on populations or the supply chain itself. Security here is no longer restricted to protecting against the traditional threat of "loss of cargo shipments through theft of misrouting," but is instead focused on both *imminent* and *immanent* threat that moves across the globe hidden within shipping containers that enter nations through ports. The security strategy here corresponds to what Melinda Cooper analyzes as the preemptive strategies conditioning, in part, the emergence of bioterror.[68] Following the work of François Ewald, Cooper identifies the *catastrophe event* as "the defining predicament of the neoliberal politics of security."[69] In the case of maritime industries and their global supply chains, logistics is identified by RAND as the topology of risk that can be related to the discourse on the catastrophe event. Such an event, explains Cooper, provokes "not so much fear (of an identifiable threat) as a state of alertness, without foreseeable end" in which the "only possible response to the emergent crisis (of whatever kind—biomedical, environmental, economic) is one of speculative preemption."[70] There is great business to be found, after all, in

Introduction—Logistical Media Theory **15**

such a speculative environment of permanent preemption. And RAND has always been alert to such opportunities that come in the form of consultancy to business communities and governmental administrations.

At once appraising and questioning the security efforts of maritime and port authorities such as the International Maritime Organization (IMO) and supporting U.S. legislation such as the Maritime Transportation Security Act of 2002 (MTSA), which designated authority to the U.S. Coast Guard for compliance and enforcement of security measures across the U.S. ports, the RAND authors extend their assessment of maritime actors to have initiated security responses to include the World Customs Organization, the World Shipping Council, the Pacific Maritime Association, the United Nations Council on Trade and Development, U.S. Customs and Border Protection, and the Transportation Security Administration, along with all 361 U.S. ports and most international ports.[71] The report expresses doubt over the capacity of the security efforts of such organizations to fully address the scope of the security problem, due largely to the oversight of policies of the networked logic that defines the movement of people and things. The authors highlight "fault tolerance" and "resilience" as particular omissions in securitization policy in the maritime industries. The former refers to the capacity of logistics to "respond to disruptions and failures of isolated components without bringing the entire system to a grinding halt." The latter refers to the "design function" of a system and its ability "to return to normal operating conditions quickly after the failure of one or more of its components." Both are identified as important to the efficiency and security of a system "under both normal and emergency operating conditions."[72] In these terms—that is, "fault tolerance" and "resilience"—logistics is returned to cybernetics as an "open" system that accommodates the feedback of noise as a corrective operation, stabilizing the system in a state of "dynamic equilibrium."

The list of recommendations in the report illuminates the scope of the securitization discourse as it manifests within the maritime industries and its logistics, transaction, and oversight layers whose network of relations compose the governance of global supply chains. Along with recommendations for public sector management (which for RAND means the U.S. federal government) of fault tolerance and resilience of global container supply chains—and not, interestingly, the private sector due to potential market failures of providing what the authors assign as a "public good"—special attention is given to research and development that targets "new technologies for low-cost, high-volume remote sensing and scanning."[73] Here, a wide range of options are canvassed, including anti-tamper seal technology designed to detect port of entry of containers and protect against either fraud or terrorism; x-ray and gamma-ray scanning of cargo shipments in order to make transparent illegal or dangerous cargo such as weapons; and radiation pages, portal sensors, and remote monitoring to detect weapons of mass destruction.[74]

Recommendations are also made for the use of RFID technology, which registers the geographic position of ships and goods and assists in the management of

16 Introduction—Logistical Media Theory

inventories and the efficiency of supply chains. While largely used as a tracking and data storage device, the surveillance of labor through the use of RFID tags is already under way in some service and health industries. The regulation of labor in the maritime industries is, for the time being, left to other digital systems of control such as ERP and KPI software, as discussed earlier.

Coextensive with this political economy and militarization of logistics is the at times radical and increasingly mainstream culture and business of open source software developers. Never celebrated, as far as I am aware, by the open source geeks and critics that inhabit the global circuit of media arts festivals, mailing lists, and hacker labs, ERP software has in recent years also found open source developers willing to expend their "free labor" in providing nonproprietary applications for the logistics industry.[75] The free labor of open source software development finds another manifestation in websites that plot the location of commercial, leisure, and unidentified vessels as they move across international waters. MarineTraffic.com is one such example of sites used to identify the position of maritime vessels as they traverse the planet's coastlines.[76] Hosted by the Department of Product and Systems Design Engineering, University of the Aegean, the site is a community-driven project hooked on providing real-time simulations of vessel movements. Once equipped with an Automatic Identification System (AIS) receiver attached to a computer with an Internet connection and a standard VHF roof antenna, users within ten miles of the sea are able to identify the coordinates of a vessel's position and then upload the data to a central database.

This type of activity is highly banal at one level, and is a kind of nerdy digital cousin of those CB radio nuts getting off on "free airwaves" or train-spotting obsessives stalking the railway transport systems of the industrial Fordist era, where a fascination in the efficiencies of time-tabling is multiplied from workplace to leisure. As easy as it is to dismiss such phenomena of freewheeling tech innovation, I find it nonetheless indicative of the spectrum of formal to informal interests that collectively work on making visible the movement of things. In their production of an informational commons, projects such as these function at a benign level with their provision of information on ships, port traffic, navigation aids, and so forth. They start to become more enmeshed with biopolitical practices of governmentality, however, as they feed into logistical machines and are adopted within the maritime industries as securitization practices whose ultimate ambition is to make visible and knowable the movement of everything. And of course such transparency is inseparable from economic interests, and belongs to what Thrift notes as the "geography of calculation" attending the political economy of logistics.

In terms of biopolitical technologies of control, there is much research to be done that analyzes the role of software in governing the activities of labor within the field of logistics. The calculation of risk that Foucault attributes to postwar American neoliberalism can be seen to manifest in the social-technical systems of contemporary logistics. Securitization of global supply chains is a central concern here, as set out in the policy-shaping efforts of think tanks such as RAND Corporation. The type of technological processes and protocols put forward by RAND take global supply chains and port security as the key systems and spaces at risk of attack.[77] But there is not a great gap between this sort of infrastructural and systemic targets of securitization and the biopolitical control of labor. The discussion of standard software systems currently used in the maritime industry and logistics to monitor and regulate efficiencies with supply chains shows well that labor also belongs to the field of risk assessment and securitization.

Biopolitical Calculations

If this diverse array of conditions, practices, and social-technical systems is any indication of the future-present of sovereign states and biopolitical technologies of population control, then it would seem that labor that is able to operate outside of the software devices special to logistics and its global supply chains might correspond with a life that is at once free, and economically impoverished. Logistics provides a key to understanding the future-present of state sovereignty and the biopolitical management of populations.

If Foucault's interest in biopolitics moved around the indistinction within a neoliberal paradigm between labor and life, production and reproduction, then it follows that the labor of research might share something with the life of labor. Both subsist within what Foucault identified as the "milieu" or environment within which the life of species-beings is addressed and constituted by power.[78] Perhaps even more forcefully, does the analytic rubric turn to the "biopolitics of experience" when labor and life are constitutively indistinct?[79] No doubt one could say that experience has always been subject to regimes of governance that manage labor and life—the church, for instance, exercised its power over life through the ritual of prayer and worship and the social practice of congregation for Mass. But the real subsumption of labor by capital in a post-Fordist era renders the organization of experience in novel ways. Within network societies and data economies, experience presents itself as one of those last frontiers of capture in the economization of life. Think, for instance, of search engines such as Google and the way economies of data mining derive profit from the aggregation of the seemingly inane activity of users clicking from one site to the next, or from the accumulation of the trivial taste on social networking sites.

Across his lectures on biopolitics, Foucault returns to a core definition of biopolitics, only to then take further "detours" in his elaboration of the relationship between territoriality, governmentality, security, populations, and economy. "Biopolitics deals with the population, with the population as a political problem, as a problem that is at once scientific and political, as a biological problem and as power's problem."[80] This book does not set out to problematize or critique Foucault's work on biopolitics. That work is best left to those with more theoretical insight into such matters. Rather, I engage the biopolitical writings of Foucault

18 Introduction—Logistical Media Theory

as a point of departure in order to find some kind of critical and theoretical traction in elaborating the connections between logistics, labor, and life as they figure in and around logistical industries vis-à-vis the constitution of geopolitics and the economization of life.

What, for instance, is the population or species-being operating or constituted as a "problem" in the maritime industries? For logistics, the problem emerges in the interruption of global supply chains—what RAND Corporation terms "fault tolerance" (a technocratic term suitably emptied of political substance and subjectivity).[81] The biopolitical problem, or population, for maritime logistics includes: the pirate, the stowaway, the sex worker, the "illegal migrant," the disobedient worker, the disruption of organized labor, and the like. But what of the production of knowledge on such populations? How is the population of academics, NGO researchers, health professionals, policy makers, and think-tank consultants managed and organized? What are the techniques of calculus by which these diverse populations, subsumed into the category of "fault tolerance," are identified and managed in the interests of securitization? Such questions concern the human as the species-being of biopower. But what of the population of software applications and technological devices that, to varying degrees, are a species-being of computational life increasingly able to self-manage, auto-correct, and internally propagate as they process the informatized status of people and things? Technologies such as these would also belong to an analysis of the biopolitics of contemporary labor and life.

These are questions I pursue throughout this book in an analysis of how logistics intersects with contemporary institutional, social, and technological practices, situating logistics alongside cybernetics as a biopolitical technology of governance. With its use of customized software to manage the movement of people and things, contemporary logistics shares something with the genre of science fiction insofar as it comprises a thought experiment in the future-present of the relations between territory, populations, and security.

The political challenge today is to devise techniques and strategies that operate both within and outside the territory of control exerted by logistics technologies and their software algorithms that shape how practices of knowledge production are organized, which in turn shapes the conditions and experiences of contemporary labor. As much as the emergent field of software studies celebrates the collective innovation of open source initiatives and radical gestures of hacker cultures, there is a much more profound and substantive technological impact exerted upon labor-power in the formal and informal economies concomitant with the global logistics industries that has not yet received critical attention in analyses of the cultures of code. The challenge of political organization within the logistics industries is steep. Not only are unionized forms of labor organization marginal, where they do exist—in the maritime industries of some countries, for instance—there is great pressure for workers and their representatives to conform to ever-increasing demands for greater workplace productivity and enhanced efficiency modulated by computational systems that manage KPIs.

Soft Infrastructure

One consequence of such computational power can be seen in the way logistical infrastructure not only manifests in particular locations and material forms but also has the capacity to scale across geographic registers, technological systems, and social, political, economic, and cultural settings. Scale is calibrated according to real-time systems of measure and performance special to just-in-time regimes of labor productivity and commodity assemblages. Software management systems that oversee transport and communications infrastructure may be located in remote settings at considerable distances from the metropolitan scenes of activity, registering a shift from Saskia Sassen's concept of the "global city" of finance centers to one predicated on the peripheral operations of the "logistical city" (chapter 2).[82] It is in this sense that infrastructure takes on a quality of "liquid modernity," making possible organization at a distance.[83] Algorithmic architectures are thus central to logistical operations and indeed to global service-based markets and value-adding systems.

The software applications special to logistics visualize and organize these mobilities, producing knowledge about the world in transit. Software-driven systems generate protocols and standards that shape social, economic, and cross-institutional relations within the global logistics industries. Such operations result in the production of new regimes of knowledge within an organizational paradigm. The logistical industries that drive supply chain capitalism consist of different infrastructural aspects of the expanding sector of logistics: transport, communications, warehousing, procurement, and ports.

Soft infrastructure may be understood in four key ways: First, as algorithmic architectures (software platforms and code) operating transport and communications infrastructure that connect global supply chains to the managerial science of logistics. Second, as communications and transport infrastructure that materializes algorithmic agency (or the shaping power of code and software) and serves as a central "problem" for R&D and policy making in the logistics industries. Third, in terms of formal and informal labor sectors that adopt different and often conflicting algorithmic architectures operating within supply chain capitalism. And fourth, as models of governance or "protocological control" (Galloway) that draw on "big data" to organize and manage the mobility of people, finance, and things within infrastructure systems on local and transnational scales.

Once combined, these features of soft infrastructure provide the basis for developing a theory of logistical media. As I discuss in chapter 3, a theory of logistical media derived from a study of logistical software developer SAP can be organized around the following headings: securitization, coordination, control, simulation, models, algorithmic architectures, the Internet of Things, protocols, standards, and parameters. Although there is no question that logistical systems can facilitate greater workplace productivity and improve supply chain management, it is also the case that the seamless interoperability sought by policy makers

20 Introduction—Logistical Media Theory

and technologists is often disrupted by labor struggles, software glitches, bottlenecks in transport and computer network traffic, infrastructural breakdowns, inventory blowouts, sabotage of supply chains, and the like.

The political geography of data centers (also known as colocation centers, server farms, and the cloud) instantiates a new form of infrastructural governance on a planetary scale. The technical level of data center governance is defined by low-latency, network interoperability, packet switching, and load capacity. As digital infrastructures they comprise server racks, fiber-optic cables, cooling equipment, and secure facilities. The growth in data centers over the past decade indexes the society of tracking as it bears upon the accumulation of surplus information within an economy of algorithmic capitalism. As an apparatus that governs the storage, processing, and transmission of data, the data center extracts value from the social and economic life of connection. As such, the data center is also a crucial infrastructural component to logistical operations, and I examine it further in this book's final chapters. In elaborating an account in chapter 7 of data centers as key infrastructures of planetary governance and economy, this book rounds out its analysis by asking how such an infrastructural form elucidates the labor dimension that underscores the operation of societies of tracking. A study of the infrastructure of data centers begins to make clear how computational economies consist of diverse regimes of governance that include not only technical operations but also forms of sovereign power distributed across state and non-state entities.

Notes

1. See Thomas Schulz, "Global Crisis Hits Shipping Industry Hard," *Spiegel International*, December 5, 2008, http://www.spiegel.de/international/business/0,1518,594710,00. html. See also Leo Lewis, "Worldwide Shipping Rates Set to Tumble 74%," *The Times*, April 8, 2009, http://business.timesonline.co.uk/tol/business/industry_sectors/transport/article6058358.ece.
2. Lewis, "Worldwide Shipping Rates Set to Tumble 74%."
3. Schulz, "Global Crisis Hits Shipping Industry Hard."
4. Lewis, "Worldwide Shipping Rates Set to Tumble 74%."
5. See "Ship-Breaking Ordered Shut," *The Daily Star*, March 18, 2009, http://www.ban. org/ban_news/2009/090318_shipbreaking_ordered_shut.html.
6. Schulz, "Global Crisis Hits Shipping Industry Hard."
7. Quoted in Tyler Durden, "Global Trade Just Snapped: Container Freight Rates Plummet 70% in 3 Weeks," *Zero Hedge*, November 21, 2015, http://www.zerohedge.com/news/2015–11–21/global-trade-just-snapped-container-freight-rates-plummet-70–3-weeks. All further references in this paragraph to Durden's report.
8. See Luciana Parisi, "Algorithmic Architecture," in Carolin Wiedemann and Soenke Zehle, eds., *Depletion Design: A Glossary of Network Ecologies* (Amsterdam: XMLab and the Institute for Network Cultures, 2012), 7–10. See also Parisi's *Contagious Architecture: Computation, Aesthetics and Space* (Cambridge, MA: MIT Press, 2013).
9. I take the term "logistical modernities" from Benjamin Bratton's introduction, "Logistics of Habitable Circulation," to Paul Virilio, *Speed and Politics*, trans. Marc Polizzotti

(Los Angeles: Semiotext(e), 2006), 7–25. See also Patrick Crogan, *Gameplay Mode: War, Simulation, and Technoculture* (Minneapolis: University of Minnesota Press, 2011) and John Durham Peters and Jeremy Packer, "Becoming Mollusk: A Conversation with John Durham Peters about Media, Materiality, and Matters of History," in Jeremy Packer and Stephen B. Crofts Wiley, eds., *Communication Matters: Materialist Approaches to Media, Mobility and Networks* (New York: Routledge, 2012), 35–50. John Durham Peters, "Calendar, Clock, Tower," in Jeremy Stolow, ed., *Deus in Machina: Religion, Technology, and the Things in Between* (New York: Fordham University Press, 2013), 25–42.

10. Peters and Packer, "Becoming Mollusk," 43.
11. John Durham Peters, *The Marvelous Clouds: Toward a Philosophy of Elemental Media* (Chicago and London: University of Chicago Press, 2015).
12. Judd A. Case, "Logistical Media: Fragments from Radar's Prehistory," *Canadian Journal of Communication* 38, no. 3 (2013): 379–95, http://www.cjc-online.ca/index.php/journal/article/view/2735/2389.
13. Peters, *The Marvelous Clouds*, 37.
14. Ibid.
15. Ibid.
16. http://www.ge.com/stories/industrial-internet.
17. Anna Tsing, "Supply Chains and the Human Condition," *Rethinking Marxism* 2 (2009): 148–76.
18. Katie Hepworth, "Enacting Logistical Geographies," *Environment and Planning D: Society and Space* 32, no. 6 (2014): 1130.
19. See Brett Neilson and Ned Rossiter, "Still Waiting, Still Moving: On Migration, Logistics and Maritime Industries," in David Bissell and Gillian Fuller, eds., *Stillness in a Mobile World* (London and New York: Routledge, 2011), 51–68.
20. Hepworth, "Enacting Logistical Geographies," 1128.
21. Ibid.
22. Friedrich A. Kittler, *Gramophone, Film, Typewriter*, trans. Geoffrey Winthrop-Young and Michael Wutz (Stanford: Stanford University Press, 1999), xxxix.
23. Stefan Heidenreich, "The Situation after Media," in Eleni Ikoniadou and Scott Wilson, eds., *Media after Kittler* (London and New York: Roman & Littlefield, 2015), 138.
24. See Harold A. Innis, *The Bias of Communication* (Toronto: University of Toronto Press, 1951); Lewis Mumford, *Technics and Civilization* (New York: Harcourt, Brace & Co., 1934); Manuel Castells, *The Rise of the Network Society* (Oxford: Blackwell, 1996); Manuel Castells, *Communication Power* (Oxford: Oxford University Press, 2009); Friedrich A. Kittler, "There Is No Software," in *Literature, Media, Information Systems*, ed. John Johnston (Amsterdam: G+B Arts International, 1997), 147–55; Kittler, *Gramophone, Film, Typewriter*; Lisa Parks, *Cultures in Orbit: Satellites and the Televisual* (Durham: Duke University Press, 2005); and John Durham Peters, "Calendar, Clock, Tower," in Jeremy Stolow, ed., *Deus in Machina: Religion and Technology in Historical Perspective* (New York: Fordham University Press, 2012), 25–42.
25. James Carey, "Technology and Ideology: The Case of the Telegraph," in *Communication as Culture: Essays on Media and Society* (Boston: Unwin and Hyman, 1989), 204. Quoted in Mimi Sheller, "Materializing U.S.-Caribbean Borders: Airports as Technologies of Communication, Coordination and Control," in Packer and Wiley, *Communication Matters*, 233.
26. See Packer and Wiley, *Communication Matters*; David Morley, "For a Materialist, Non-Media-centric Media Studies," *Television & New Media* 10, no. 1 (2009): 114–16; Gerard

22 Introduction—Logistical Media Theory

Goggin, *Global Mobile Media* (Oxon: Routledge, 2011); Larissa Hjorth, *Mobile Media in the Asia-Pacific: Gender and The Art of Being Mobile* (Oxon: Routledge, 2009); and Mark Andrejevic, "Media and Mobility," in John Nerone, ed., *Media History and the Foundations of Media Studies, The International Encyclopedia of Media Studies, Vol. 1* (Cambridge and Malden, MA: Wiley-Blackwell, 2013), 521–35.

27. Sheller, "Materializing U.S.-Caribbean Borders," 233.

28. Lisa Parks, "Infrastructural Changeovers: The US Digital TV Transition and Media Futures," in Kelly Gates, ed., *Media Studies Futures, The International Encyclopedia of Media Studies, Vol. 5* (Cambridge and Malden, MA: Wiley-Blackwell, 2013), 296–317.

29. Ibid.

30. See Matthew G. Kirschenbaum, *Mechanisms: New Media and the Forensic Imagination* (Cambridge, MA: MIT Press, 2008); Anne Balsamo, *Designing Culture: The Technological Imagination at Work* (Durham: Duke University Press, 2011); N. Katherine Hayles, *How We Think: Digital Media and Contemporary Technogenesis* (Chicago: University of Chicago Press, 2012); and Jussi Parikka, *A Geology of Media* (Minneapolis: University of Minnesota Press, 2015).

31. See, respectively, Lev Manovich, *Software Takes Command* (New York: Bloomsbury Academic, 2013); Alexander R. Galloway, *Protocol: How Control Exists after Decentralization* (Cambridge, MA: MIT Press, 2004); Matthew Fuller, *Media Ecologies: Materialist Energies in Art and Technoculture* (Cambridge, MA: MIT Press, 2005); Wendy Hui Kyong Chun, *Programmed Visions: Software and Memory* (Cambridge, MA: MIT Press, 2011); and Erkki Huhtamo and Jussi Parikka, eds., *Media Archaeology: Approaches, Applications and Implications* (Berkeley: University of California Press, 2011).

32. See Lev Manovich, "Cultural Analytics: Visualizing Cultural Patterns in the Era of 'More Media,'" 2011, http://manovich.net; and Keller Easterling, *Enduring Innocence: Global Architecture and its Political Masquerades* (Cambridge, MA: MIT Press, 2005).

33. Anja Kanngieser, "Tracking and Tracing: Geographies of Logistical Governance and Labouring Bodies," *Environment and Planning D: Society and Space* 34, no. 4 (2013): 598. The remainder of my account of RFID, GPS, and Voice Picking technologies in this paragraph draws on research in Kanngieser's article.

34. The question of authorship and ownership of data produced through the use of locative media is one raised in an article written around the period that saw the first wave of critical research on locational-aware technologies. See Anne Galloway and Matt Ward, "Locative Media as Socialising and Spatializing Practice: Learning from Archaeology," *Leonardo Electronic Almanac* 14, nos. 3–4 (2006), http://www.leoalmanac.org/leonardo-electronic-almanac-volume-14-no-3-4-june-july-2006/.

35. Adriana de Souza e Silva and Jordan Frith, "Location-Aware Technologies: Control and Privacy in Hybrid Spaces," in Packer and Wiley, *Communication Matters*, 266.

36. See Alexander Galloway, "Protocol," *Theory, Culture & Society* 23, nos. 2–3 (2006): 317. See also Galloway, *Protocol*.

37. The work of David Golumbia is one notable exception. He sets out a critique of spreadsheets and ERP systems in the chapter "Computationalism, Striation and Cultural Authority." Golumbia gives special attention to the healthcare sector and its adoption of customer relationship management (CRM) software developed by ERP vendors such as SAP, Oracle, and Microsoft, among others. While aspects of his critique and analysis are relevant to an analysis of ERP systems in logistical industries, Golumbia does not focus on the relationship between software and labor, nor does he raise the question of method (which I address in chapter 3) as a research practice informed by ERP systems as an architecture whose abstract presence prompts the need for alternative visualizations that

begin to register the relation between software, labor, and research methods. See David Golumbia, *The Cultural Logic of Computation* (Cambridge, MA: Harvard University Press, 2009).

38. See https://play.google.com/store/apps/details?id=moocsmentor.com.

39. See Anonymous, *The Debt Resistors' Operations Manual: A Project of Strike Debt/Occupy. Wall Street*, New York, September, 2012, http://www.scribd.com. See also Maurizio Lazzarato, *The Making of Indebted Man: An Essay on the Neoliberal Condition*, trans. Joshua David Jordan (Los Angeles: Semiotext(e), 2012); Andrew Ross, "The Rise of the Global University," in *Nice Work if You Can Get It: Life and Labor in Precarious Times* (New York: New York University Press, 2009), 189–205; and Andrew Ross, *Creditocracy and the Case for Debt Refusal* (New York: OR Books, 2014).

40. See Martin Christopher, *Logistics and Supply Chain Management*, 4th edition (Harlow: Pearson, 2011); and Donald Waters, ed., *Global Logistics: New Directions in Supply Chain Management* (London: Kogan Page, 2010).

41. Martin van Creveld, *Supplying War: Logistics from Wallenstein to Patton* (Cambridge: Cambridge University Press, 1977); and Paul Virilio, *War and Cinema: The Logistics of Perception* (London: Verso, 1989).

42. Deborah Cowen, "A Geography of Logistics: Market Authority and the Security of Supply Chains," *Annals of the Association of American Geographers* 100 (2010): 600–20; and Craig Martin, "Desperate Mobilities: Logistics, Security and the Extra-Logistical Knowledge of 'Appropriation,'" *Geopolitics* 17, no. 2 (2012): 355–76.

43. See Carl von Clausewitz, *On War* (Oxford: Oxford University Press, 2007). See also Brett Neilson, "Five Theses on Understanding Logistics as Power," *Distinktion: Scandinavian Journal of Social Theory* 13, no. 3 (2012): 323–40.

44. See Manuel DeLanda, *War in the Age of Intelligent Machines* (New York: Zone Books, 1991).

45. Alexander Klose, *The Container Principle: How a Box Changes the Way We Think*, trans. Charles Marcrum II (Cambridge, MA: MIT Press, 2015), 165.

46. See http://en.wikipedia.org/wiki/Cold_War.

47. Deborah Cowen undertakes a thorough analysis of the convergence of materials management and physical distribution in "The Revolution in Logistics: 'America's Last Dark 'Continent',"in *The Deadly Life of Logistics: Mapping Violence in Global Trade* (Minneapolis: University of Minnesota Press, 2014), 23–52.

48. Brian Holmes, "Guattari's Schizoanalytic Cartographies; or, the Pathic Core at the Heart of Cybernetics," *Continental Drift: The Other Side of Neoliberal Globalization*, February 27, 2009, http://brianholmes.wordpress.com/2009/02/27/guattaris-schizoanalytic-cartographies/.

49. Edna Bonacich and Jake B. Wilson, *Getting the Goods: Ports, Labor and the Logistics Revolution* (Ithaca: Cornell University Press, 2008).

50. Ibid., 6–22.

51. Ibid., 4–5.

52. Nigel Thrift, *Knowing Capitalism* (London: Sage, 2005), 219.

53. Cowen, *The Deadly Life of Logistics*, 40.

54. Antoine Bousquet, *The Scientific Way of Warfare: Order and Chaos on the Battlefields of Modernity* (London: Hurst Publishers, 2009), 124. See also Paul N. Edwards, *The Closed World: Computers and the Politics of Discourse in Cold War America* (Cambridge, MA: MIT Press, 1996).

55. Ibid., 130.

56. For a fascinating account of these debates, see Jean-Pierre Dupuy, *The Mechanization of the Mind: On the Origins of Cognitive Science*, trans. M. B. DeBevoise (Princeton: Princeton

24 Introduction—Logistical Media Theory

University Press, 2000). See also Claus Pias, ed., *Cybernetics—Kybernetik: The Macy Conferences, 1946–1953, Volume 1: Transactions* (Zürich-Berlin: Diaphenes, 2003). A more informal and highly personalized account of the Macy Conferences on cybernetics can be found in Mary Catherine Bateson, *Our Own Metaphor: A Personal Account of a Conference on the Effects of Conscious Purpose on Human Adaptation* (Washington and London: Smithsonian Institution Press, 1972).

57. Holmes, "Guattari's Schizoanalytic Cartographies; or, the Pathic Core at the Heart of Cybernetics." For the back-end of these ideas, see the following threads provoked by initial essays by Holmes on the Nettime mailing list: "Cybernetics and the Control Society," September 14, 2007; "Cybernetics and the Internet," October 17, 2008 and March 2009, http://www.nettime.org. See also Brian Holmes, "Future Map," *Continental Drift*, September 9, 2007, http://brianholmes.wordpress.com/2007/09/09/future-map.

58. Holmes, "Guattari's Schizoanalytic Cartographies; or, the Pathic Core at the Heart of Cybernetics."

59. Again, see Brian Holmes's text on Adam Curtis's documentary *The Century of the Self* (2002) and Edward Bernays, "Neolib Goes Neocon: Adam Curtis; or, Cultural Critique in the 21st Century," June 27, 2007, http://brianholmes.wordpress.com/2007/06/25/neolib-goes-neocon.

60. Edward L. Bernays, *Propaganda* (London: Routledge, 1928), 18.

61. Ibid.

62. Brian Holmes, "Cybernetics and the Internet," posting to Nettime mailing list, October 16, 2008, http://www.nettime.org.

63. Michel Foucault, *The Birth of Biopolitics: Lectures at the Collège de France, 1978–1979*, Michel Senellart, ed., trans. Graham Burchell (Basingstoke: Palgrave Macmillan, 2008), 144, 131, 176.

64. Ibid., 192–93.

65. Ibid., 221–23.

66. Henry H. Willis and David S. Ortiz, *Evaluating the Security of the Global Containerized Supply Chain* (Santa Monica, CA: RAND Corporation, 2004), http://www.rand.org/pubs/technical_reports/2004/RAND_TR214.pdf.

67. For an extended analysis of supply chain security, see Cowen, *The Deadly Life of Logistics*, 76–90.

68. Melinda Cooper, *Life as Surplus: Biotechnology and Capitalism in the Neoliberal Era* (Seattle: University of Washington Press, 2008), 74–100.

69. Ibid., 83.

70. Ibid.

71. Willis and Ortiz, *Evaluating the Security of the Global Containerized Supply Chain*, 2. For critiques of resilience as a discourse, see Jeremy Walker and Melinda Cooper, "Genealogies of Resilience: From Systems Ecology to the Political Economy of Crisis Adaptation," *Security Dialogue* 42, no. 2 (2011): 143–60; and Danny MacKinnon and Kate Driscoll Derickson, "From Resilience to Resourcefulness: A Critique of Resilience Policy and Activism," *Progress in Human Geography* 37, no. 2 (2012): 253–70.

72. Cf. chapter 2, note 60.

73. Willis and Ortiz, *Evaluating the Security of the Global Containerized Supply Chain*, xiii.

74. Ibid., 21–3.

75. See http://www.erpsoftware-news.com/open_source_erp/. On the concept of "free labor," see Tiziana Terranova, "Free Labor: Producing Culture for the Digital Economy," *Social Text* 18, no. 2 (2000): 33–58.

76. See http://www.marinetraffic.com.
77. See Willis and Ortiz, *Evaluating the Security of the Global Containerized Supply Chain*. See also Neilson and Rossiter, "Still Waiting, Still Moving."
78. Michel Foucault, *Society Must Be Defended: Lectures at the Collège de France, 1975–76*, trans. David Macey (London: Allen Lane, 2003), 245.
79. For an examination of the biopolitics of experience, see Jon Solomon, "The Experience of Culture: Eurocentric Limits and Openings in Foucault," *Transeuropeénnes: Review Internationale de Pensée Critique*, November, 2009, http://www.transeuropeennes.eu/en/articles/108/The_Experience_of_Culture_Eurocentric_Limits_and_Openings_in_Foucault.
80. Foucault, *Society Must Be Defended*, 245.
81. See Willis and Ortiz, *Evaluating the Security of the Global Containerized Supply Chain*.
82. Saskia Sassen, *The Global City* (Princeton: Princeton University Press, 1991). See also Brett Neilson and Ned Rossiter, "The Logistical City," *Transit Labour: Circuits, Regions, Borders* 3 (August, 2011): 2–5, http://transitlabour.asia/documentation/.
83. Zygmunt Bauman, *Liquid Modernity* (Cambridge: Polity, 2000).

2
LOGISTICAL WORLDS

The unruly worker, the software glitch, willful acts of laziness, sabotage and refusal, traffic gridlock, inventory blowouts, customs zealots, flash strikes, protocological conflicts and proliferating standards. Disruption generates logistical nightmares for the smooth-world operations of "supply-chain capitalism."[1] Contingency prompts control to reroute distribution channels and outsource labor to more business-friendly client-states and corporations. Enterprise resource planning (ERP) software parameters are adjusted to calibrate key performance indicators (KPIs) in ways that demonstrate enhanced productivity and economic efficiencies. Peasants revolt across IT special economic zones in West Bengal and the infrastructural transformation of farming land comes to a grinding halt. Global architectural firms export Chinese visions of high-speed economies coupled with new-world urban integration and social utopias. Shipping-container yards and warehouses coordinate the movement of people and things via technologies of remote control. Wharf-side loading and unloading of cargo become increasingly automated with labor displaced by algorithmic tracking devices and human oversight of machine operations.

These are possible scenarios of *Logistical Worlds*, a computer game that does not as yet exist. Set against operational fantasies of real-time labor management and the governance of things within logistical industries, this chapter registers code as a site of struggle for labor and life. Located somewhere between *SimCity* and the *Grand Theft Auto* series, *Logistical Worlds* envisages a multiuser game environment within which players collectively stage wildcat strikes at port facilities, misplace consignments in container yards, or write code for patches that mess with models of supply-chain integration by rerouting stock to warehouses already burdened with excess inventory. Whether it is a technical process or operative principle, *Logistical Worlds* explores code as a system of the future-present in which living labor must reckon with logistical regimes of governance and control.

Parameters of Play

If, as Heidegger proposed, cybernetics now takes the place of philosophy, then we might inquire into how the body and brain are enmeshed into circuits of data mediated by infrastructures of communication.[2] Concept production becomes integrated with algorithmic architectures and politics is played out, in part, on the horizon of parameters, protocols, and standards. The "management cybernetics" of Stafford Beer in the late 1950s is today manifest in logistical systems of coordination, communication, and control.[3] A "numerical imaginary" is required for the workings of the brain to be tied to infrastructures of mediation.[4] The "foundational indeterminacies of counting" provide technocratic reason with a parametric logic that makes both matter and experience calculable entities. Metrics function as the new mediators of our machinic relation to material phenomena and the modulation of desire. Despite the determining architecture of algorithmic capitalism, there is, as Reinhold Martin notes, also a variational scope to numbers grafted to matter. Numbers don't always stick. In the case of the logistical fantasy of seamless interoperability across global supply chains, numerous conflicts emerge at the level of protocols, sabotage, labor disputes, excess inventory, and so forth.

Such variables comprise the properties special to what Keller Easterling defines as the *disposition*—a "tendency," "capacity," or "propensity"—of infrastructure space.[5] The mathematical grammar that underlies algorithmic architectures, in other words, should not be seen as totalizing in force, even if it does hold a determining capacity to shape outcomes, including how experience is modulated and made productive within digital economies. Rather than assuming at the outset that forms of agency that cannot be folded into a politics of representation lie beyond the scope of the political, part of the question of a data politics is how we engage the disposition of these new technical systems in ways that acknowledge the actuality of machinic agency.

When we hear or speak of social catastrophes, ecological catastrophes, institutional catastrophes, or even the private catastrophes of our own lives, we have some idea of what the catastrophe is. But what is an algorithmic catastrophe? As Yuk Hui deduces, "All catastrophes are algorithmic, even the natural ones, when we consider the universe to be governed by regular and automated laws of motion and principles of emergence."[6] As much as the Flash Crash of 2010 was attributed to an algorithmic catastrophe, the verdict is still undecided among the world's best programmers. How, then, to manifest or invent the accident within algorithmic regimes in ways that alter the contours of control? Can games do this in a preparatory way by foregrounding the politics of parameters?

Any substantial intervention into the power of algorithmic capitalism requires disruption across multiple scales, institutional settings, and economic sectors. Within an algorithmic milieu, it is not clear how a project such as J. K. Gibson-Graham's "post-capitalist politics" is going to cut it, no matter how many micro-alternative economies it spawns.[7] Jodi Dean is particularly scathing in her critique of Gibson-Graham's vision of post-capitalism, which she considers a disavowal of communism and typical of a leftist eschewal of militant anticapitalism.[8] Although perhaps there is something in Massumi's call for an affective politics harnessed to the inductive capacity of bodies attuned to the constitution of a situation.[9] The intersection of such a micro-politics with macro-structures may signal a collective contagion of the event—think, for example, of the effect of distributed social panic in the stock market. Prices come tumbling, banks foreclose, states are crippled.

One chief algorithmic catastrophe looming on the horizon of the future-present consists of the quantified self movement. The catastrophic dimension to this movement cannot be attributed to the algorithm alone, as if that predetermines the constitution of subjectivity. Rather, the descent into collective submission to the interpenetration of architectures of control with biotechnical pulsations is, of course, as much social as computational. There is a powerful social desire predicated on the vanity of the self that willingly subjects the body to processes of datafication. But there are also pernicious institutional and industrial forces at work. It is not a leap of imagination to manifest a world in which insurance agencies hit you with higher premiums because you refuse to wear your life-tracking device that provides a real-time risk assessment of your body as it moves about its daily routines. The quantified self movement indexes the computational measure of performance as it bears upon labor regimes and the experience of daily life.

The logic of gameplay proceeds through the exploration and testing of functional rules. In this respect, one might concur with McKenzie Wark that a correspondence exists between how we experience daily life and the "fully realized neo-liberal utopia" of certain games (think the *Sims* or the *Grand Theft Auto* series).[10] Can cracks in the system still be made politically operational? Most certainly. The world is still far from being formatted in ways that conform to the technics of gameworlds. The neoliberal utopia described by Wark and others finds its correlate within geocultural worlds specific to advanced economies that incorporate the debris of other times, socialities, classes, economies, and so forth. In such spaces, it may make some sense for activists, programmers, designers, and theorists to invent new parametric horizons. This would entail an alteration of not just the game, but also the borders of thought and expression. There is no question that the world of work and stuff of life are infinitely more complex, nuanced, and varied than universes of play within video games. Nonetheless, the phenomenon of the quantified self and the gamification of life through apps and dashboards would seem to support such a claim. The commercialization of data generated through such devices, and from the technification of the body, also registers the financialization of biopower.

The tension between the capacity of computational systems to govern in non-representational ways through the rule of code and the various contingencies special to living labor will serve as an analytical architecture in an ongoing study of global supply chains. Initiated by the Transit Labour project, our intention was for *Logistical Worlds* to help draw out aspects of these tensions within the parameters of a video game. The term "parameter" is invoked in two key ways in this chapter and throughout this book. First, as a border concept that delimits the range of activity and action. And second, I draw on the field of computer science in which a parameter is understood as a function, command, or "formal argument" that establishes the reference for an "actual argument," which then executes the command of the parameter.[11] A change in parameters thus alters the operation of a program, model, or simulation. In the case of *Logistical Worlds*, the play of the game is specific to the values that define the functions of parameters. This suggests that gameplay is determined by parametric rules, and here one always wants to keep in mind that, within game space, rules are accompanied and perhaps preconditioned by the possibility of breaking and remaking the rules through the aid of cheat codes and "mods" (game modifications).[12] The ability to cheat the system is central to the gameplay of *Logistical Worlds*. Registered through the contingency of the event as it arises through the disruptive force or interpenetration of the constitutive outside, the capacity to break the rules serves to test the stability of global supply chains and logistical operations as they rub against labor practices.

Logistical Worlds hopes to be a game that both disseminates a critical analysis of supply chain capitalism and logistical labor, while also shaping the practices and methods of collective forms of research.[13] How, for instance, might digital video games be understood and analyzed for the ways in which they inform the remodeling of urban spaces and labor conditions? Such a question can also tell us something about how urban spaces are regulated within the topological space of the game. The game and its parameters of play, in other words, become the empirical ground upon which methods are designed, concepts are produced, and analysis emerges.[14] One key reason for this has to do with the way in which the Internet and rise of big data aggregation, predictive analysis, and social network mediation produce algorithmically determined coordinates that modulate our desire and quantify our experience of the world.[15] As distilled in an essay by Fenwick McKelvey, Matthew Tiessen, and Luke Simcoe, such operations are underscored by a political economy of data: "The collective activity of humanity provides the data that informs the decision making processes of algorithmic systems such as high-frequency trading and aggregated news services that, in turn, are owned by those who wield global power and control: banks, corporations, governments."[16]

Within the play of *Logistical Worlds*, part of our plan is to design counterstrategies along the lines of what Brian Holmes identifies as "Critical communities of deviant subjectivity, forming at the site of the eviscerated private/public divide, [which] are not subcultural frivolities but attempts to reinvent the very basis of the political."[17] As Holmes then notes, "What's at stake is the elaboration of different functional rules for our collective games, which in today's society cannot be put into effect without the language of technology." While Holmes is speaking of games here in the more collective social sense of a hack or political intervention, there is nonetheless something to be taken from this idea of using video games as a site for testing an ensemble of functional rules or parameters specific to the

30 Logistical Worlds

operation of global logistics industries and their supply chains. The development of a serious video game such as *Logistical Worlds* might then work as a mediating device through which to think the politics of logistical systems that increasingly govern labor and life, finance and things.

Falling within the genre of serious games (variously known as educational, critical, tactical, and activist games), *Logistical Worlds* will be an exercise in modeling a range of logistical settings such as ports, warehouses, shipping, and transport routes in order to draw attention to complex material relations between logistics, computing, and labor. The genre of serious or activist games within digital formats has a short but venerable history. Examples like *Escape from Woomera* (2002) and Molleindustria's various tactical games come most immediately to mind. With their interest in social and political critique of government policy on migrant detention, the experience and condition of precarious labor, electronic waste, media concentration, and globalized fast-food production and consumption chains, such games can broadly be grouped within the culture of the counter-globalization movement as it was emerging at the time. Serious games such as *Third World Farmer* (2005/2006), *Darfur Is Dying* (2006), and *Climate Challenge* (2007) hold a less radical agenda, and instead aim to educate players about civil society concerns and ecological challenges.

In *Games of Empire: Global Capitalism and Video Games*, Nick Dyer-Witheford and Greig de Peuter argue that "Games not only cultivate the imagination of alternative social possibilities; they also present practical tools that may be useful for its actualization."[18] They go on to observe:

> Tactical games, polity simulators, and also the self-organized worlds of MMOs [massively multiplayer online games] all emerge as part of a wider autoludic culture in which the ability to code, change, and copy digital culture is diffusing.[19]

These, in a sense, are obvious points of reference for anyone interested in designing critical, activist games. Perhaps less apparent is the resonance with the animated equivalent of "grey literature": the myriad corporate training videos that simulate picking and packing in warehouses, the automation of port operations, and the transit of rail and trucks across urban settings—all of which contribute to the production of a subject special to logistics: namely the training of the organization man, a persona first encapsulated in William H. Whyte's best-selling book published in 1956.[20] With the advent of transnational capitalism and the informatization of organizational practices, particularly since the 1990s, logistics marks a shift away from the bureaucratization of society reproduced through the institutional settings of the firm or government agency. This did not result in the passing of the organization man so much as his transformation into multiethnic and gendered subjects whose once secure and now perpetually uncertain employment is beholden to the interpenetrative power of code. Nor could we say that society has become any less bureaucratic. Our everyday activities are monitored and data-mined like never before, though in ways more abstracted and obscure than previously. One thing that particularly stands out in the logistical paradigm is the ways in which labor and workers' knowledge is increasingly transferred to the algorithmic agency of machines and code.

The algorithmic action of logistical optimization translates contingency as that which is contained, rerouted, absorbed, adding value. For Matthew Fuller and Andrew Goffey, "there is a sense that a decision that is mediated through a series of obviously disinterested data-crunching algorithms has greater trustworthiness than decisions mediated through the representations of greedy, lazy, whining employees."[21] The "stupidity" that Fuller and Goffey attribute to the "concrete closure" invested upon the empirical verisimilitude of data might be offset to some extent by the irrationality of experience, if only experience was not so often absorbed into metrics that quantify our encounters with the cloud. The question of decision requires a mediation of relation that separates the refusal of optimization (contingency) from the incorporation of desire (logistical control). At stake is the "authority to act" and with it the question of action itself.[22] How game design brings user experience and acts of play together with programming data on labor productivity that becomes corruptible upon extraction by commercial machines could function as a technique of dissimulation in the development of *Logistical Worlds*. Acts of play become acts of deception.

Logistical Knowledge

Since the Cold War game theory and systems analysis have been at the core of the managerial science of logistics. Computational models of conflict scenarios within procurement networks and supply chains have played a key role in the technocratic management of people and things. Patrick Crogan's *Gameplay Mode: War, Simulation and Technoculture* situates game development firmly within the military-industrial complex.[23] From World War II, the military apparatus organized itself around models of preemption in the form of logistical simulation games that strive to "foreclose the future" in "the war on contingency."[24] The problematic of contingency—or the "incalculability of tactical space"—has origins in the writings of Prussian soldier and military theorist Carl von Clausewitz,[25] while the technocratic or administrative aspects of military operations dates back to the War of the Spanish Succession (1701–14), where Friedrich Wilhelm I realized the need for "officials with cameralistic skills" in order to mobilize supplies and fresh troops for standing armies. Officers equipped with such skills "opened up the possibility . . . to switch from a purely military career to an administrative one,"[26] thus instantiating the conjunction of theaters of war with the management of civilian life.[27] War games mirrored this intersection between the military and society.

In his study of logistical catastrophes, Manuel DeLanda is preoccupied with logistics as a war machine. According to DeLanda, the military sought a

32 Logistical Worlds

rationalization of labor, "beginning in early nineteenth-century armories and culminating a century later in the time-and-motion studies and scientific management theories of Frederick Taylor, the product of his experiences in U.S. arsenals."[28] DeLanda notes that, "To lessen its dependence on manpower, the military increasingly effected a transference of knowledge from the worker's body to the hardware of machines and to the software of management practices."[29] Within the context of capitalist globalization, however, the "command structure" of logistics is not tied to theaters of war or the military-industrial complex in any exclusive manner. Nonetheless DeLanda's observation here remains relevant. The transfer of knowledge from labor to machines and code results in workers within the logistical industries having a segmented, compartmentalized, and often partial understanding of how supply chains are composed and the effects disruption or blockages in one part of the distribution system may have elsewhere. A comprehension of how supply chains operate may enable forms of political organization and cross-sectoral modes of workers' solidarity.

Already available social media networking software such as Facebook or Twitter might be one option that facilitates a political knowledge on the part of workers of integrated supply chains. But these software systems are designed primarily for chatting, even if we have seen them put to use in the mobilization of political populations, as was the case with the Arab Spring and the Occupy movement. The more informal sectors of logistics industries rely on such software to manage their own supply chain operations. But they face a protocological barrier when informal supply chains meet the computational architecture of the world's dominant logistical software developers: SAP, Oracle, Infor, MS Dynamics AX, Descartes Systems Group, to name some of the leading players. Either way, the capacity to remodel parameters of proprietary logistics software packages is out of the question and existing social media software will lock workers into silos of Friends and Groups. Both are insufficient for workers seeking a comprehensive overview of logistical operations.

The materiality of communication technology and transport infrastructure provide key sites from which to begin assembling a political knowledge of logistics organized in part through algorithmic architectures. Such an analytical focus involves studying not just the infrastructure of logistics and the ways in which subjectivity is produced. It also includes a study of how logistics organizes labor as an abstraction within the parameters of software. Modeling these spaces and operations within the genre of a serious video game provides an experimental sandbox to articulate conditions that otherwise manifest as disconnected, discrete sectors within global supply chains.

The logistical university is another sector increasingly enmeshed in the smooth-world fantasy of just-in-time services and education commodities delivered within informatized institutional settings and across the world's network of providers and consumers. The penultimate technocratic fantasy within the logistical university is to manage labor away from annual performance reviews, which everyone knows full well are a gestural exercise amounting to vague affirmation of the managerial apparatus and its primary persona: the knowledge manager.[30] The logistical technocrat extends the meddling reign of the knowledge manager (whose earlier incarnation was the organization man), seeking to measure the productivity of labor through software that provides ongoing feedback of activity, review, and command within real-time systems of measurement.[31]

In a column published in the *London Review of Books*, Will Self reminisced about the "large resident population of evil archetypes" that inhabited many of the video games he played in his youth.[32] In the case of *Logistical Worlds*, that character is filled less by humans and more by communication machines, organizational systems, and algorithmic processes related to techniques of governance. The logistical technocrat is not the epicenter of control so much as its earnest functionary. Frequently fragile and inept, the logistical technocrat requires their own real-time measures of reassurance and appraisal. The primary trade of the logistical university becomes organized less around the delivery of educational services and products, and more aligned with the economy of big data. Here, we begin to see a continuum across the aggregation of data and its commercial exchange mastered by social media network corporations such as Facebook, the back-end maintenance of client's data operations by enterprise resource planning software providers such as Germany's world-leading company SAP, the United States' National Security Agency and its PRISM data surveillance program, and the use of customer relationship management (CRM) software by universities keen to supplement their student fee-driven economies with the prospect of data goldmines open for transaction with undisclosed third party clients. Welcome to the economy of "lifestream logistics." For Soenke Zehle, lifestream logistics "include the datascapes generated by our modes of communicative relation and the network architectures that sustain them."[33] As biolinguistic and affective technologies of capture, lifestream logistics subsume living labor within patent-protected clouds of control.

Game as Method

The development of a video game can also shape the design of research methods for a project interested in the study of transnational circuits of labor, life, and infrastructure special to logistics and supply chain capitalism. Far from enthralled by the prospect of the lone theorist strapped to their keyboard, nor enticed by the anthropologist spending extended time in the field, we found ourselves having to take seriously the problem of method within university settings that no longer support the possibility for either of these intellectual personas, even if they were desirable. Certainly within the accelerated technocratic culture that defines much of the higher education sector, the time of thought is secondary to the generation of publications and external funding whose registration as "research quantum" in annual performance databases and spreadsheets determine the calculation of research workloads. With highly compressed economies of academic production there is a certain default rationale of institutional survival that attends the decision to undertake collective forms of research. This is especially the case for large-scale transnational projects in which partial knowledge defines for many the situation of encounter.

Accompanying this social dimension to collective modes of knowledge production is a media arrangement that integrates our world of experience with technologies of calculation.[34] Just as cinema organized perception through the logic of genre coupled with the technics of light and sound, so the social ubiquity of the game interface informs the production of knowledge through the protocols of play. This is not to go down the formalist path of media continuity proposed by Lev Manovich, but rather to foreground how the properties and qualities special to media of communication prompt singular universes of possibility. McKelvey, Tiessen, and Simcoe frame media of simulation as technologies of calculation:

> The Internet is no longer a space primarily of communication, but of simulation. By simulation, we do not mean a reproduction of reality "as it is out there," but rather a sort of reality-in-parallel, one that generates its own sets of tangible quanta and its own "realities"-to-be-calculated.[35]

When gameplay crosses with research practices in global logistics industries, the serious game *Phone Story* developed by Italian tech-critique outfit Molleindustria is a standout example of how games can register a critique of the dark life of technology consumption and production. Designed for smart phone devices, *Phone Story* is set across four stages of the manufacturing and supply chain process, making "the player symbolically complicit in coltan extraction in Congo, outsourced labor in China, e-waste in Pakistan and gadget consumerism in the West."[36] With its satirical depiction of Chinese factory workers leaping to their death, it was no surprise that the tactical media stunt of *Phone Story* was removed within hours of its release on Apple's App Store. Yet despite the efforts of *Phone Story* to connect the play of users to issues of ecological destruction and human rights abuse associated with smart phone supply chains, Sy Taffel notes that the capacity for action in ways that produce any substantive change remains highly circumscribed: "The user may still be caught within the trap of representation."[37]

For *Logistical Worlds*, the scene of global supply chains, logistical processes, software control, and labor conditions comprise the central elements around which play unfolds. How this ensemble of relations will serve as the backdrop for play more specifically is a narrative yet to be decided. More significant is the design of the game in terms of the relation between the game as a conceit for the collection of data on labor conditions and logistical operations in order to enhance users' gameplay, and the game as interface for target audiences and players from corporate, union, and activist sectors.[38] Needless to say, it is possible to reflect on how the game as a medium of expression might feed into the method of researching aspects of supply chain capitalism. New York media theorist Alexander Galloway goes so far as to say we are now in a period of "ludic capitalism"—an economy of play—that fuses the poetry of romanticism with the design of cybernetic systems theory as a "juridico-geometric sublime" whose online interfaces extract value from our labor of play.[39] Galloway's allegory of protocological control manifest in computer interfaces is suggestive of how the aesthetic events of multilayered data can "reveal something about the medium and about contemporary life."[40] Just when you might have thought that theory these days was all about nonrepresentational relations and post-human agency, we see here a return to the problem of representation and hermeneutics, where code is the new grammar awaiting interpretation.

Without a doubt there is importance in the critical capacity to read the correspondence between the programmer's language of code and its shaping effects on social, cultural, and economic life—or what Galloway, in dialogue with Wendy Hui Kyong Chun, refers to as functionality embedded in software and ideology.[41] But in studying global logistical industries, much of the software used to manage supply chains and the mobility of people and things is beyond the reach of the critical theorist. As mentioned earlier and discussed further in chapter 3, the software developed by companies such as SAP and Oracle are under proprietary control and are highly expensive. Even with a knowledge of programming, it is far from straightforward to get a look under the hood. Moreover, the data generated on logistical operations related to supply chain management, procurement, warehousing, and labor productivity from this software is commercially valuable information and therefore far from easy to incorporate into the parameters of a game. In the absence of code as a discernible thing, the materiality of transport and communications infrastructure found in the logistical city offers some contours of reference to design how algorithmic architectures govern much of labor and life.

Gaming the Logistical City

In many respects the logistical industries that drive supply chain capitalism already present themselves as a game to the millions who work in transport, communications, warehousing, procurement, and ports—all of which comprise the key infrastructural sites of the logistical city. The logistical city is a city of peripheries. These peripheries are occupied by intermodal transport terminals, warehouses, IT infrastructure, container parks, and shipping ports. Such logistical facilities do not stand isolated, of course, but are interspersed with suburbs, green belts, roads, railways, water systems, and barren land. The interconnection of peripheries on a transnational scale comprises a special kind of globality, one in which the complex network of distribution systems—roads, rail, shipping, aviation—makes concrete the otherwise mysterious abstractions of capitalist operations. Yet for all this materiality, the logistical city goes largely unnoticed in the metropolitan imaginary precisely because the margins of cities tend to be overlooked and made invisible by more spectacular elements—magisterial feats of architecture, harbor views, cultural

36 Logistical Worlds

festivals, and so forth. We long ago resigned ourselves to not needing to know how things work or where things come from. And we are in no rush for a reminder. The logistical city ticks along in the background as we get on with our busy daily lives.

While the logistical city traverses the outskirts of urban spaces, it is not suburban *per se* since it is nestled between and beyond residential zones. The logistical city is distinct from the global city, which is characterized by financial services located in CBDs and cosmopolitan populations whose ethnic peculiarities are integrated more or less seamlessly into the flow of global economies. The logistical city also differs from the industrial city, which is defined by class stratifications across urban spaces and an economy based on the manufacturing of goods. Like the global city, the logistical city is a city of services, but these services are driven by computational systems oriented around managing the mobility of things produced by the industrial city. Servicing the services of the global city, the logistical city is one whose borders are porous and elastic. Scale is calibrated according to real-time systems of measure and performance special to just-in-time regimes of labor productivity and commodity assemblages. Composed with infrastructure that is frequently coded and managed by computational systems, the logistical city can be understood as something akin to the contemporary urban settings Rob Kitchin and Martin Dodge call "code/space" in which "software and the spatiality of everyday life become mutually constituted."[42] The digital coding of space—or the making soft of infrastructure—has impacts on how labor is managed and how subjectivities are produced when the time of life and action of bodies is increasingly overseen and governed by computational systems of control and regulation.

Thirty years ago the L.A. School of planners, geographers, sociologists, and historians identified many of the features of the logistical city just described, especially "the emergence of information-age 'edge cities,' and the hypermobility of international capital and labor flows," as recounted by Steven Erie in his book *Globalizing L.A.: Trade, Infrastructure and Regional Development.*[43] The logistical city nevertheless stands out as a new urban form for the ways in which it stitches together diverse cities and regions across the global North and South, continuously reconfiguring connections according to just-in-time demands of supply chains and contingencies that disrupt their smooth operation. Whenever a new diagram of relations is set into play, a new logistical world is created in which difference must either be displaced or absorbed. This spatiotemporal elasticity and capacity to adapt to changing conditions marks the logistical city as particularly distinct from other urban forms. Always searching for enhanced efficiencies across its circuits of distribution, the logistical city is an urban laboratory ripe in experimentation.

The logistical city can also be understood in terms of what architect Reinhold Martin calls an "organizational complex," which consists of technocratic and aesthetic systems designed to modulate the world as "an organized, informatic pattern" in flexible ways.[44] Not constrained by sovereign rule or national borders, the logistical city is a recombinatory form that attempts to standardize capital accumulation from the micro level of algorithmic apparatuses to the macro level of global infrastructures. Standards are crucial to the universal logic of interoperability across software platforms and infrastructural components. Without them, cargo containers could not transfer with such ease from ship to truck, software operating systems could not exchange data across platforms, and circuit boards could not be manufactured to fit and function in multiple computational devices.

Whoever sets the standard rules the world. Yet standards change and develop over time. New standards are always being established, though only some percolate to the top and become universally adopted. This is where innovation meets political economy. The desire for a trans-scalar smooth world, however, is accompanied by any number of contingencies: labor strikes, software glitches, inventory blowouts and traffic gridlock, to mention just a few that come to mind. In principle, the topological parameter of "fault tolerance" incorporates such disruptions to make anew the seamlessness of logistical worlds. But there can be no denying that contingency is the nightmare of logistics.

Logistical nightmares can be found across the cities investigated in the Transit Labour project, which examined how circuits of labor are reshaping the contours of regions while coming up against, testing, and transforming a multiplicity of borders. Rajarhat New Town is a development under way since the late 1990s on the northeast fringes of Kolkata, situated between the airport and on the edge of Sector V, an IT park developed in the 1970s as an industrial extension of Kolkata's Salt Lake township. The government legislation that authorized both of these developments is complex and fraught with political conflicts and social tensions. Chief among these was the West Bengal Housing Infrastructure Development Corporation's (HIDCO) invocation of a colonial administrative remnant, the Land Acquisition Act of 1894. When combined with a China-inspired neoliberal legislation, the Special Economic Zone (SEZ) Act of 2005, HIDCO was able to legally conjure a zoning technology for Rajarhat designed to attract foreign capital to finance the transformation of fertile agricultural land and fisheries into nonagricultural use. The economic and social displacement of peasant populations numbering in their tens of thousands recalls for Ranabir Samaddar and his colleagues at the Calcutta Research Group the Marxian critique of "primitive accumulation,"[45] or what David Harvey prefers instead to term "accumulation by dispossession."[46] In the case of Rajarhat, the expropriation of land and the partial remobilization of peasant labor forced by HIDCO into "service villages" are the conditions of possibility for the logistical city and its information economy (Figure 2.1).

Following an initial surge, which saw the installment of fiber-optic cable and a skeletal road system, a number of international and national IT firms opened for business in Rajarhat, including Wipro, Accenture, Unitech, IBM, and Tata Consultancy Services. Graduates of computing and IT programs working in these firms

FIGURE 2.1 Rajarhat "New Town," Kolkata. Photograph by Ned Rossiter, 2011.

are largely undertaking beta testing of new software or business process outsourcing (BPO) work, doing basic data entry and accounting tasks for financial, medical, and insurance companies based in Europe and North America. Indeed, the work of BPO has become a staple economy across much of the IT sector in India. Servicing the needs of data entry in the medical, insurance, logistical, and finance sectors for both large multinational companies and small and medium enterprises (SMEs), BPO work is secure as long as wages remain suppressed. Like the circuit board that never tires, BPO work and its affective correlate found in call centers is 24/7. Both offer a form of "sensory impoverishment" that dulls perception and dissipates any reserves of energy that might be harnessed into forms of labor organizing.[47]

With the rise of "smart cities" one finds an increasing feedback operation in which "all that is solid" modulates forms of algorithmic governance and vice-versa. Adaptation and transformation are a mutually constitutive process contained, retrieved, and acted upon within the parameters of the database that is now oriented toward an architecture of service delivery. It is worth noting that a logistical city like Rajarhat registers an uneven geography of information that goes one step beyond the international division of labor running along the global North and South axes. Most of the IT-related work in Rajarhat, as well as Sector V, is a secondary form of outsourcing internal to the nation state. Parent firms based in Mumbai, Chennai, Bangalore, and Hyderabad undertake the more interesting R&D and management-related work, while IT workers with similar qualifications are lumped with menial informatic tasks.

With India's elevation in these sorts of high-skill sectors of the information economy, it is hard not to assume a substantial loss of similar jobs in the global North accompanying forms of outsourcing internal to the space of the nation within India. In Australia in recent years, there has been quite extensive reporting about how the aviation and finance industries are also planning to outsource data-entry and general service-related work. Whether it is the global or national scale, the key driver behind these decisions is, of course, the lower cost of labor coupled with cheaper land leases for IT service firms located on the peripheries. And this is where logistical cities such as Rajarhat find their rationale for existence.

Since 2008, however, the rate of development in Rajarhat has slowed considerably due to the effects of the global financial crisis. Partially built apartment towers stand isolated against a backdrop of now arid land dotted with surveyors' pegs and the occasional grazing cattle. Many of the complete residential complexes remain empty as investment owners are located in other Indian cities or live overseas. A number of IT firms are operating, but their workers are often commuting from elsewhere in Kolkata, as do many of the owners of the makeshift teahouses and eateries servicing the IT workers during their breaks. As Ishita Dey's research has made clear, some of the women find employment as domestic labor, but for most of the men security and construction work is considered semiskilled and usually contracted out to migrant workers residing elsewhere in India.[48] Following some initial work filling in the wetlands, this only leaves low-skill construction jobs and teahouses as sources of income for men. No wonder, then, that Rajarhat New Town is the scene of regular acts of infrastructural sabotage, social unrest, and political conflict. Not only is the logistical city distant from metropolitan imaginaries, it suffers the intrusion of materiality in ways that unsettle the abstraction of information.

The logistical city is also at the cutting edge of labor reform. Technologies of automation are transforming shipping ports across Australia and elsewhere in the world, shifting the work of wharfies from the dockside to the screen where the oversight of robotic operations is duplicated by human labor clicking through the interface of software applications. Whether machine or flesh, performance indicators are finely calibrated against time and volume. The logistical city does away with the biological and social rhythms of urban life so beloved by Henri Lefebvre,[49] and instead operates by the cold sword of code that measures productivity and worth in real-time. The logistical city is caught between expediency and contingency. The machine dream of absolute efficiency runs counter to the unruliness of labor and life. The elasticity of logistical time and space must nevertheless contend with the materialities of society and place, particles, and power. Even if the logistical city could overcome the protocological asymmetries across software platforms that prevent cross-sector and global interoperability, it could never entirely eradicate the constituent power of refusal. The logistical city is cold, and without employment. The work has been done, elsewhere, sometimes hundreds if not thousands of kilometers away.

40 Logistical Worlds

Logistical Time, or, Calculations of Performance

Logistics robs living labor of time. At the level of labor management, logistics registers the calculation of time against the performance of tasks and movement of things. This is where Marcel Mauss's techniques of the body and related early twentieth-century studies in body-motion and their technologies of capture (principally the chronophotography of Etienne-Jules Marey) provide the preconditions for labor efficiencies—or what Anson Rabinach terms a "physiognomy of labour power"[50]—in industrial and, later, informational market economies. More recently, Jonathan Crary diagnoses the "injuring of sleep" by the rapacious force of capitalism.[51] The 24/7 just-in-time, flexible mode of capital accumulation critiqued by Crary is coincident with the real-time regime of logistics managed through ERP software interfaces. How does one play against the all-pervasive temporality of logistical regimes? And to recast Crary, how does the society of living labor protect and defend itself when logistical time externalizes "the individual into a site of non-stop scrutiny and regulation"?[52]

Within the space of warehouses and transport industries, the movement of workers is increasingly regulated by GPS vehicle tracking, RFID tags that profile workers within database time, and voice directed order picking technologies "that manage the passage and pace of workers through the workplace with the aim of maximising efficiencies."[53] The automated coordination and control of workers results in higher levels of productivity accompanied by increased demands and pressures upon the laboring body. Such technologies of governance correspond with the rise of what I would term "informatized sovereignty," which takes on particular hues in logistical techniques associated with transportation industries. Code is King.

Enterprise resource planning databases are standard platforms used within logistics in combination with customized software applications to manage global supply chains, organizational conditions, and labor efficiencies. Key performance indicators are software interfaces built into ERP databases to measure worker and organizational efficiencies, meeting of target quotas, financial performance, real-time status of global supply chains, and the capacity of the organization to adapt to changing circumstances. These are all quantitative indicators that register performance with a numerical value, however, and are not able to accommodate more affective factors such as a worker's feelings and level of motivation and enthusiasm. It would seem logistics software is still to address the biological spectrum special to the species-being of human life. Yet it in another sense, such qualities of labor and life are coded into the quantitative parameters of KPIs through the brute force of instrumentality or calculation: No matter how a worker might feel, quotas have to be met and global supply chains must not be adversely affected.

The coded materiality of fulfilling performance quotas and ensuring the smooth operation of supply chains subsists within its own universe of auto-affirmation. The relationship between logistics software and self-regulation by workers assumes closure in the circuit of governance. An operator working in the logistics of new and secondhand equipment transportation for a Shanghai-based U.S. automotive company put it this way: "As per our broker's management experience, every staff is trained to use their internal ERP software to reflect every movement of their work. Moreover, the data from ERP software is also used as a tool or KPI to evaluate staff's performance, thus making them work more efficiently."[54] This ready inculcation of both disciplinary practices and the logic of control within the organizational culture of the company and its workers is quite confronting. Certainly, the managerial culture of universities has more than its share of whacky acronyms that constitute a new planetary grammar coextensive with the governance of labor. And the bizarre interpellation of academics into the pseudo-corporate audit regimes predicated on performance outcomes and accountability measures presents some novel terrain for theories of subjectivity and desire.

The industry of logistics further amplifies such biopolitical technologies, where the labor control regime is programmed into the logistics chain at the level of code. A standard operation procedure (SOP) is incorporated into the KPI of workers.[55] The SOP describes the status of specific job, dividing it "into measurable control points." My informant in Shanghai provided this example: "For instance, we would set [the] SOP to our broker, which may require them to finish custom clearance of a normal shipment within 3 working days, if they fail to hit it, their KPI will be influenced and thus influence their payment."[56]

There is a sense here of how logistics software internalizes the movement of labor as the fulfillment of assigned tasks over a set period of time. This sort of labor performance measure is reproduced across many workplace settings. What makes it noteworthy here is the way in which the governance of labor is informatized in such a way that the border between undertaking a task and reporting its completion has become closed or indistinct. There is no longer a temporal delay between the execution of duties and their statistical measure. There is little scope for the worker to "fudge" their reporting of tasks some days or even months after the event, as in the case of academia and its increasing adoption of annual performance reviews, where a simple cut and paste of the previous year's forecast of anticipated outputs with a shift to the retrospective tense is usually sufficient. The Žižek factory tuned in early to the genre of labor performance indicators, with this account of lessons learnt while working at the Institute of Sociology in Ljubljana: "Every three years I write a research proposal. Then I subdivide it into three one-sentence paragraphs, which I call my yearly projects. At the end of each year I change the research proposal's future-tense verbs into the past tense and then call it my final report."[57] Any academic who hasn't been totally subsumed into the drone-like persona found in audit-land learns this technique of sanity management early in their career. But with the rise of data sovereignty, biopolitical control is immanent to the time of living labor and labor-power.[58]

To find out more about the role of software in logistics, I got in touch with two logistics workers in China—one employed by a U.S. automotive company based in Shanghai and the other studying at Shanghai Maritime University, having previously worked in container stowage at the Shanghai Port. Both placed an emphasis on the importance of efficiencies in logistics, with one noting that "Well

42 Logistical Worlds

organized and highly-efficient workers can eliminate the risk and cost of logistics activities and provide added value service to customer." This automaton-like response is embodied in software standards for logistics. The following account describes the use of ERP software to evaluate the KPIs of workers:

> Each employee is asked to mark it in the ERP system when they finish their required work. There are two advantages for it: 1) If they fail to finish the logistics activity within SOP time, they check in the ERP system to find which employee did not complete his/her time according to SOP, which help measure employee's performance. 2) Every employee could track in the ERP system to know about the current status/movement of the logistics activities. In short, ERP software visualizes the movement of logistics activities by efforts of every link in the logistics chain.[59]

If ERP software were a game interface, one counter-challenge for the worker-as-player would be to score against time-based performance measures and the visibility of movement. But as noted earlier, ERP software is a quantitative system, and as a closed cybernetic model it refuses the feedback or noise of more affective forces such as workers' attitudes, feelings, and levels of motivation that would have disruptive effects.[60] Although a more sophisticated software environment would calculate in such variables precisely because their modulating power operates in a replenishing way, such is the parasitical logic of capital and the organic *modus operandi* of life. As it stands, the metaphor of global supply chains signals a totalizing vision in which everything can be accounted for, measured, and ascribed an economic value. Yet as Sandro Mezzadra and Brett Neilson note in *Border as Method*, "the notion of the chain, though it carries a sense of ligature or bondage that should not be discounted or diminished, suggests the linkage or articulation of multiple units into a single linear system."[61]

In the case of logistics, there is an institutional, discursive, and political-economic investment in securitization and risk assessment that underscores the need for such linear systems of control. Linearity and closure are always going to be the condition of undoing for a system that rests on stasis, consistency, and control without incorporating contingency and complexity that define the "far from equilibrium" conditions of life-worlds as understood in more advanced cybernetics.[62] As we have been reminded in countless news media reports on the global financial crisis, all limits or failures of capital present new opportunities for its ongoing reproduction. The algorithmic mining of big data is just one of various horizons of acquisition for capital in its tireless movement. The extent to which standards determine the mobility of people, finance, and things can be registered, in part, through a study of global infrastructures of transport and communication. My interest in this chapter has been to ask how the design of a video game can contribute to such analytical and, perhaps occasionally, political work.

Coda

In the later part of 2014 the Logistical Worlds project finally found the right confluence of circumstances to begin the work on producing a video game. For various reasons we were not able to get this happening in Sydney. Our designer shifted into a job with a different intensity of demand, the game developer we were looking to work with had some health struggles, and we found ourselves scraping for time and feeling a bit bereft of ideas. The platform research undertaken in Athens provided the necessary crystallization of thought and urgency of deadlines. We were invited to present this game that did not exist at the Transmediale—Capture All media arts festival in Berlin early in the new year of 2015.[63] In collaboration with Ilias Mamaras and Anna Lascari, we were able to produce a demo of the video game based on the logistical operations in and around the port of Piraeus.

For centuries shipping ports have been a key marker of imperial power. This is no less the case in the age of supply chain capitalism, where standardization enables—in principle—the integration of global spaces through the infrastructure of containerization and enterprise management software. Despite the growing trend toward automation, the restless body of labor persists as a subject to govern in the interests of capital accumulation. Yet this is a body that also refuses control, that cherishes dreams and desires, and holds the capacity to extract value in unexpected ways from the margins of capital. The demo-game *Cargonauts* envisions a logistical world of infrastructure, of transport economies, of zones and concessions, of nocturnal possibilities for sabotage and revenge (Figure 2.2).[64]

FIGURE 2.2 *Cargonauts* demo game, 2014. http://cargonauts.net

44 Logistical Worlds

The imperial infrastructure of logistical apparatuses—ports, railways, warehouses, software—inspire unforeseen acts of sabotage, which gives rise to an informal economy of scrap metal work. The subject of labor escapes regimes of measure special to software operations designed to extract value through the calculation of movement on global scales. The borders of the concession within which port activity is governed begin to unravel. New subjectivities of labor and politics are produced. Territory is redefined in ways external to interstate and commercial agreements. This is how infrastructure makes worlds.

There are currently three piers at Piraeus. Pier 1 is, for the time being, operated by the Piraeus Port Authority (OLP), the existing Greek organization vested with control of the port in its entirety up until 2009 when the concession agreement was signed with Cosco Pacific, a subsidiary of Cosco Holdings whose majority shareholder is the Chinese (PRC) state-owned enterprise Cosco Group. As part of the austerity reforms agreed to by the Syriza-led government, the Greek government announced in January 2016 that Cosco was the preferred bidder in the further privatization of the port, taking out a 67 percent shareholding in OLP and giving it control of Pier 1.[65] With a 35-year lease of Piers II and III, Cosco's Piraeus Container Terminal (PCT) runs its port operations, planning, and management using CATOS, a software system developed by the Korean-based maritime logistics solution company Total Soft Bank. At Pier 1 OLP coordinates activities with NAVIS SPARCS N4, a U.S.-developed terminal operating system (TOS).[66]

In principle these two systems are interoperable and have the technical capacity to coordinate different activities across the piers. Yet the movement of transshipment containers from the PCT to OLP piers, for example, is clocked in manually. The coincidence of dockwork and paperwork reintroduces a media apparatus that asserts a regime of governance no longer accountable to the digital logic of search and calculation that define the event logs of terminal operating systems. "Paperwork syncopates the state's rhythms" (Kafka).[67] And, in the case of Piraeus, it invites minor technical errors that result in misplaced consignments and missing containers. Prone to human mistake and physical deterioration over time, there is also a certain autonomy of labor upheld by the media of paper files that nowadays appears strange, paradoxical, even quaint yet decidedly effective when set against real-time media of command and control. Perhaps more than anything paperwork recalls a form of "sovereign media" (Adilkno) beyond the attention of political theorists and seemingly disconnected from architectures of algorithmic governance.[68] For all this, the use of paper files to mediate the passage of containers between PCT and OLP piers signals a suspicion toward optimization as performed by terminal operating systems. Open to unaccountability, paper guards against digital technologies defined by the extraction of value from social relations concentrated around activities of the port.

Korea's Total Soft Bank is currently promoting its TOS as a technology suited to process mining within port settings. Using data generated through event logs that record port activity and organizational operations, process mining is a computational form of knowledge extraction designed to garner information on the timing and potential correlation of events in order to lever productivity and organizational transformation. Port infrastructure becomes animated not just by the movement of machines, but through patterns of data. Whether through the configuration of yard systems, the stacking sequence of containers, the oversight of customs procedures, or the calculation of labor efficiencies, the making of port spaces according to computational transactions instantiates the economic potential of algorithmic governance.

Our collective research in Athens, led by Nelli Kambouris and Pavlos Hatzopoulos, highlights the many ways in which territory exceeds the national or continental state, while also remaining very much a force of capital whose coordinates manifest in very particular and often localized ways. Think, for example, of the Roma families residing in the Newly Builts (dwellings without permits) situated on the hillside along the rail line connecting Piraeus to a freight and intermodal terminal currently under construction in Thriassion. Historically diasporic, the Romani people are frequently stripped of the right to property and denied the many privileges of citizenship. The scrap metal industry has availed Roma families with a line of income, though even this has come under increasing pressure as rival scrap metal collectors and Golden Dawn thugs mete out violence and threats of housing demolition in an effort to exert economic and social-political control.

The combination of European Union transport policies, austerity politics in Greece, and investment from Cosco coalesces in the construction of new Ikonion-Thriassion rail line (Figure 2.3).[69] This as yet unused piece of infrastructure traverses

FIGURE 2.3 Site for Thriassion freight center and rail line to Piraeus port. Photograph by Ned Rossiter, 2013.

46 Logistical Worlds

an area whose economy in scrap metal prizes industrial cables rich in copper. Such items in turn are eventually sold on commodity markets whose prices are shaped significantly by the strong demand for metals in China. In the economy of copper, territory is a spatial arrangement encompassing the geography of rail infrastructure, the movements of scrap metal workers, and the algorithmic architectures of commodity markets. This elasticity of space is accompanied by modulations of time whose rhythms, pulses, and vibrations are synchronized with the financialization of labor and life. The logistical worlds of Piraeus are many and varied. Their scalar dimensions stretch around the Athens basin and glide across oceanic trade routes.

Notes

1. Anna Tsing, "Supply Chains and the Human Condition," *Rethinking Marxism* 21, no. 2 (2009): 148–76.
2. Martin Heidegger, "Only a God Can Save Us," *Spiegel* (1981) cited in Andrew Pickering, *The Cybernetic Brain: Sketches of Another Future* (Chicago: Chicago University Press, 2010), 390. See also Friedrich Kittler, "Martin Heidegger, Media and the Gods of Greece: De-Severance Heralds the Approach of the Gods," in *The Truth of the Technological World: Essays on the Genealogy of Presence,* trans. Erik Butler (Stanford, CA: Stanford University Press, 2014), 290–302.
3. On "management cybernetics," see Pickering, *The Cybernetic Brain,* 9. See also Eden Medina, *Cybernetic Revolutionaries: Technology and Politics in Allende's Chile* (Cambridge, MA: MIT Press, 2011), 24–9.
4. Reinhold Martin, *Mediators: Aesthetics, Politics and the City* (Minneapolis: University of Minnesota Press, 2014), 1.
5. Keller Easterling, *Extrastatecraft: The Power of Infrastructure Space* (London and New York: Verso, 2014), 71–93.
6. Yuk Hui, "Algorithmic Catastrophe: The Revenge of Contingency," *Parrhesia* 23 (2015): 122.
7. J. K. Gibson-Graham, *A Postcapitalist Politics* (Minneapolis: University of Minnesota Press, 1996).
8. Jodi Dean, *The Communist Horizon* (London and New York: Verso, 2012), 3–5.
9. Brian Massumi, *The Power of the End of the Economy* (Durham and London: Duke University Press, 2015), 108–9.
10. Marc Garrett and Ruth Catlow, "Capture All Play: An Interview with McKenzie Wark," *Furtherfield,* January 27, 2015, http://www.furtherfield.org/features/interviews/capture-allplay-interview-mckenzie-wark.
11. See Foldoc: Free On-Line Dictionary of Computing, http://foldoc.org/. Within object-oriented design and programming, formal generic parameters may be accompanied by a class of arbitrary types: "A routine may have formal arguments, representing values which the routine's clients will provide in each call. The literature commonly uses the term parameter (formal, actual) as a synonym for argument (formal, actual). There is nothing wrong in principle with either term, but if we have both routines and genericity we need a clear convention to avoid any misunderstanding. The convention will be to use 'argument' for routines only, and 'parameter' (usually in the form 'generic parameter' for further clarification) for generic modules only." Bertrand Meyer, *Object-Oriented Software Construction,* 2nd edition (Santa Barbara: ICE Inc., 2000), 96. Thanks to Yuk Hui for his guidance here.

12. See Julian Kücklich, "Seki: Ruledness and the Logical Structure of Game Space," in Stephan Günzel, Michael Liebe, and Dieter Mersch, eds., *Logic and Structure of the Computer Game*, DIGAREC Series 4 (Potsdam: Potsdam University Press, 2010), 36–56.

13. For a statement on collective research methods that also includes a critique of social theories of digital methods, see Anja Kanngieser, Brett Neilson, and Ned Rossiter, "What Is a Research Platform? Mapping Methods, Mobilities and Subjectivities," *Media, Culture & Society* 36, no. 3 (2014): 302–18.

14. Such an understanding of topology, sociality, and knowledge production shares something with the notion of topological space and time as the conjoining of difference through the relationality of borders within spatiotemporal dynamics understood as intrinsic as distinct from extrinsic. See Celia Lury, Luciana Parisi, and Tiziana Terranova, "Introduction: The Becoming Topological of Culture," *Theory, Culture & Society* 29, nos. 4–5 (2012): 3–35. It also privileges an empiricist process of concept production, as outlined in Scott Lash's proposition of topological operations of space and time as *a posteriori* (empiricist) rather than *a priori* (rationalist). See Scott Lash, "Afterword: In Praise of the *A Posteriori* Sociology and the Empirical," *European Journal of Social Thought* 12, no. 1 (2009): 175–87. A conceptual affiliation could also be drawn between topology and mediation as developed by medium theorists such as Harold Innis who hold an interest in how the material properties of communications media and transport technologies shape time and space.

15. See Fenwick McKelvey, Matthew Tiessen, and Luke Simcoe, "We Are What We Tweet: The Problem with a Big Data World When Everything You Say Is Data," Culture Digitally: Examining Contemporary Cultural Production, June 3, 2013, http://culturedigitally. org/2013/06/we-are-what-we-tweet-the-problem-with-a-big-data-world-when-everything-you-say-is-data-mined/. Such scenarios of digitally modulated social control are reminiscent of a raft of science-fiction stories (think J.G. Ballard and Phillip K. Dick) along with the advertising and political campaign strategies devised by Edward Burneys and his team of public relations consultants, as discussed in the Introduction. See Adam Curtis's documentary, *The Century of the Self* (2002) and Brian Holmes, "Neolib Goes Neocon: Adam Curtis; or, Cultural Critique in the 21st Century," June 25, 2007, http://brianholmes.wordpress.com/2007/06/25/neolib-goes-neocon.

16. McKelvey, Tiessen and Simcoe, "We Are What We Tweet."

17. Brian Holmes, "Future Map; or, How the Cyborgs Learned to Stop Worrying and Love Surveillance," *Continental Drift*, September 9, 2007, http://brianholmes.wordpress. com/2007/09/09/future-map.

18. Nick Dyer-Witheford and Greig de Peuter, *Games of Empire: Global Capitalism and Video Games* (Minneapolis: University of Minnesota Press, 2009), 213.

19. Ibid.

20. William H. Whyte, *The Organization Man* (Philadelphia: University of Pennsylvania Press, 2002 [1956]). On the topic of grey literature, I am thinking of the work on intellectual property, postal records, and archives by Esther Milne, "The Archive: Informality and Intellectual Property," *Data, Memory, Territory*, Digital Media Research, no. 1 (2012): 25–7.

21. Matthew Fuller and Andrew Goffey, *Evil Media* (Cambridge, MA: MIT Press, 2012), 135–36.

22. For an example of such a gloomy extrapolation of contemporary trends, see Jonathan Zittrain, *The Future of the Internet—and How to Stop It* (New Haven and London: Yale University Press, 2008). Needless to say, such an explicit exaggeration of contemporary trends is not meant to obscure the many creative uses to which such infrastructures have

been put, or deny that corporate and military infrastructures can also provide public goods, but to counter the unbearable evangelism of decentralization-as-democratization. As Benkler notes: "For the first time since the industrial revolution, the most important inputs into the core economic activities of the most advanced economies are widely distributed in the population. Creativity and innovation are directly tied to the radical decentralization of the practical capability to act, on the one hand, and of the authority to act, on the other. The critical policy questions of the networked environment revolve round the battles between the decentralization of technology and the push of policy to moderate that decentralization by limiting the distribution of authority to act." Yochai Benkler, "For the First Time Since the Industrial Revolution," in Richard N. Katz, ed., *The Tower and the Cloud: Higher Education in the Age of Cloud Computing* (Boulder, CO: EduCause, 2008), 52, http://www.educause.edu/thetowerandthecloud. This footnote and the sentence to which it refers is taken from Ned Rossiter and Soenke Zehle, "Acts of Translation: Organized Networks as Algorithmic Technologies of the Common," in Trebor Scholz, ed., *Digital Labor: The Internet as Playground and Factory* (New York: Routledge, 2013), 225–39.

23. Patrick Crogan, *Gameplay Mode: War, Simulation and Technoculture* (Minneapolis: University of Minnesota Press, 2011).

24. Ibid., xxi. On the shift within the U.S. military from the state-centered doctrine of mutual deterrence to more dispersed strategies of preemption designed to anticipate biological contagion, network terrorism and insurgency, and finance capitalism, see also Melinda Cooper, "Pre-Empting Emergence: The Biological Turn in the War on Terror," *Theory, Culture & Society* 23, no. 4 (2006): 113–35.

25. Philipp von Hilgers, *War Games: A History of War on Paper*, trans. Ross Benjamin (Cambridge, MA: MIT Press, 2012), 32.

26. Ibid., 31.

27. The militarization of civil society is a thesis spread across the writings of Paul Virilio, and informs much of Crogan's argument. Arguably logistics in post–World War II settings is no longer beholden to or progeny of military operations in the first instance and obscures what Brett Neilson notes as "the sense in which logistics has actively formed a new terrain of politics on which struggles are and will continue to be played out." Think, for instance, of any number of labor struggles arising along global supply chains, border disputes around migration, food contamination, faulty commodities, and consumer backlash against child workers assembling electronic goods or working in severe conditions. Such examples all stem from logistical operations. We could even include privacy debates emerging around the use of data generated within workplace settings or out of daily social media practices. See Brett Neilson, "Five Theses on Understanding Logistics as Power," *Distinktion: Scandinavian Journal of Social Theory* 13, no. 3 (2012): 324.

28. Manuel DeLanda, *War in the Age of Intelligent Machines* (New York: Zone Books, 1991), 106.

29. Ibid.

30. For an account of the rise of this persona, see Christopher Newfield, *Unmaking the Public University: The Forty Year Assault on the Middle Class* (Cambridge, MA: Harvard University Press, 2008), 129.

31. Such is the view of some executives of a company providing cloud software to universities. See Kristi Erickson, "Continuous Feedback: It May Be a Better Approach Than the Annual Review," *TLNT: The Business of HR*, August 22, 2012, http://www.tlnt. com/2012/08/22/continuous-feedback-it-may-be-a-better-approach-than-the-annual-review/.

32. Will Self, "Diary," *London Review of Books* 34, no. 21 (November, 2012): 46.

33. Soenke Zehle, "The Autonomy of Gesture: Of Lifestream Logistics and Playful Profanations," *Distinktion: Scandinavian Journal of Social Theory* 13, no. 3 (2012): 341–54.

34. There is some parallel here with what Jussi Parikka terms "medianature." See Jussi Parikka, "New Materialism as Media Theory: Medianatures and Dirty Matter," *Communication and Critical/Cultural Studies* 9, no. 1 (2012): 95–100; "Insects and Canaries: Medianatures and the Aesthetics of the Invisible," *Angelaki: The Journal of Theoretical Humanities* 18, no. 1 (2013): 107–19 and the edited collection, *Medianatures: The Materiality of Information Technologies and Electronic Waste*, Living Books about Life (Ann Arbor: Open Humanities Press, 2011), http://www.livingbooksaboutlife.org/books/Medianatures.

35. McKelvey, Tiessen, and Simcoe, "We Are What We Tweet."

36. http://www.phonestory.org/.

37. Sy Taffel, "Scalar Entanglement in Digital Media Ecologies," *NECSUS: European Journal of Media Studies* 3 (Spring, 2013), http://www.necsus-ejms.org/scalar-entanglement-in-digital-media-ecologies/.

38. Thanks to Sean Dockray for part of this phrasing.

39. Alexander R. Galloway, *The Interface Effect* (Cambridge: Polity, 2012), 28–9.

40. Ibid., 44–5.

41. Galloway, "Software and Ideology," *The Interface Effect*, 54–77.

42. Rob Kitchin and Martin Dodge, *Code/Space: Software and Everyday Life* (Cambridge, MA: MIT Press, 2011), 16.

43. Steven P. Erie, *Globalizing L.A.: Trade, Infrastructure and Regional Development* (Stanford, CA: Stanford University Press, 2004), 205.

44. Reinhold Martin, *The Organizational Complex: Architecture, Media and Corporate Space* (Cambridge, MA: MIT Press, 2003), 10.

45. Ranabir Samaddar, "Rajarhat, the Urban Dystopia," *Transit Labour: Circuits, Regions, Borders*, Digest no. 3 (August, 2011): 14–16, http://transitlabour.asia/documentation/. See also Ishita Dey, Ranbir Samaddar, and Suhit K. Sen, *Beyond Kolkata: Rajarhat and the Dystopia of Urban Imagination* (New Dehli: Routledge, 2013).

46. David Harvey, *The New Imperialism* (Oxford: Oxford University Press, 2003).

47. See Jonathan Crary, *24/7: Late Capitalism and the Ends of Sleep* (London and New York: Verso, 2013), 33, 105.

48. Ishita Dey, "New Town and Labour in Transit," *Transit Labour: Circuits, Regions, Borders*, Digest no. 3 (August, 2011): 10–13, http://transitlabour.asia/documentation/.

49. Henri Lefebvre, *Rhythmanalysis: Space, Time and Everyday Life*, trans. Stuart Elden and Gerald Moore (London and New York: Continuum, 2004).

50. Rabinach, quoted in Martin, *The Organizational Complex*, 17.

51. Crary, *24/7*, 18.

52. Ibid., 32.

53. Anja Kanngieser, "Tracking and Tracing: Geographies of Logistical Governance and Labouring Bodies," *Environment and Planning D: Society and Space* 31, no. 4 (2013): 601.

54. Email correspondence, Shanghai, May 30, 2009.

55. Standard operation procedure also refers, of course, to the routine practices of torture adopted by the U.S. military, supposedly as a technique of interrogation. The shared terminology here should come as no surprise, given the origins of logistics within the military-industrial complex.

56. Email correspondence, Shanghai, May 31, 2009.

57. See Robert S. Boyton, "Enjoy Your Zizek! An Excitable Slovenian Philosopher Examines the Obscene Practices of Everyday Life, Including His Own," *Lingua Franca* 8, no. 7 (October, 1998), http://www.lacan.com/zizek-enjoy.htm.

58. See also Tiziana Terranova, "What we seem to have then is definition of a new biopolitical plane that can be organized through the deployment of *immanent control*, which operates directly within the productive power of the multitude and the clinamen," *Network Cultures: Politics for the Information Age* (London: Pluto, 2004), 122.

59. Email correspondence, Shanghai, May 31, 2009.

60. Since logistics software operates as a closed environment that does not accommodate feedback as a correctional process through the modification of form, it is not properly a cybernetic system, as developed by Norbert Wiener in his book *Cybernetics; or, Control and Communication in the Human Animal and the Machine* (Cambridge, MA: MIT Press, 1948). As Reinhold Martin notes in his account of Wiener's work on cybernetics, "The second law of thermodynamics [which Wiener drew on in his study of 'systems of information measurement and management'] holds that the overall level of entropy, or disorder, tends to probabilistically to increase in any closed system." It is in this respect that one wonders how logistics does not break down into frequent chaos. See Martin, *The Organizational Complex*, 21.

61. Sandro Mezzadra and Brett Neilson, *Border as Method, or, the Multiplication of Labor* (Durham: Duke University Press, 2013), 95.

62. See Terranova, *Network Cultures*, 122. See also Ned Rossiter, *Organized Networks: Media Theory, Creative Labour, New Institutions* (Rotterdam: NAi Publishers, 2006), 166–95.

63. http://transmediale.de/past/2015.

64. *Cargonauts*, http://cargonauts.net.

65. See Kerin Hope, "Greece Picks China's Cosco in Port Deal," *Financial Times*, January 20, 2016, http://www.ft.com/intl/cms/s/0/d65aa7c4-bfb1–11e5–846f-79b0e3d20eaf.html.

66. For an extended analysis of terminal software and labor regimes operating in Piraeus, see Pavlos Hatzopoulos, "Software, Machines, People and Things as Tangled Species," Logistical Worlds: Infrastructure, Software, Labour, December 14, 2014, http://logisticalworlds.org/blogs/software-machines-people.

67. Ben Kafka, *The Demon of Writing: Powers and Failures of Paperwork* (New York: Zone Books, 2012), 10.

68. Adilkno, *The Media Archive: World Edition* (New York: Autonomedia, 1998), 12–15. I elaborate Adilkno's concept of sovereign media in chapter 8.

69. See Anna Lascari, "The New Ikonian-Thriassion Rail Line," Logistical Worlds: Infrastructure, Software, Labour, December 16, 2014, http://logisticalworlds.org/blogs/new-ikonion.

3

INTO THE CLOUD

"We Help the World Run Better and Improve People's Lives" (SAP)

The German-based company SAP is one of the largest developers of software that drives global economies, offering leading enterprise software solutions that make possible movements of people, finance, and things that coalesce as global trade. In its 2012 Annual Report with the not especially modest title, *Helping the World Run Better*, SAP declares that "63% of the world's transaction revenue touches an SAP system."[1] SAP specializes in software development and web-based services associated with enterprise resource planning (ERP) systems in the logistics industries among many others, including mining, health, finance, medical, insurance, oil and gas, retail, and higher education. This means companies can integrate and automate the majority of their business practices in real-time environments that share common data. So goes the sales pitch.

A 2013 report placed SAP as holding 25 percent of the worldwide market share in enterprise resource planning revenue. SAP's closest competitor, Oracle, held 13 percent of market share at the time of the report in 2013.[2] Given their market and institutional reach, it is therefore not a stretch to say that the power of SAP rivals that of the Murdoch empire. Yet SAP's ERP and logistics software generally remain a black box to most. Even those who use the software have little idea of how it works. For this reason SAP's supply chain software can be considered a form of imaginary media.[3] We might ask how much—or to what extent—does imagination shape protocols? You choose what you want to put into that imagined space, because if you don't, then others certainly will. Another tech report went so far as to say SAP "poisons networks." And then continued with this dire warning: "SAP's expensive business software, which no one knows what it does, and is so esoteric that no one ever bothers to upgrade it, could be a ticking security bomb."[4] So what is supply chain

52 Into the Cloud

software and what does it do? Why don't we have it installed on our PCs and laptops? Why are we so utterly unaware of its very existence, let alone its influence in our daily lives and capacity to coordinate the world within its own tangled nightmare?

Given the enormous influence and widespread industry use of SAP software, we need to ask why this company and its products are so unknown by scholars in the fields of media studies, digital humanities, software studies, and network cultures. In part the answer to this question can be explained with reference to the objects of study that tend to define these fields, especially those of software studies and network cultures that more often valorize open source initiatives, tactical media interventions, and experimental media culture in general. Less clear is the case of media studies. Broad as the field is, one might expect research into the political economy of media industries to pay some attention to the technology and infrastructure underpinning the global exchange of finance and commodities.[5] Yet this is not the case. Why such an omission looms so large in critical studies of media culture and industries may also have something to do with the fact that logistical software is an aesthetically unattractive and closed proprietary system, even if the logistical infrastructures special to transport and communication hold a particular aesthetic allure, which occasionally tips over to the sublime.[6] It would appear that media theory remains largely unaware of the existence of enterprise resource planning systems. Software studies is all too often bewitched by the utopia of the open source movement, and digital humanities is struggling to lift itself out of the archives, even if there is a scramble for methods. A theory of logistical media is a theory of software, infrastructure, and global supply chains crossed with the labor of bodies and brains.

Jangling in the background of this chapter is an interest in developing a theory of logistical media. Given the elusiveness of logistical software as an object of encounter, in this chapter I instead shadow such logistical media by tracing the history and vision of SAP with recourse to digital visualizations of logistical operations. My interest is to situate SAP within the field of media theory and debates in digital humanities and software studies as they bear upon the question of method. I emphasize how the digital visualizations developed in the Transit Labour project are not just a method of aggregating disparate datasets into a new synthetic form that provides insight into conditions of labor; they also work as a mediating apparatus in terms of the sociality and design of research. In other words, the visualizations mediate the relation between people, organization, and things. By exploring these interrelations, I suggest that the visualizations offer digital humanities an opportunity to extend research into the politics of labor as it meets the logistical force of supply chain governance and technologies of control.

SAP and the Birth of Global Logistics Software

The opportunity to begin unraveling the mystery of SAP and its software arose during a period of research in Germany during the first half of 2013. Standing around chatting late one evening in the renovated villa accommodating the

Medienkulturen der Computersimulation (MECS) program at Leuphana University, Lüneburg, Christoph Engemann offered an intriguing story to my puzzlement over SAP's supply chain software. He suggested that the origins of SAP's global domination might best be found in the modern rise of double-entry bookkeeping. I sensed a Kittlerian moment in action and found it somewhat unnerving. How was I to trace the media archive of SAP—one that I barely knew beyond a Wikipedia entry—back to a pre-digital, indeed mediaeval, accounting technology? I was struck by the possibility of an accounting class able to install double entry bookkeeping as a worldwide institutional standard with the advent of neoliberal capitalism. Former British Prime Minister Margaret Thatcher was presented by Engemann as the catalyst of contemporary audit cultures. But it was the technical capacity of an accounting tool able to filter through corporate and government systems that I found more intriguing.

The rise of the card catalogue as a technology of information management could be placed as another reference to the prehistory of SAP software. John Durham Peters makes note of Bernhard Stiegert's study of "nascent merchant capitalism in thirteenth- and fourteenth-century Europe" in which "Double-entry bookkeeping makes it possible for the merchant to substitute control of a large area with control of calculating operations on paper."[7] Nowadays double-entry book-keeping and file cards seem decidedly quaint when set against the vast array of ERP modules available from logistical software developers such as SAP. Though it is worth noting that SAP does not stand alone here: IBM, Microsoft, and Oracle are other key players in ERP systems, while companies such as Amazon and, up until 2010, Walmart develop their own in-house versions to manage logistical operations. The enormous scope of SAP in terms of organizational culture, product variation, technical systems, economic impact, and the division and multiplication of labor presents numerous challenges in terms of analysis.

Logistical media are shifting to cloud computing services, which in many countries are a national policy priority in an effort to increase productivity, innovation, and trade. At stake for governments and commercial entities alike is the extent to which labor embedded in global value chains will tie economic and social prosperity into competitive digital economies. One indication of such a perspective was recently reported on in the IT and business pages of AllAfrica, which noted the push of German software developer SAP to drive innovation at universities and research centers in Kenya:

> "Professors and students are on the forefront of innovation, so to accelerate research and co-innovation on SAP HANA, we are opening the platform to academia," said Bernd Welz, executive vice president and global head of Solution and Knowledge Packaging, SAP. "Faculty and students working in diverse fields such as computer science, artificial intelligence, healthcare, national security, environmental sciences and smart cities will be able to advance their research and demonstrate new and innovative approaches to

> create a world where the Internet of Things is harnessed in real time to improve people's lives."[8]

The Internet of Things (IoT) integrates ubiquitous computing within urban settings, producing a city of calculation and measure. Forever generating data from the movement of people and things, the computational power of embedded technologies is geared toward the economy of efficiency. Data analytics emanating from IoT needs to be tested within the laboratory of media theory, interrogating the precepts that claim to know objects liberated from epistemology.

The digital humanities and software studies may have something to contribute by way of response to how enterprise planning systems are transforming the world. But both would need to radically shift their focus away from a general mission to digitize the humanities archive and conduct exotic sorties into the fringes of network cultures. These are important enough activities, but they tell us little about how big power works. First of all we need to enter the imaginary world of SAP. We need to pose critical questions based not on our disciplinary predilections and intellectual whimsies, but rather on the object of inquiry—computational power, interface aesthetics (what so many drearily and uncritically refer to these days as "usability"), algorithmic architectures, and the politics of parameters. What is required is a truly transdisciplinary collective investigation into the increasingly mysterious centers of power in the age of big data. This would involve work between media theorists, organizational studies, computer scientists, programmers, and designers to open up the black box of SAP and the products of similar software developers, identifying how their algorithmic architectures are constructed, what their business models are, and how they use data extracted from the back end of mostly unwitting clients. What is the vision of SAP beyond the PR machine? According to one SAP consultant, it is 1 billion SAP users by the year 2020. What does SAP's management Hasso Plattner & Co. see as the limit horizon for extracting value from the world? These questions matter because whether or not we personally use this software our lives are becoming increasingly subsumed by logistical operations.

SAP is renowned for its real-time ERP software, beginning with the R/1 financial accounting system, which was developed in the early 1970s. This was soon followed in the late seventies by the text-based R/2 software—"a mainframe based business application suite" able to handle multi-currencies and multi-language requirements. Making use of relational databases such as Oracle (SAP's main competitor), R/3 was launched in 1992 with a graphical user interface based on three-tier client-server architecture able to scale and integrate multiple operating systems.[9] In November 2010 the SAP HANA product was released. This was SAP's response to the challenge of big data. As the product spiel on SAP's site reads: "SAP HANA can help you dramatically accelerate analytics, business processes, predictive analysis, and sentiment data processing—all on a single in-memory computing platform."[10] More recently SAP is dealing with the computational (security) and market challenge of cloud computing, with ventures into the world of educational courseware such as MOOCs (massive open online courses).

One of the keys to SAP's success has been the development of modules within the ERP systems that can handle multiple aspects of business operations. Some of these modules include human resource management, finance and accounting, sales and distribution, production planning, warehousing, procurement, supply chain management, and logistics. SAP's money is made through a combination of license fees, consultation, customized implementation of ERP packages, and ongoing maintenance of modules within the operational context of its clients. The cost for companies is enormous, reaching into the hundreds of millions for large corporations and into the tens of millions for small and medium enterprises (SMEs). The exact cost for companies varies considerably, with pricing made highly flexible and negotiable depending on the extent of customization required and the geographic and national location of the organization wishing to adopt SAP's ERP system. Ten years ago SAP education and training was another profitable line of revenue, but since the global financial crisis hotels have been empty for SAP education sessions.[11]

Through its widespread application in a variety of industries with around 29 million users worldwide, SAP software not only shapes business practice but profoundly affects people and the planet. Along with providing the dominant interface for managing our global economies engaged in planetary obliteration, SAP scrutinizes the experience and conditions of labor in the fairly unforgiving regime of real-time performance measures. It would seem obvious, then, for SAP software to constitute an important object of inquiry not only for business and management or computing, but equally for social, political, and cultural analysis. My interest in this chapter, however, is a bit more specific: What does SAP have to contribute to a theory of logistical media?

A theory of logistical media might begin with a critical analysis of software, focusing specifically on how SAP logistics software is designed in ways that govern both labor and global supply chains. Beyond the need for some quite sophisticated programming knowledge, a key obstacle to such an undertaking concerns the prohibitive pricing of SAP software (which runs into the millions to install and maintain), its corporate secrecy, and the commercial value of the data it collects. Despite these very real constraints for software critique, one notable intervention into SAP's prison house of code occurred in 1996 in Dortmund, Germany, when anarchist programmers affiliated with LabourNet—a network of labor unions— cracked SAP software.[12] The motivation, according to LabourNet's Helmut Weiss, was to identify specific lines of code within SAP software that would affect workplace activity in detrimental ways.[13] Algorithmic parameters became the basis for union negotiations.

Yet despite this quite exceptional feat of code breaking, Weiss notes that "[n]ot a single union accepted our proposal (as the media-workers union)" to develop this further as a topic of political research.[14] Weiss went on to explain two key reasons for this disinterest on the part of unions in addressing the technical parameters of labor control that impact on their constituencies: "First the traditional approach of German unionism towards technology—always in favor of new technologies, despite not knowing anything about them. (A position widely shared even by the left wing unionists)." Second: "They all (at that time it was, practically speaking, mainly the metalworkers union IG Metall and public services union ÖTV who had to deal with SAP) were afraid of 'illegal action' so they distanced themselves from our initiative." Even though the media-workers union had a collective agreement in 1990 on "lifelong learning," where one of the goals was "to enable a critical analysis of all tools we use while working," the everyday practice according to Weiss never matched up with such a principle, especially as employer associations went on the attack in the early nineties. Over two decades have passed since this earlier attempt to bring a political knowledge of code to address labor conditions for those working in supply chain capitalism.

Scaling Software

The scalar dimension of software is dependent on the interoperability of protocols and the hegemony of standards. As David Dixon, the SAP program manager for the U.K. supermarket chain Asda (a subsidiary of Walmart) notes, "The main rationale [behind the SAP rollout] was to have a 'one version of the truth' approach, to standardize and gain a degree of control around the world."[15] Put another way, the market penetration of software is without doubt shaped by its capacity to communicate with a wide range of software applications and hardware devices. Of course this is only part of the story; nevertheless, interoperability is key to the political economy of software. Once universalized across the vertical distribution of organizations, from large corporations to SMEs, an ERP system designed by a developer such as SAP has the power to determine whom you do business with by the fact that transactions are simply easier when your trading partner is on the same platform. In other words, a monopoly effect arises from the trans-scalar integration of SAP's ERP systems across organizational settings. This may seem to be overstating the fact of interoperability among competing ERP systems, but from what I have been told by various people working in the world of SAP, the tendency is for companies to give preference to other businesses also on the SAP system. Indeed, companies are encouraged by SAP to spread the good word of SAP. I have no idea what sort of commission or negotiated adoption fees companies might attract for such advocacy work.

Enabling the communication of objects, the Internet of Things has also become central media components to the logistical industries.[16] Consisting of RFID tags, sensors, 3-D printing, mobile devices, and software or robotic actuators, the IoT and expansion of communication standards offers a network effect to the silo models of machine-to-machine communication (M2M). New regimes of value and the scalability of data are key attractions that the IoT brings to logistical operations, although for a company like SAP the communication of objects would be likely to occur not over the public Internet but rather through private networks in the interests of data securitization and economies of scarcity. For advocates of a public IoT, this makes the battle over open source standards a central issue. Without them, the capacity for trans-scalar and multi-platform interoperability would be severely circumscribed. As Fenwick McKelvey, Matthew Tiessen, and Luke Simcoe note, "the growing mediation of everyday life by the Internet and social media, coupled with Big Data mining and predictive analytics, is turning the Internet into a simulation machine."[17]

At stake here is the question of accessibility to communications infrastructure, or what Sheller terms "new forms of infrastructural exclusivity,"[18] once logistical firms such as SAP become the drivers of developing the Internet of Things. We might also ask, what sort of simulation machine do we wish to inhabit?

In further developing a logistical media theory, I would suggest that three key dimensions of the materiality of communication might serve as framing devices for ongoing research. First, *the materiality of concrete things* (the infrastructure of ports, IT zones, rail and road transportation, container yards, warehouses). Second, *the materiality of communication itself* (the spatial, temporal, and aesthetic properties of digital communication technologies and software). And third, *the materiality of practices that condition the possibility of communication* (the labor of coding and design in developing algorithmic architectures coupled with labor experiences and conditions across sectors within the logistics industries).[19]

Logistical media theory understood within these analytical and material coordinates also holds relevance for research into both the conceptualization and analysis of practices special to digital humanities research. Whether it is RFID tags, GPS devices, or Voice Picking technologies, these ubiquitous media of location associated with the Internet of Things assume—like logistics—a world of seamless interoperability. But we know this to be a fantasy of technologists, policy makers, and advertising agencies. Struggles over communication protocols, infrastructural standards, mobile populations, and expressions of refusal by labor are just some of the glitches that always accompany the operation of logistical media.

What would the critical practice of digital humanities research consist of in the study of big data? How might such practices be designed on transnational scales involving networks of collaborative constitution? What are some of the particular problems surrounding the politics of depletion that come to bear both in the method of digital humanities research and the datasets under scrutiny? Where is the dirt that unravels the pretense of smooth-world systems so common within industry, IT, and state discourses around global economies and their supply chains? And can disruption be understood as a political tension and form of conflictual constitution?

58 Into the Cloud

Within cybernetics, "noise" is a force of ambivalence, interference, and disruption, refusing easy incorporation within prevailing regimes of measure. Constituent forms of subjectivity and the ontology of things often subsist as noise. Undetected, without identity, and seemingly beyond control, noise is the "difference which makes a difference."[20] Digital humanities research would do well to diagram the relations of force and transformation operative within ecologies of noise populated by unruly subjects, persistent objects, and algorithmic cultures. A form of critique is required that is not simply an extension of classical political economy into the realm of digital labor, as exemplified by the work of Christian Fuchs.[21] Logistical media theory is one possible alternative that brings method and critique together in ways sufficient to the task of examining how algorithmic capitalism shapes the experience and condition of labor.

Digital Humanities and the Problem of Method

The digital humanities is a diverse and emerging field that harbors different kinds of innovation and eclecticism. By and large, however, the digital humanities has been notable for its adherence to traditional research objects and rehashing of old methods following the integration of new forms of computational power within institutional settings. Historical literary texts are digitized to revise assumed economic patterns and social forces. Geographers scan topographic maps to produce information layers and digital elevations that reveal new frontiers for research. Google Earth is traversed to uncover obscure archaeological curiosities in a dirt-free manner. Even cutting-edge research in the field of digital media cultures tends to transpose established humanities and social science methods to conduct ethnographies of Facebook, complex visualizations of networks, and content analyses of the Twittersphere.

To simply import existing methods (surveys, interviews, questionnaires, focus groups) from the humanities and social sciences and then use digital technology as a technique of enhancement is not really sufficient for the invention of new methods situated within computational architectures (*media form*). Methods developed from within media of communication—including graphic design and digital visualization—can assist in understanding, for example, how software architectures operate as key technologies for governing labor within logistical industries. This does not mean producing bar graphs and pie charts using routine applications such as Excel, PowerPoint, or Microsoft Word; nor does it involve undertaking geospatial mapping using Google Earth in order to represent the territorial distribution or location of datasets. Likewise, software used in quantitative research such as SPSS that codes questionnaire data for statistical analysis does little to inform research interested in the ways software itself at once shapes and emerges out of material conditions (social relations, economic forces, cultural dynamics).

Such methods fit largely in what David Berry and others have identified as the first wave of digital humanities research, with its focus on the digitization of archives and artifacts along with developing infrastructure associated with digital repositories and expanding research agendas.[22] This wave also involved the scramble for funding that consumes much energy in academics, albeit with a high degree of variation across different national settings. The digital humanities presented humanities academics with the occasion to start scratching at the edges of high-stakes funding and infrastructural needs more often commandeered by disciplines in science, technology, engineering, and medicine.

By Jeffrey Schnapp and Todd Presner's account, the so-called second wave of digital humanities is characterized by "born-digital" methods of analysis and modes of curated knowledge generated from within the media of communication.[23] Berry posits an emergent third wave of digital humanities research, which is interested in how software and code set computational parameters to the production of knowledge.[24] Central to such an approach is a critique of the assumption within much humanities research that its organizing concepts and methodological practices are somehow independent of algorithmic architectures or computational cultures. While Berry isn't direct in saying so, the specter of technological determinism lurks in the background here. After around three decades of research in literary, media, and cultural studies on the agency of audiences, readers, and fan cultures, the pervasiveness of digital media warrants a serious review of how technical systems and computational code format cultural expression and social practices. A further step would examine how the integration of digital technology into economic and social life is transforming neurological processes and biological systems.[25]

Another key line of investigation attending Berry's call for a "computational turn" would include a taxonomy and political economy of software applications and the cultures of code operative within institutional settings across the world. Such an undertaking might begin a critique of the extent to which knowledge production and the management of university routines and their economies are formatted in ways specific to computational regimes of communication. I analyze such operations in chapters 5 and 6, and consider them as relevant to future research within digital humanities. Needless to say, I present aspects of such an undertaking in this chapter—namely, an interest in how economies of code broaden the question of method and production of concepts beyond what is normally assumed of digital humanities research.

Cutting-edge digital humanities research requires an invention of methods developed through the use of digital media technologies. Methods situated within media of communication—including graphic design, game development, and digital visualization—can assist in understanding how the rules special to "algorithmic architectures" structure the organization and analysis of data.[26] Algorithmic architectures are computational systems of governance that hold a variable relation between the mathematical execution of code and an "external" environment defined through arrangements of data.[27] The capacity of algorithmic architectures to organize and analyze data on labor productivity in real-time, for

60 Into the Cloud

instance, means that they function as technologies for governing labor within logistical industries. Moreover, algorithmic architectures constitute a key site of intervention for digital humanities research interested in the relations between knowledge, power, and computational systems.

Methods developed within the digital humanities also have an important role to play in the critique of logistical power. Rather than turn to established humanities methods, or even those developed from within the digital humanities proper, this chapter outlines how the process of devising questions and the problem of method coextensive with research on logistics industries lends digital humanities an occasion to reorient research methods as well as the production of concepts. I explore such possibilities for digital humanities research with reference to the material dimensions of software systems operative within global logistics industries. Particular focus is given to transport and shipping activities undertaken at Port Botany in Sydney in order to highlight the multiplicity of logistical forces exerted upon labor. The development of a digital visualization drawing on data from productivity reports of the port is foregrounded to register the relation between design and research practice with regard to the question of method within digital humanities research. While the aesthetic logic of the visualization is not markedly different from the many visualizations developed in digital humanities, it is nonetheless distinct for the way in which it brings to the fore the practice of method through the process of designing a visualization. In the case of the Port Botany study, the visualization served two key purposes: first, as a methodological device in the practice of transdisciplinary research, and second, as a media form that made visible the pressures on labor within the shipping and transport industries. Both aspects of the visualization enable a critique of logistics, with the visualization providing a kind of substitute interface in the absence of access to the software actually used in logistical industries.

Big Data, Disciplinarity, and the Absence of Critique

The emergent field of digital humanities has sought to develop digital tools such as geographical information systems (GIS), simulation, data mining, and network analysis to assist the humanities and social sciences in an attempt to formulate new research questions and techniques of analysis. More often these tools take the form of software applications able to "capture, manage, and process" large datasets, or what computer scientists and industry refer to as "big data."[28] This may include transactional data such as web searches and mobile phone records, along with digital books, newspapers, statistics, photographs, music, interviews, and their supporting information architecture of tags, traces, and comments.

There is a concept-free zeal about the capacity for digital methods to verify some kind of hitherto unobtainable empirical truth.[29] In part, this stems from a fidelity in the correlation between data, its referent, and the material world. In the database economy derived from content management systems, ERP software, and social network media cultures, data has indeed become the new empiric. Displacing earlier analogue methods such as focus groups, phone surveys, and questionnaires designed to measure audience taste and consumer behaviors, digitally encoded data has a capacity to scale, recombine, and granulate the micro-practices of people, finance, and things in ways to which pre-digital methods could only aspire.

Needless to say, the frequently assumed empirical dimension of data is better understood in terms of its self-referentiality than its correspondence with an external material world. Once such a claim is accepted, the capacity for data to be modeled in ways that generate what Foucault termed regimes of truth is—at least, I find—less objectionable at a theoretical level. This is not to say that data is without empirical substance, nor is it to valorize analog objects or offline worlds as imbued with greater materiality or analytical verisimilitude.[30] Rather, the emphasis is to acknowledge the role of protocols, standards, norms, and parameters special to software platforms and their political economy that define the contours of expression through which data is made intelligible. Moreover, when data is understood to operate within, and indeed constitute, regimes of truth, a secondary empirical quality emerges in the shaping of social practices and material conditions in ways not so dissimilar from how policies of various kinds result in forms of action. Let's keep in mind that such moves occur within a context of data analytics and a certain neo-positivist epistemological and institutional anxiety around the production of "evidence-based" research and the economies it fuels.

Consider the rhetorical power of climate modeling, which refers to itself as a technical system while impacting on the economic cost, if not the rate, of greenhouse gas emissions. As McKenzie Wark demonstrates in *Molecular Red*, one can mine a long line of historical examples pertaining to data analytics that foreground the inconsistencies and incompatibilities of diverse data sets based on divergent standards and "intrusions" from the "outside" during the process of data collection. Wark makes note of how models on climate change over periods of decades are faulty precisely at the level of some basic irregularities in method along with a tendency to mistake the phenomenon of changing weather patterns for more complex transformations in climate over longer periods of time: "The problem with climate data is that most of it is actually weather data. It was collected for the purposes of short-run predictions, not long-run modeling. There is no consistent metadata attached to the data."[31] And then there are irregularities in methods of data collection: "There are not always records of what instruments were used, or if there were changes in the conditions of their use, nor are there always calibrations of a new instrument against the one it replaces." Drawing on Paul Edwards's research on computational models of climate data, Wark recounts how sea temperature variation may have much to do with how water has been collected and even national cultures of collection—in 1945 British scientists were content with water sampled using a bucket over the side of a ship, while Americans gathered data based on engine intake water. It should be no surprise, then, that historical models on shifting patterns in ocean water temperature might be dramatically different. But without this sort of historical anthropology of method, we—and this includes scientists and policy makers—are confronted with another kind of invisible global weather infrastructure, which as John Durham Peters notes is also a form of logistical media with its tendency to "statistically normalize" that which is experienced as sensory perception.[32]

In the process of drawing connections within or across datasets, old or existing research objects are remodeled in new ways. Unsurprisingly, business also has a strong interest in devising new techniques for extracting economic value using tools that produce meaning from the process of data recombination and governance. As a report from the *Economist* put it 2010, the proliferation of data "makes it possible to do many things that previously could not be done: spot business trends, prevent diseases, combat crime and so on. Managed well, the data can be used to unlock new sources of economic value, provide fresh insights into science and hold governments to account."[33] That the *Economist* hitches a neoliberal democratic ethos or agenda to the market potential of data management should come as no surprise. While not especially novel or insightful, the *Economist* foresees problems with the rise of big data, including data storage availability and privacy and security issues. The digital humanities could contribute to these debates in ways that address, for example, cultural and social dimensions wrought by the accumulation of big data.

For the digital humanities, the problems presented by digitalization and, to a lesser extent, big data are quite different. With its tendency toward text-based analysis using digital tools (parsing the Shakespeare archive to reveal grammatical variation, for example), the digital humanities is arguably at a formative stage in terms of developing critical methods and concepts that can address cultural, social, and political phenomena and challenges in the world at large.[34] Alan Liu signals this current impasse with precision in his critique of digital humanities: "the digital humanities are not ready to take up their full responsibility because the field does not yet possess an adequate critical awareness of the larger social, economic, and cultural issues at stake."[35] It is almost as though nothing happened after New Criticism in literary theory and positivism in the social sciences. Broadly speaking, there seems to be a studious avoidance of inventing digital research methods outside disciplinary comfort zones. Nor is there any substantive academic engagement with the politics of data as it intersects with labor and life. Critical studies involved in research on virtual work or digital labor tend to reduce the experience and condition of labor to people working in the cultural and media industries, rather than identify how diverse sectors of the economy and society are affected—often in conflictual yet mutually constitutive ways—by the expansion of information economies and their attendant technologies.[36]

Referring to the absence of canonical figures in the digital humanities compared with those generated within the early years of cultural studies, Andrew Prescott is quite scathing in his characterization of the field: "the focus of much digital humanities work has been on the creation of online projects anchored in conventional subjects."[37] While Prescott's desire for a canon seems to linger as a form of nostalgia for the days when cultural and media studies "branch[ed] out into new fields in the way the work of (say) Hoggart did," it is not something he sees as necessary or even possible for the digital humanities.[38] Indeed, whether the orientation of research in digital humanities, irrespective of its substance, has the capacity to produce canonical works is doubtful. Projects situated within or alongside digital humanities are largely conducted independently of each other as a result of their diverse global and geocultural distribution. As a consequence, a certain disciplinary, institutional, and geocultural fragmentation ensues that does not lend itself to the production of disciplinary canons. There are too many small, unreplicated one-off software development projects that don't go far enough toward the development of new methods, let alone new methodologies. At the very least, canon formation requires both a distillation and articulation of shared ideas and energies across a broad range of inquiries. One might also debate the need or relevance for a shared theoretical point of reference in order to advance conceptual apparatuses and methodological practices. But this is less Prescott's point. More urgent for Prescott is the need within digital humanities to give attention to theorizing and critical reflection with reference to digital technologies and objects of research.

At the level of disciplinarity, the digital humanities often finds itself set against institutional structures that corral projects into disciplinary silos that are incapable of communicating with each other. Just go to a large-scale digital humanities association meeting and you will know what I mean. In a similar vein, Liu argues that "the underlying issue is disciplinary identity not of the digital humanities but of the humanities themselves."[39] More straightforwardly, disciplines have disciplinary interests irrespective of whether they have undertaken a computational turn. Art historians probe computationally generated patterns in visual archives, linguists develop speech analysis tools, literary scholars build databases to survey the history of book industries, mediaevalists reconstruct the Middle Ages through digital cartographies. As a consequence, new research questions in the fields of digital humanities, software studies, and sociological digital research are often posed in terms of how to tackle larger-scale datasets rather than address a material world underscored by complex problems.

The work on digital methods by sociologist Noortje Marres is emblematic of such an approach. Like Richard Rogers, Marres's advocacy of digital methods has an interest in how "natively digital" research tools "take advantage of the analytic and empirical capacities that are 'embedded in online media.'"[40] Their approaches contrast with those developed in the digital visualization of Port Botany discussed below. In focusing on the empirics of data as it is generated through algorithmic operations of search tools such as Issue Crawler, the analysis of political issues, discourses, and actors become displaced from the material conditions from which they arise.[41] As it turns out, "method as intervention" for Marres is a fairly exclusive online undertaking no matter that it might involve a "redistribution of research" and "transfer" of knowledge among diverse actors.[42] Search data and its visualization become the universe of critique. The subject of labor is divided between humans and technology in the practice of method but not the interface between politics, economy, subjects and objects, and the material and technical conditions from which they emerge.

In the social science and humanities disciplines undertaking transnational and transcultural research using digital methods for collecting and sampling large-scale datasets, there is a tendency for analyses to formulate a universal system of questions to ensure maximum consistency in generating usable data. In adopting such methodological and analytical approaches, the disparity between the particularities of the object of study and the abstraction of knowledge becomes even further amplified than might be the case in, for example, more traditional methods of practice in anthropological fieldwork. Alternatively, abstraction itself becomes the object of study, which is the direction taken in Franco Moretti's quantitative method of "distant reading" of literary history.[43]

An additional and rarely addressed problem can arise with projects international in scope that place a priority on modeling, visualizing, aggregating, and analyzing large datasets. The underlying method within many "global" approaches to comparative research in media, social, and cultural research often seeks to integrate and make uniform data that is nonassimilable due to protocological conflicts, parametric irregularities, qualitative differences, and the like. In doing so, such approaches reproduce some of the central assumptions of area studies—namely, that the study of geocultural difference is predicated on equivalent systems of measure that demonstrate difference in terms of self-contained areas or territories and civilizational continuities often conforming to the borders of the nation-state. Yet it is a mistake to suppose that cultural variation can be distinguished in terms of national cultures, at least in any exclusive sense. In the case of transnational research on logistics industries (and, more broadly, any research project taking a global perspective), digital methods of comparative research need to be alert to the asymmetrical composition of datasets on transport and communication industries and labor performance, which upsets any desire for equivalent units consistent across time and space that might provide the basis for comparison.

The challenge of digital methods and critique is not about integrating historical or archival data into ever larger sets, but involves finding meaningful ways to accept and work across variable, uneven, and often incomplete datasets. Here the fantasy of logistical industries of creating interoperability through protocols of electronic data interchange (EDI) and ERP software platforms hits its limits. Designed to track the movement of people and things, EDI and ERP architectures are intended to function as real-time registrations of labor productivity and the efficiency of distribution systems. Yet these technologies of optimization frequently rub up against any number of disruptions in the form of labor struggles, infrastructural damage, software glitches, supply chain problems, and so forth. This discrepancy between the calculus of the plan and the world as it happens suggests that the most interesting sites to study are those where interoperability breaks down and methods of organization external to logistics' software routines are instituted in an attempt to smooth out the transfer of data and material goods.[44]

Technologies of logistical governance external to software architectures may include border regimes such as special economic zones (SEZs), territorial concessions, and trade corridors. They may also manifest as juridical power in the form of labor laws or extra-state forms of governance, such as manufacturing and industrial design standards, communication protocols, and the politics of affect as it modulates the diagram or relations special to subjectivity. Borders, in short, proliferate, multiply, and at times overlap.[45] Studying such an expanse of governmental techniques is beyond my scope in this chapter and is not the focus of this book. But the techniques are important to note by way of signaling that the digital is not as ubiquitous as is often claimed or assumed. And this has implications for the design of methods within digital humanities; chief among these is an "invention of new knowledge practices and methods that intervene in the world."[46]

A study of logistical media begins to address some of these issues. Given the focus on digital methods in this chapter, I limit my comments here to the relation between logistical media critique and software studies. The program of "cultural analytics," headed by Lev Manovich and his Software Studies Initiative labs at the University of California—San Diego and City University of New York (CUNY), summarizes its project in ways that essentially transpose already existing techniques rather than invent new methods *per se*: "Today sciences, business, governments and other agencies rely on computer-based analysis and visualization of large datasets and data flows. They employ statistical data analysis, data mining, information visualization, scientific visualization, visual analytics, and simulation. We propose to begin systematically applying these techniques to contemporary cultural data."[47]

By contrast, a study of software within the global logistics industries prompts the question of method with regard to how to research the relation between software and the management of labor; the role of logistics infrastructure and the reconfiguration of urban, rural, and geopolitical spaces; and the production of new regimes of knowledge within an organizational paradigm. Software systems operative within global logistics industries such as SAP or Oracle generate protocols and standards that shape social, economic, and cross-institutional relations within and beyond the global logistics industries. How such governing forces and material conditions are captured and made intelligible through the use of digitally modified data is, in part, the challenge of method.

Data, Method, Labor

In elaborating digital methods developed out of logistical operations, I refer to the Transit Labour project, which examined how circuits of labor are reshaping the contours of regions while coming up against, testing, and transforming a multiplicity of borders.[48] Our work around digital methods within this project builds upon international research we have been conducting on labor, logistics, and the production of subjectivity in Shanghai, Kolkata, and Sydney. A second iteration of research on China led globalization began with the Logistical Worlds project in 2013 in the Athens port of Piraeus, with current research taking place on Chile's port at Valparaíso, the old and new ports of Kolkata, and the transport hub of Siliguri in northeast India.[49] After an initial interest in labor in the cultural industries, we quickly realized how labor mobilities that condition the possibility of cultural labor cannot be reduced to the cultural sector alone. Indeed, we found that logistics is key to forms of "differential inclusion" such as SEZs, land acquisition policies, residential permits, software protocols, and manufacturing standards.[50] Along with cultural and social borders, these kinds of devices or apparatuses that modulate inclusion and movement within logistical industries also function to govern labor and supply chains in the informational economies.

I emphasize the need for politically inflected research here for the obvious reason that technology and software shape how practices of knowledge production are organized and how labor is governed. And I register such research as a challenge due to the difficulty, among others, of producing—let alone even identifying—counter-logistical worlds. Needless to say, researchers can make a start. The study of how databases, supply chain software, GPS, Voice Picking, and RFID technologies affect work in the logistics industries contributes to a politicized conception of humanities and social research.[51] Furthermore, the incorporation of digital methods into critical research on logistics can facilitate and inform the politics of data, which I would suggest is also a politics of labor and life, borders and movement, knowledge production, and infrastructural implementation.

Relevant here for the development of digital methods is the question of how labor performativity is incorporated into the computational design of visualizations as distinct from decision-making undertaken by machines. Given that the body of labor is at the center of logistical calculations of productivity and efficiency, it is also the least visible for those not directly working within logistical industries or involved in developing and implementing parameters for supply chain software. Thus, one of the key reasons why a critical study of logistics is going to devise quite different computational and design methods than, say, Manovich's program on cultural analytics has to do with the difficulty of obtaining datasets due to commercial confidentiality agreements along with the politically sensitive nature of some of this data. Statistics on labor productivity are especially protected across the institutional spectrum in the case of Australia's ports, which have been marked by industrial dispute between the MUA (Maritime Union of Australia) and stevedoring companies in recent years (to say nothing of the long history of struggles). In the formal, high-end sectors of the logistics industries, it is particularly difficult to research the actual software used to oversee supply chains and measure labor performativity in real-time. One reason is prohibitively expensive proprietary licenses that enclose the computational operations of logistical firms, coupled with the highly guarded ways in which companies and authorities regulate access to this software and the data it generates. As a result, other processes and techniques of computational research are required in order to model logistical worlds, foregrounding the labor dimension of "supply chain capitalism."

Based on publicly available datasets published in *Waterline* reports from the Australian government's Department of Infrastructure and Transport, the pilot study we conducted on logistics operations at Port Botany in Sydney aimed to digitally visualize the relations between container loading/unloading times, truck turnaround times, and the pressures that come to bear upon labor productivity and efficiency.[52] These government reports provide statistics on a set of parameters designed to measure wharfside productivity (loading and unloading of containers) and landside performance (truck turnaround times upon entering and exiting the port). The report's statistics are compiled from data supplied by port authorities (Sydney Ports) and stevedoring companies (DP World, Patricks) operating around the country. While the reports provide a range of productivity indicators, they do not provide data on labor performance even though they indicate that "elapsed labour time" was one of the measures used to calculate the vessel working rate (or number of containers handled per hour). Container loading and unloading times, and indeed truck turnaround times, can therefore be read as a substitute for labor productivity (see Figure 3.1).

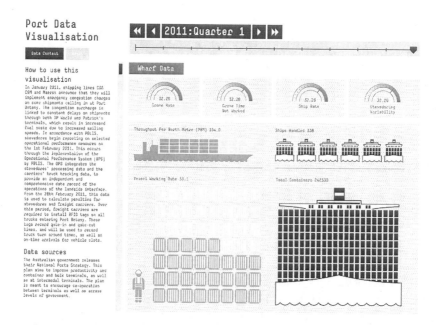

FIGURE 3.1 Port Botany wharf data visualization, 2012. Design: Kernow Craig; research: Katie Hepworth; visual analytics programming: Quang Vinh Nyugen; concept: Brett Neilson and Ned Rossiter.

Source: http://transitlabour.asia/documentation/

Unsurprisingly, the genre of the reports is unable to register the various tensions that underlie performance measures that seek to smooth over glitches between the movement of trucks throughout the port area and the unloading of containers from ships.[53] Port authorities attempt to regulate traffic problems landside through the use of RFID vehicle tracking and online "vehicle booking slots" (VBS), which determine when a truck enters the port and the time it has to be serviced by the stevedore and exit without incurring penalty. Following the introduction of VBS at Port Botany in 1999, Katie Hepworth notes, "the VBS became the site of intervention by the ports authority into the operations of its leaseholders, DP World and Patrick Stevedores; the slot became the means of reorganizing the operators' relationships with various terminal users."[54] Yet it also resulted in conflicts between data systems through governance methods quite different from data transaction protocols (EDI, ERP, and so on). Extra booking slots would be made available online for trucks during periods when the port was less busy, for example, or warehouses able to receive goods may not have been operating while containers were being loaded on the wharf. Traffic congestion across the urban road network intervenes as another contingency unable to be accommodated within the circumscribed universe of the vehicle booking slot system. Time and space, in other words, upset interoperability in multiple ways.

Through the more traditional humanities and social science method of conducting interviews and site research, the Port Botany research identified data sources usually not subject to critical digital humanities analysis. Much data on logistics industries is frequently not publicly accessible on websites or available through search engines. The Port Botany project showed that datasets often only become known about in the instance of discussion with informants. Data on the impact of technology on labor practices and conditions, for example, is something many unions collect for the purpose of internal analysis. And typical of more anthropological modes of investigation, we found that unions are willing to make that data available to university researchers once a relationship of trust has been established. Along with productivity figures obtained from publicly accessible government and industry reports, such data on workplace productivity can then serve as analytical parameters in the digital visualizations of logistical operations.

A technology report from 2012 noted that "data must be broken out of silos in order to be mined, and the organization must learn how to communicate and interpret the results of analysis."[55] With most high-end logistical software systems only available through prohibitively expensive proprietary licenses, the Port Botany project sought to remodel publicly and commercially available datasets as digital visualizations that assist in the analysis of logistics, infrastructure, and labor. In this respect, a key outcome of this study involved understanding that the "art and practice of visualizing data is becoming ever more important in bridging the human–computer gap to mediate analytical insight in a meaningful way."[56] The central analytical framework for designing and interpreting the digital visualizations consists of translating the data (for example, on labor productivity, container movements, truck turnaround times in ports, supply chain volumes, and so on) with a view to understanding how the combination of infrastructure and algorithmic architectures function as technologies that govern logistical labor. The digital visualizations effect their own algorithmic architecture (or rules of code) distinct from those available through proprietary licenses. Obviously the visualizations are not software applications that coordinate supply chains; rather, the digital visualizations begin to offer an analytical medium through which to register the interrelations between logistical infrastructure, algorithmic rules, labor practices, and supply chain assemblages.

To be clear, the animated digital visualizations that the Transit Labour project developed in collaboration with colleagues in computer science and design do not profess to represent in any veridical manner the conditions and experiences of labor. Nor do they assume to be particularly innovative at the level of design, method, or conceptualization when compared to other visualizations of temporality in digital humanities projects. Rather, the visualizations make a claim for research on the politics of labor and logistics within the field of digital humanities. Again, such research can be distinguished from work done on virtual or digital labor, which, like the digital sociology of Marres and others, takes the online world as its milieu of action at the expense of studying how online worlds or digital apparatuses and the methods we bring to them are entangled with material conditions of possibility. In contrast to such approaches, the visualizations indicate a diagram of relations special to logistical operations at Port Botany and, more generally, to logistical worlds. Simple as it may seem, to chart a ten-year period of truck turnaround times and loading and unloading times at Port Botany begins to make visible some of the forces around labor productivity (see Figure 3.2). Moreover, the visualization begins to suggest that logistics is substantially removed from the all-pervasive smooth-world fantasy upheld by industry, government, and the IT sector in which complex operations move across a seamless continuum of control and order. Logistical operations are better understood as event processes underscored by conflict, dispute, glitches, and contingency.

Here, we can think about the waterfront disputes heating up in Australia and New Zealand, where labor flexibility and demands for increasing productivity are key issues in concert with managerial drives for enhanced automation technologies. Such developments stem in part from the 1988 waterfront dispute, which was the iconic strike of the Howard-era government and took a defining toll across many other areas of labor in Australia, shaping the form of the current resource-driven economy (fly-in-fly-out workers, along with the offshoring of labor within both the mining industry and more recently across a range of service industries on the eastern seaboard of the country).

An announcement by Patrick in 2012 explains that the 44 AutoStrads (automated straddles not requiring human operation) ordered for delivery at Port Botany in 2013–2014 "will operate unmanned, using radar and laser guidance technology to navigate the straddles around the yard, moving and stacking containers from the quay line into the holding yards, onto vehicles and back to the

70 Into the Cloud

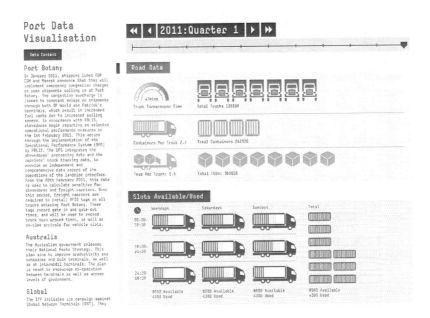

FIGURE 3.2 Port Botany road data visualization, 2012. Design: Kernow Craig; research: Katie Hepworth; visual analytics programming: Quang Vinh Nyugen; concept: Brett Neilson and Ned Rossiter.

Source: http://transitlabour.asia/documentation/

quay cranes with pinpoint accuracy of better than 2cm."[57] Automation thus presents an index of industrial dispute as maritime labor confronts stevedores such as Patrick (whose container ports were acquired by Asciano in 2007 following a restructure of Toll Holdings), DP World, and Hutchinson, which are all set to increase productivity rates across the country's container terminals through unmanned straddle carriers. While efficiency gains are the prime motivation behind such technological upgrading, an obvious cost occurs in terms of labor redundancies. Labor on Sydney's ports, in short, is set to be transformed in terms of new modes of work following the introduction of automation.

Another example of the centrality of labor to logistics can be drawn from Occupy Oakland, which concentrated on port blockades in an attempt to disrupt global supply chains of capital accumulation.[58] As with many disputes, there are frequently internal lines of division. In this case, the tactic of port blockades ran afoul of local unions and at least some of their members, who claimed that the occupation resulted in workers and their families suffering economic hardship due to loss of income. We could also see this as an interesting contest over the right to intervene by different organizational forms.

The remarkable thing about logistics is its capacity to incorporate these sorts of disruptions within ever expanding parameters through the rubric of "fault tolerance." While labor struggles, infrastructural breakdowns, supply chain blockages, natural disasters, and local conditions and events may have significant effects, they also prompt logistics to reorient shipping routes, relocate warehouses and factories, search for economic zones with more favorable labor regulations and better tax incentives, and so on. Contingency, in short, conditions the reproduction of logistics.[59] This flexible dynamic of absorbing disturbances to produce new regimes of coordination and control lends a high degree of temporariness and partiality to attempts to diagram logistical relations through the design of visualizations.

The digital visualizations produced in the Transit Labour project point to the undulations and irregularities of seemingly mechanical functions that can be better understood when situated in broader economic and political contexts that encompass local, national, regional, and global scales. The transdisciplinary practice of collectively producing the visualizations corresponds with Willard McCarty's notion of the "model" and "modeling," which he understands as "the process seen in and by means of a developing product, not the definitive achievement."[60] At the level of method, Transit Labour's visualizations operate as models by feeding back into a research process and constellation of practices, prompting a revision of research questions and pointing to institutional settings and relevant experts for follow-up engagements that may well take the form of more traditional humanities research methods such as interviews, discussions, and site visits.

The visualizations also signal that data aesthetics has a central role to play in devising suitable methods for research projects that cut across the otherwise smooth relation assumed between labor, software, infrastructure, and economic growth. Data aesthetics bring critique together with design in the invention of method. Or as Liu writes, "Seeing design in data is a method for knowing meaning in the digital humanities."[61] At stake, I would suggest, is not only the development of novel methods shaped by the social-technical dynamics of digital media but the constitution of subjectivity itself. Since software and technology are transforming how we do work, there is an opportunity here to alter the parameters and thus topological horizons of machine intelligence and its increasing governance of labor and life.

Politics of Parameters

Digital humanities is in danger of becoming stuck at the level of the digitalization of existing archive material, producing visualizations of these and other so-called big data. By shifting the object of research beyond traditional areas of study (literary archives, datasets of artworks, and museum collections, etc.), digital humanities research becomes relevant to broader social and political concerns that place great emphasis upon economic activities and associated infrastructure. Digital methods can address political issues and the routines and institutions that sit between people and states, labor and capital, borders and subjectivity. Digital humanities research at the current conjuncture might decide to investigate how circuits of capital connect with the constituent force of labor, life, and things, shaping the production of time, space, and economy in a variety of ways. With an interest in making visible

72 Into the Cloud

the new subjectivities of logistics and the politics of parameters, I have positioned research on logistical media and "supply chain capitalism" within the digital humanities, not the social sciences.

In the age of big data, everything and anything is or has the capacity to become digitally encoded. Datasets are everywhere, residing as a standing reserve awaiting incorporation as topological parameters into analytical models and capital expropriation. As Paul Edwards notes, "Parameterization illustrates the interaction of computational friction with the limits of human knowledge."[62] Within a topological horizon, the politics of parameters amounts to a battle around epistemological and social legitimacy in the form of measure. Parameters are also a matter of protocols, which Alexander Galloway understands as "the technology of organization and control operating in distributed networks."[63] Parameters and protocols are both rules that govern systems. If a person, thing, or phenomenon is without rule or measure, it might just as well not exist. In assembling datasets, selection is predicated on the poverty of excess, which is data gone to waste. This, at least, is the doxa of a logistical worldview where everything is about accountability, efficiency, and productivity calibrated in systems of real-time. Data produces and is accompanied by other forms of waste, forms more insidious than the economist's "wasted opportunity."

The social production of value and the algorithmic mining of data seem the last frontiers of economic extraction. But so often we're talking about a social milieu and informational economy that is profoundly abstracted from the multiple informal economies and geocultural settings engaged in secondary forms of value extraction. A substantial portion of the latter are associated with economies of electronic waste, with the global South structurally and historically consigned the role of manufacturing and later dispersion of discarded ICTs and consumer electronics. Both the production and dismantling of e-waste exposes "workers and ecosystems to a morass of toxic components."[64] With Internet transmissions long ago exceeding measure, and annual increments in computational power ensuring planned obsolescence, analytical capacity and consumer desire both become destined to their own forms of obsolescence. Jennifer Gabrys writes, "Obsolescence is not so much innovation in reverse as it is the ongoing maintenance of a sense of technological development."[65] On the sidelines of speed, digital humanities research might seem left pondering the disaster as a program beyond control.

Notes

1. SAP, *Helping the World Run Better*, Annual Report, 2012, 4.
2. See Louis Columbia, "2013 ERP Market Share Update: SAP Solidifies Market Leadership," *Forbes*, May 12, 2013, http://www.forbes.com/sites/louiscolumbus/2013/05/12/2013-erp-market-share-update-sap-solidifies-market-leadership/.
3. See Erik Kluitenberg, ed., *Book of Imaginary Media: Excavating the Dream of the Ultimate Communication Medium* (Rotterdam: NAi Publishers, 2006).

4. Nick Farrell, "Ancient SAP Software Poisons Networks," *TechEye*, June 18, 2013, http://news.techeye.net/security/ancient-sap-software-poisons-networks.

5. An exception to these tendencies can be found in the adjacent field of science and technology studies (STS). See Neil Pollock and Robin Williams, *Software and Organisations: The Biography of the Enterprise-Wide System, or, How SAP Conquered the World* (Oxon and New York: Routledge, 2009).

6. See the photographs and documentary films of Edward Burtynsky, for example: *Manufactured Landscapes* (Ottawa and New Haven: National Gallery of Canada and Yale University Press, 2003); and *China: The Photographs of Edward Burtynsky* (London: Steidl, 2005). See also Soenke Zehle, "Dispatches from the Depletion Zone: Edward Burtynsky and the Documentary Sublime," *Media International Australia* 127 (May, 2008): 109–15.

7. Bernhard Siegert, *Passage des Digitalen: Zeichenpraktiken der neuzeitlichen Wissenschaften, 1500–1900* (Berlin: Brinkmann und Bose, 2003), 43. Quoted in John Durham Peters, "Technology and Ideology: The Case of the Telegraph Revisited," in Jeremy Packer and Craig Robertson, eds., *Thinking with James Carey: Essays on Communications, Transportation, History* (New York: Peter Lang, 2006), 147. See also Markus Krajewski, *Paper Machines: About Cards & Catalogues, 1548–1929*, trans. Peter Krapp (Cambridge, MA: MIT Press, 2011).

8. Lilian Mutegi, "Kenya: SAP Launches Program to Drive Innovation at Universities and Research Centres," *AllAfrica*, May 29, 2014, http://allafrica.com/stories/201405300329.html.

9. Technical details taken from the "SAP R/3" entry on Wikipedia, with additional reference to the SAP Community Network thread on R/2 and R/3, http://scn.sap.com/thread/282002.

10. http://www.sap.com/solutions/technology/in-memory-computing-platform/hana/overview/index.epx.

11. Details on these SAP operations have been gleaned from discussions in Germany in 2013 with professionals working in SAP securitization, market analysis, and global project management. In order to obtain some insight into the corporate practices of SAP and its software interface for supply chain coordination, organizational culture, data economies, and event processing, further discussions about the SAP Human Capital Management (HCM) Module were held with SAP consultant Michael Hellmich followed by an introduction to the SAP Supply Chain Management (SCM) Modules by Anselm Roth, a Solution Architect at SAP Germany. These formed part of an international workshop on SAP, software, and labor I organized with Götz Bachmann, Armin Beverungen, and Timon Beyes at Leuphana University's Centre for Digital Cultures: "Logistics of Soft Control: SAP, Labour, Organization," Lüneburg, June 20–21, 2013, https://www.leuphana.de/zentren/cdc/aktuell/termine/archiv/ansicht/datum/2013/06/20/workshop-logistics-of-soft-control-sap-labour-organization.html.

12. http://www.labournet.de/.

13. Many thanks to Helmut Weiss for his discussions during the Leuphana workshop on SAP, and for this account in particular of union research in IT within Germany.

14. Helmut Weiss, email communication, July 9, 2013.

15. Quoted in Anh Nguyen, "Walmart Pushes Ahead with SAP Rollout after Asda Pilot Success," *Computer World UK: The Voice of IT Management*, August 23, 2010, http://www.computerworlduk.com/news/it-business/3236348/walmart-pushes-ahead-with-sap-rollout-after-asda-pilot-success/.

16. For an overview of IoT, see Rob van Kranenburg, *The Internet of Things: A Critique of Ambient Technology and the All-Seeing Network of RFID*, Network Notebooks no. 2

(Amsterdam: Institute of Network Cultures, 2008), http://www.networkcultures.org/_uploads/notebook2_theinternetofthings.pdf.

17. Fenwick McKelvey, Matthew Tiessen, and Luke Simcoe, "We Are What We Tweet: The Problem with a Big Data World When Everything You Say Is Data," Culture Digitally: Examining Contemporary Cultural Production, June 3, 2013, http://culturedigitally.org/2013/06/we-are-what-we-tweet-the-problem-with-a-big-data-world-when-everything-you-say-is-data-mined/.

18. Sheller, "Materializing U.S.-Caribbean Borders," 238.

19. The first two of these categories are adapted from Packer and Wiley, "Introduction: The Materiality of Communication," *Communication Matters*, 3. The third dimension to the materiality of communication is one that I see as both a precondition for and coincident with the former two.

20. Gregory Bateson, *Steps to an Ecology of Mind* (New York: Ballantine Books, 1972).

21. See, for example, Christian Fuchs, *Internet and Society: Social Theory in the Information Age* (New York: Routledge, 2008); and Christian Fuchs, *Digital Labour and Karl Marx* (New York: Routledge, 2014).

22. David M. Berry, "The Computational Turn: Thinking about the Digital Humanities," *Culture Machine* 12 (2011): 1–22, http://culturemachine.net. This essay was reprinted in a slightly modified form in David M. Berry, ed., *Understanding the Digital Humanities* (Basingstoke and New York: Palgrave MacMillan, 2012). See also Leighton Evans and Sian Rees, "An Interpretation of Digital Humanities," in Berry, *Understanding the Digital Humanities*, 21–41.

23. Jeffrey Schnapp and Todd Presner, "The Digital Humanities Manifesto 2.0," 2009, http://www.humanitiesblast.com/manifesto/Manifesto_V2.pdf cited in Berry, "The Computational Turn."

24. Berry, "The Computational Turn," 12.

25. There is, indeed, a growing body of research interested in the relation between technology and neurological processes. At the more populist end, a very crude form of technological determinism pervades the claims made by the likes of neurologist Susan Greenfield in her various writings, including *ID: The Quest for Identity in the 21st Century* (London: Sceptre, 2008) and technology commentator Nicholas Carr's *The Shallows: What the Internet Is Doing to Our Brains* (New York: W. W. Norton, 2010). Such psychologically driven accounts can be offset by more critical and technically astute studies such as Anna Munster, *An Aesthesia of Networks: Conjunctive Experience in Art and Technology* (Cambridge, MA: MIT Press, 2013). For an overview of literature related to the "neurological turn" in Internet criticism, see also Geert Lovink, "MyBrain.net: The Colonization of Real-Time and Other Trends in Web2.0," *Eurozine*, April 18, 2010, http://www.eurozine.com/articles/2010–03–18-lovink-en.html.

26. Kostas Terzidis, *Algorithmic Architecture* (Oxford: Architectural Press, 2006).

27. Luciana Parisi, "Algorithmic Architecture," in Carolin Wiedemann and Soenke Zehle, eds., *Depletion Design: A Glossary of Network Ecologies* (Amsterdam: XMLab and the Institute for Network Cultures, 2012), 7–10.

28. See Lev Manovich, "Trending: The Promises and the Challenges of Big Social Data," 2011, http://www.manovich.net/DOCS/Manovich_trending_paper.pdf.

29. For literary studies critiques of this position, see Willard McCarty, "Knowing: Modeling in Literary Studies," in Susan Schreibman and Ray Siemens, eds., *A Companion to Digital Literary Studies* (Oxford: Blackwell, 2008). See also Katherine Bode, *Reading by Numbers: Recalibrating the Literary Field* (London: Anthem Press, 2012). For a critique of the empirics of big data, see danah boyd and Kate Crawford, "Critical Questions for Big

Data: Provocations for a Cultural, Technological, and Scholarly Phenomenon," *Information, Communication, and Society* 15, no. 5 (2012): 662–79.

30. Thanks to Mark Coté for pushing this line of thought further.

31. McKenzie Wark, *Molecular Red: Theory for the Anthropocene* (London and New York: Verso, 2015), 178.

32. John Durham Peters, *The Marvelous Clouds: Toward a Philosophy of Elemental Media* (Chicago and London: University of Chicago Press, 2015), 251–2.

33. "Data, Data Everywhere (interview with Kenneth Cukier)," *The Economist*, February 25, 2010, http://www.economist.com/node/15557443.

34. See, for example, Hugh Craig and Arthur F. Kinney, eds., *Shakespeare, Computers, and the Mystery of Authorship* (Cambridge: Cambridge University Press, 2009).

35. Alan Liu, "The State of the Digital Humanities: A Report and a Critique," *Arts & Humanities in Higher Education* 11, nos. 1–2 (2012): 11.

36. See, for example, David Hesmondhalgh and Sarah Baker, *Creative Labour: Media Work in Three Cultural Industries* (Oxon: Routledge, 2011); Mark Deuze, *Media Work* (Cambridge: Polity, 2007); and Trebor Scholz, ed., *Digital Labor: The Internet as Playground and Factory* (New York: Routledge, 2013). I would emphasize that I consider all the above titles fine studies and do not exempt myself from this criticism, having contributed in the past to various debates around creative and digital labor. Since around 2006–07, it has nonetheless become clear to me that an account of the constitutive outside of cultural industries in the form of migrant workers and informal economies such as electronic waste industries highlights the conditions of possibility for cultural economies.

37. Andrew Prescott, "Consumers, Creators, or Commentators? Problems of Audience and Mission in the Digital Humanities," *Arts and Humanities in Higher Education* 11, nos. 1–2 (2012): 72.

38. Ibid.

39. Alan Liu, "The Meaning of the Digital Humanities," *PMLA* 126, no. 2 (2013): 410.

40. Noortje Marres, "The Redistribution of Methods: On Intervention in Digital Social Research Broadly Conceived," *Sociological Review* 60 (2012): 151.

41. See Anja Kanngieser, Brett Neilson and Ned Rossiter, "What Is a Research Platform? Mapping Methods, Mobilities, and Subjectivities," *Media, Culture & Society* 36, no. 3 (2014): 302–18.

42. See also Richard Rogers, *Digital Methods* (Cambridge, MA: MIT Press, 2013).

43. See Bode, *Reading by Numbers*, 9.

44. Brett Neilson, "Beyond Kulturkritik: Along the Supply Chain of Contemporary Capitalism," *Culture Unbound: Journal of Current Cultural Research* 6 (2014): 77–93, http://www.cultureunbound.ep.liu.se.

45. See Sandro Mezzadra and Brett Neilson, *Border as Method, or, the Multiplication of Labor* (Durham: Duke University Press, 2013).

46. Neilson, "Beyond Kulturkritik," 79.

47. Lev Manovich, "Cultural Analytics: Visualizing Cultural Patterns in the Era of 'More Media'," 2011, http://www.manovich.net. See also Manovich, "Trending," http://www.manovich.net and Lev Manovich, *Software Takes Command* (New York: Bloomsbury Academic, 2013). For research generated out of the Software Studies Initiative, see http://lab.softwarestudies.com/.

48. Transit Labour: Circuits, Regions, Borders, http://transitlabour.asia.

49. Logistical Worlds: Infrastructure, Software, Labour, http://logisticalworlds.org/.

50. See Mezzadra and Neilson, *Border as Method*.

76 Into the Cloud

51. See Anja Kanngieser, "Tracking and Tracing: Geographies of Logistical Governance and Labouring Bodies," *Environment and Planning D: Society and Space* 31, no. 4 (2013): 594–610.
52. The animated digital visualizations produced for the Transit Labour study of Port Botany can be found at http://transitlabour.asia/documentation. Visual analytics programming by Vinh Nguyen, design by Kernow Craig, and background research by Katie Hepworth.
53. Katie Hepworth, "Enacting Logistical Geographies," *Environment and Planning D: Society and Space* 32, no. 6 (2014): 1120–34.
54. Ibid.
55. Edd Dumbill, "What Is Big Data? An Introduction to the Big Data Landscape," *O'Reilly Radar*, January 19, 2012, http://radar.oreilly.com/2012/01/what-is-big-data.html.
56. Ibid.
57. Patrick, "Asciano Signs Contract for Automated Straddles for Port Botany," September 3, 2012, http://www.patrick.com.au/asciano-signs-contract-for-automated-straddles-for/w1/i1003881/.
58. Occupy Oakland, http://occupyoakland.org.
59. In this respect, logistics shares with neoliberalism the capacity to incorporate crises. As Philip Mirowski notes, "Crises is the preferred field of action for neoliberals, since that offers more latitude for [the] introduction of bold experimental 'reforms' that only precipitate further crises down the road." See Philip Mirowski, *Never Let a Serious Crisis Go to Waste: How Neoliberalism Survived the Financial Meltdown* (London: Verso, 2013), 53.
60. Willard McCarty, *Humanities Computing* (Basingstoke: Palgrave Macmillan, 2005), 22.
61. Liu, "The Meaning of the Digital Humanities," 416.
62. Paul N. Edwards, *A Vast Machine: Computer Models, Climate Data, and the Politics of Global Warming* (Cambridge, MA: MIT Press, 2010), 338.
63. Alexander Galloway, "Protocol," *Theory, Culture & Society* 23, nos. 2–3 (2006): 317.
64. Richard Maxwell and Toby Miller, *Greening the Media* (New York: Oxford University Press, 2012), 3.
65. Jennifer Gabrys, *Digital Rubbish: A Natural History of Electronics* (Ann Arbor: University of Michigan Press, 2011), 116.

4

ECONOMIES OF WASTE

"As long as there are people on this planet, the waste industries will never die. So we're not worried about the future of the industry."
—*Owner of a small e-waste processing business in Ningbo, China, 2009*

"Dirt is the stuff that makes a system jump."
—*Born, Furján, and Jencks,* Dirt, *2012*

In the northern summer of 2010 we began our research in Shanghai for the Transit Labour project.[1] Collective field trip visits to two seemingly incongruous settings—an IT facility on the outskirts of Shanghai and Baoshan market for electronic waste, secondhand products, and fake gadgets—provided an index of how both regions and social mobilization are configured as singularities within a larger constellation of relations. Following earlier waves of manufacturing across East Asia where "Made in Japan" and, later, "Made in Taiwan" became synonymous with a range of electronic commodities and attendant mythologies of techno-cultural dystopias, over the last two decades China has become renowned as the planet's epicenter for electronic manufacturing. When purchased, one of the primary attractions of an electronic commodity is how clean it seems. The lovely smooth surfaces coated in buffed plastics or complex metal composites provide a suitable black box of mystery for their interior circuits and generation of values that betray the toxic conditions of production and their effects on workers' health and the environment. Such is the fantastic power of the commodity-form to abstract itself from the experience of labor and life.

But the index of labor, as Marx so astutely observed, is never entirely divorced from the commodity form. The relation between labor and the production of electronic commodities will of course be palpable at an IT factory in ways that can never be the case at some flagship store for global electronic brands. But even at the factory, the body is separated from the commodity form as a result of the division of labor and the centrality of machines to the manufacturing process. What we see is the factory body in its totality, a body that is at once machinic (as technical apparatus rather than social assemblage of the general intellect) while refusing complete subjugation by the machine through the assertion of special human qualities. We hear the language of dialects and notice the skin of ethnicities. Here is the most basic of anthropological encounters. Without some kind of hermeneutic device we are left in the realm of the senses—responses that nowadays are discredited within academe and its disciplinary sensitivities to the politics of the other (which arguably are more about a narcissistic politics of identity and the self). No matter how momentary or partial, we search for a cognitive model with which to render the mutability of sensation as stasis in the grid of reason. This is the problem of method.

There is another dark side to logistics, whose just-in-time economies are driven by ever increasing demands for efficiency and productivity. The waste generated by economies of consumption result in secondary economies of disposal and recycling. Frequently informal and often circumventing sovereign control, the logistics of waste provides the basis for a media theory of logistical disposal (and, in different ways, opens a route into a geomedia theory of particle aesthetics, as developed in some of Jussi Parikka's recent work).[2]

This chapter is interested in the relationship between electronic waste and emergent regimes of labor control operative within the global logistics industry. Central to logistics is the question and scope of governance—both of laboring subjects and the treatment of objects or things. The relation between labor and electronic waste constitutes a milieu (environment) and population (of human and technological life) whose communication comprises a unique multi-scalar space that severely tests techno-systems of governance. In registering the contingency of governance—its capacity for failure or oversight—this chapter inquires into the uncertainty that underpins the technics of control special to logistics.[3] At stake is the connection between the milieu and the labor of human life. How does the former give expression to working conditions and experiences of struggle within a milieu whose operational logic can be likened to what Georges Canguilhem attributes to neo-Lamarckian scientific thought in the mid-nineteenth century as "a dissolution of individualized organic syntheses into the anonymity of universal elements and movements"?[4] As arcane and distant such a notion of milieu is from the material realities of electronic waste industries in China, it does nonetheless signal an opening for analyses of governance beyond the human subject. This includes, as Sean Cubitt points out, "a biopolitical recognition that our devices have indeed evolved a life of their own."[5]

Paradoxically perhaps, conflicting governance regimes make possible the production of non-governable subjects and spaces. Electronic waste and many of those working in its informal secondary economies can be considered as occupants that reside off the grid. Such positioning in itself does not constitute a political program or articulated agency. Non-governance should not, in other words, be assumed to be synonymous with some kind of counter-political force. This would be the error of translation understood as a system of equivalence in which an *a priori* relation exists between, for instance, non-state actors and political agency. Indeed, it may even be desirable for biopolitical powers to ensure a non-governable dimension in order to manage the political, economic, and environmental problem of electronic waste—the maintenance of unregulated informality serves as one of the structural resources that sustains the current economy of waste. Since there is no globally implemented consensus or treaty and quite frequently an absence of national legislation on how to address the economic and social life of electronic waste, it helps to reflect on the question of e-waste by taking this "indifferent" status of e-waste as a point of departure—both technically within logistics software and politically within the institutional limits of the state apparatus. As I argue below, such indifference comes at a potential political and social cost, one that sees a further expansion and penetration of biopolitical technologies of control over relatively autonomous aspects of labor and life.

To complement the various hypotheses above, this chapter also addresses the relation between regions and the composition of labor in electronic waste industries in China. The multiplication of regions through practices of translation coextensive with the movement of people, language, technological protocols, and things presents a serious challenge to regions as they are defined by hegemonic orders and interests. A region such as the European Union, for example, is translated as a legitimate political, economic, and social entity through an ensemble of institutions (state governments, international institutions, universities, cultural organizations, labor unions, and so forth). While there may be numerous instances of dispute and conflict between such actors, ultimately the fact of their relation serves to mutually reaffirm the legitimacy of the European Union as a region. But to reduce the configuration of a region to such translation devices alone is to overlook the diverse practices and technics through which spaces and populations are comprised. The battle of hegemony, in this sense, is a contest over idioms of translation.

Similarly, the social practice of translation brings into question the analytical modalities that assume the existence of the region as a set of stable coordinates and coherent institutional practices that facilitate economies of depletion.[6] In the case of the global logistics industries, the rise of secondary resource flows accompanying the economy of electronic waste is coextensive with the production of non-governable subjects and spaces. The relation between these entities constitutes new regional formations that hold a range of implications for biopolitical technologies of control.

Waste and Logistics as Method

Where the IT factory's PCB circuit board—"the basic platform used to interconnect electronic components"—is part of an East Asian regional formation at a transnational scale, sites such as Baoshan electronic market in urban Shanghai combine intranational regional formations in terms of the domestic sale of second-hand commodities and electronic waste with a global traffic in the recycling of e-waste.[7] By studying the movement of e-waste, we find that electronic components—many of which have been made in China—are grafted in different ways to national and international regulations designed to govern the treatment of electronic waste. The Chinese government notionally banned the importation of e-waste in 1996.[8] Yet the informal e-waste economy is substantial and thriving in small businesses in cities along the eastern seaboard.[9] Some of these businesses located in places like Baoshan market integrate the reassembly of secondhand computer parts with a sideline in recycling e-waste purchased through domestic and transnational circuits of trade. In both instances, electronic objects belonging to the same family of parts hold a substantially different status at the spatial scale depending on their circuits of distribution.

In moving from the site of manufacturing to one that deals in the detritus of consumption, we discern the multiplication of regions. The circuit boards produced at the IT factory are part of a social life of things that become mobilized across the regional space of Asia during the process of assembly. The composition of low-wage labor also constitutes a regional formation, but one that in the case of the Shanghai IT factory is drawn from provinces set back from the special economic zones stretching along the eastern seaboard. In China's manufacturing, construction, and service industries there is a tendency for labor to assemble according to provincial filiations. The network of street-waste workers in Shanghai's Xu Hui District (or former French Concession), for example, is made of migrants from Anhui province and their self-organization of labor is predicated on provincial connections.

To take another example: Many of the workers in the e-waste and secondhand electronic markets in Ningbo, a city south of Shanghai, migrate from Jiangxi province. And in the case of Nanhai—"one of the best digital cities in Guangdong" (and one of the biggest centers for e-waste and secondhand electronics)—workers stem from Hubei province. It is worth noting that Nanhai also has a substantial ship-building industry, and it is perhaps no surprise that Guangdong province has more relaxed borders of control when it comes to the importation of illegal e-waste from overseas markets such as Japan, Europe, the United States, and Australia. Businesses in Ningbo, where border control at the port is more stringent, find alternative routes for the movement of illegal e-waste—cities such as Nanhai serve as a key source for the transit of waste from within the sovereign territory of the nation; in turn, unsold products in Ningbo's secondhand markets are considered e-waste and sold back to junk men and women from Guangdong and Taizhou.[10]

In a site visit to Shanghai's Baoshan electronic market in June 2010, one of our co-researchers, Anja Kanngieser, found that workers came from quite a wide range of cities and provinces: Suzhou, Nanjing, Henan, Jiangxi, and Anhui. Yet at another electronic market, not so far away on Fuxing Lu, workers came predominantly from Guangdong province, the center of the electronic manufacturing and waste industries. While e-waste was something on sale in the case of Baoshan with all its regional cosmopolitanism, this wasn't the case at Fuxing Lu market. Yet often e-waste is hard to see immediately, and it is a sort of sliding object or category in the sense that unsold secondhand products, which are often reassembled into hybrid objects to be sold again, then become "e-waste" when they can't be sold as commodity objects riding on brand names and are then sold on to junk men and women as waste. Junk is not junk, in other words. Or rather, the same looking junk becomes quite different junk—an object lesson on the empty signifier. Both waste and labor, then, comprise forms of social mobility that can be understood as special intranational and transnational regional formations whose borders, like the logistical city (chapter 2), are highly elastic.

In searching for an analytical method with which to make sense of these various mobilities, we have been struck by the role of logistics as a biopolitical technology of control in governing the movement, as noted throughout this book, of people, finance, and things in the interests of communication, transport, and economic efficiencies. On the question of method, Sandro Mezzadra and Brett Neilson propose the following: "We understand method to emerge precisely from the material circumstances at hand. . . . Border as method thus entails not only an epistemic viewpoint from which a whole series of strategic concepts as well as their relations can be recast. It also requires a research process that continually accounts for and reacts to the multifarious battles and negotiations, not least those concerning race, that constitute the border both as an institution and a set of social relationships."[11] What, then, might logistics as method hold for the analysis of transit labor (labor mobilities in transition) and the production of knowledge? As we note in our catalog of project concepts: "Logistical methods of organization apply to contemporary production and patterns of mobility."[12] Organization, in turn, becomes a question and practice for the arrangement of bodies and brains mobilized as labor.

Multiplication and Division

With their capacity to adapt flexibly to a range of circumstances and skill requirements, the rural migrant worker in China is arguably the exemplary post-Fordist subject rather than, as often assumed, the specialist work of the designer, architect, filmmaker, or adman attributed to the figure of cognitive, creative, or immaterial labor. Such a distinction in the body of labor-power points also to the residual class dimension of post-Fordist labor, which in this case is frequently underscored by the spatial division between rural provinces and metropolitan centers. Ethnic divisions also prevail, with the rural migrant worker often enough not belonging to the Han Chinese majority population.[13]

Fieldwork undertaken in early 2009 with my MA students in Ningbo—a second tier and major port city a few hours south of Shanghai—began to make visible

82 Economies of Waste

(at least for us) the "division and multiplication of labor" within the electronic waste industries.[14] Mezzadra and Neilson:

> By speaking of the multiplication of labor we want to point to the fact that division works in a fundamentally different way than it does in the world as constructed within the frame of the international division of labor. It tends itself to function through a continuous multiplication of control devices that correspond to the multiplication of labor regimes and the subjectivities implied by them *within* each single space constructed as separate within models of the international division of labor. Corollary to this is the presence of particular kinds of labor regimes across different global and local spaces. This leads to a situation where the division of labor must be considered within a multiplicity of overlapping sites that are themselves internally heterogeneous.[15]

And as Neilson elaborates elsewhere:

> It is crucial to note that the multiplication of labour does not exclude its division. . . . Indeed, multiplication implies division, or, even more strongly, we can say multiplication is a form of division.[16]

Hierarchies of labor separate the first stage of waste processing and storage from the initial collection of unwanted trash in the cities of China. The looped tape recording of *diannao* (computer/electronic brain) and *kongtiao* (air conditioner) rhythmically alerts locals to the arrival of the junk men and women as they move about neighborhoods on a bicycle equipped with a flat tray for the transport of waste. Situated among those at the bottom of the supply chain of electronic waste industries (others working in particularly toxic conditions include children who dissemble electronic products, stripping copper from plastic casings while inhaling poisonous fumes from incineration), the junk men and women are among the most transient in the economy of e-waste. The working life of junk men and women is one of low income and frequently changing low-skill jobs determined by the fluctuation of market economies and the informal social networks and family demands that shape the movement of populations from country to city, job to job. Here, we see the multiplying effect of labor: While hierarchically distinct from other modalities of work in the economic life of electronic waste, the job of the junk men and women is underscored by mobility and uncertain transformation. It is unlikely, in other words, that waste collection is a job for life.

A different story prevails, however, in the case of many of the small businesses that deal with the sorting of electronic waste (Figure 4.1). Like many Chinese cities, the waste collection centers dispersed across the neighborhoods and districts of Ningbo are pivotal sites in the social and economic life of electronic waste. Often run as small family businesses, these recycling centers can be divided along formal and informal lines, both with differing degrees of toxicity in terms of the type of waste materials collected. Of the thousand or so businesses with official licenses to operate in Ningbo (a legal requirement in Zhejiang province), there are many more that exist illegally. At 6000 RMB (approx. 600 euros in 2009 exchange rates), the annual license fee is a costly obstacle for many, yet it offers a level of economic and political security not afforded by the illegal collection centers. The official sites tend to have a regular network of waste suppliers based on *guanxi* (social relations or networks) and, unlike the illegal sites, do not negotiate prices. This in turn affords the junk men and women a level of guaranteed income, albeit with wildly fluctuating and typically declining prices over the past year. Trading prices for metals are set each morning according to futures markets, which are usually accessed as daily updates by mobile phone more often than through computers.

External and internal forces have placed enormous pressure on the recycling industry and labor conditions across China. The owner of one small licensed recycling company we spoke to, who had been in business for fifteen years, made note of the Chinese Labor Contract Law, which came into effect in January 2008, making it harder for companies to sack employees.[17] He offered this example as an indication of the more stable and secure working conditions for the migrants he employs from Jiangxi and Húnán provinces to the west of coastal Zhejiang.

By contrast, reports produced by various human rights NGOs and environmental monitoring organizations document numerous instances in which workers'

FIGURE 4.1 Scales in small-waste business, Ningbo. Photograph by Ned Rossiter, 2009.

rights are violated in the electronics factories and recycling industries, with excessive and often unpaid working hours, hiring of child labor, gender divisions, dangerous working conditions, suppression of efforts to organize labor and strike actions, and fines and punishments for violation of highly punitive rules (correct haircuts, smoking in designated areas, improper attire, wastage of water, making noise, posting or distributing unauthorized articles, etc.).[18] More broadly, in her assessment of the legislative reform of labor conditions, Jenny Chan notes "severe rights violations in at least three major areas: job security; the use of contingent labor; and fair, fixed-term labor contracts."[19] Worker layoffs from factories were also on the rise since the end of the 2009 Chinese new year—the social effects of this became rapidly clear, if relatively short-lived, on the streets of Shanghai and Ningbo, with increased numbers of homeless migrants and visible instances of untreated mental illnesses.

Improved labor conditions are often perceived by businesses and investors to come at a cost rather than a benefit in terms of higher productivity through workplace stability. Other economic forces impact in more immediate ways. Since January 1, 2009, recycling companies have had to absorb the cost of a 17 percent value added tax—a burden not suffered by other industries. This comes on top of an enormous drop in prices of around 50–60 percent for recyclable metals due to the global economic recession. With successive months of depressed prices, the global recycling economy is now dire. In China, this manifests in the form of massive stockpiling of waste that cannot be sold. There are additional storage costs and increased health risks associated with prolonged exposure to inventory accumulation of toxic metals, to say nothing of increased pressures on labor.

Another owner of a Ningbo recycling business, Mr. Yu, assessed the situation in the following way in early 2009:

> Metals and papers are online transactions. Copper and aluminum are sold and bought in the futures markets. For China, marketing Chinese products is fine, however, in the global market it is hard to do good business. I have to purchase and sell the waste at cheap prices. I suppose the economy will improve. Copper makes more profits, however it makes me lose more money. Now the price of copper is 17 yuan/500 grams compared with the previous price (27/28 yuan 500g)—we lose 10 yuan per 500g. We are a small business. Foreign waste such as plastic, copper, and aluminum are packaged and put into containers that are transported to Beilun dock.

The connection made here between electronic waste and the maritime industries is worth noting. Despite the fact that importation of electronic waste in China has been illegal since 1996, much of the movement of waste from North America, Europe, East Asia, and Australia is channeled through the ports of China.[20] There is a story to be told here about informal labor within the global logistics industry and how electronic waste industries obviously fit into that schematic. The potential for escape, invention, and refusal become severely compromised within such a biopolitical regime of control, one that is already dominant for millions working across the world in different industries articulated with global logistics systems. Moreover, and most oddly, it would seem that the capacity for capital to renew itself is substantially challenged within such a system: Logistics aims to diminish the force of contingency, which plays a key role in the emergence of innovation upon which the reproduction of capital depends. Do we find here, then, an instance whereby capital programs its own obsolescence?

Translation and the Battle of Standards

An important control device in the maritime industries is radio-frequency identification (RFID) technology, which registers the geographic position of ships and goods and assists in the management of inventories and the efficiency of supply chains. While RFID technologies are indifferent to the matter of things, and thus do not discern between, say, automotive parts or textiles on the one hand, and electronic waste on the other, their database logic nonetheless identifies the content of motion. In other words, the database provides a record of that which migrates from one place to another. And in the case of electronic waste, there are strict national and international regulations governing its transport and treatment. But since, as noted earlier, electronic waste is deemed an illegal import in China, it is questionable whether it falls into the purview of the database and its informatized sovereign power. Like many countries, electronic waste holds a contradictory status within the rule of law in China, with waste businesses requiring a license to operate, as mentioned previously.

In another respect, the connection between electronic waste, logistics, and software systems constitutes the battle of standards across idioms of translation. The governance of labor associated with electronic waste varies enormously depending upon whether or not the movement, economy, and treatment of e-waste is made visible by logistics software used in maritime industries, to take one example. In such a case, there are industry, state, and union standards that shape the conditions of labor and management of waste. Logistics software facilitates such relations by tracking cargo movement, registering times of passage in global supply chains, and accounting for inventory accumulation. The standards established in such an economy run into conflict, or are just modulated differently, when the circuits of labor and resource flows associated with electronic waste are translated through less formal standards found in economies not officiated by the state. The case of electronic waste in China is one of these economies. The sex trade in and across many countries and regions would be another.

Translation can be understood in one sense as the process of establishing standards expressed through a community of practice. In Naoki Sakai's terms, this is the "homolingual" operation of translation.[21] Yet such an occasion should not be seen as the end point of translation, but rather in terms of the instantiation of a particular border that promulgates new modes of practice and relation. Indeed, it is precisely the scene of conflict that attends the drive toward standardization that raises the problem of translation.[22] The example of standardization in the shipping and transport industries helps clarify this process.

Modern logistics turns around the battle of standards that accompanied containerization in the maritime industries. The standardization of shipping containers from the 1950s was accompanied by disputes between engineers, corporations, and governments over competing economic and geopolitical interests in the transport industries.[23] As geographer Deborah Cowen notes, "Containerization radically reduced the time required to load and unload ships, reducing port labor costs and enabling tremendous savings for manufactures who could reduce inventories to a bare minimum."[24] By the 1970s a global standard in containerization had been established, around the same time economic globalization came into full swing following the end of the Bretton Woods Accord in 1971 and the oil crisis of 1973. Such cursory contextualization indicates that standard containers did not alone determine or create economic accumulation (the same might be said for logistics software). Marc Levinson notes that by the late 1960s:

> The economic benefit of standardization . . . was still not clear. Containers of 10, 20, 30 and 40 feet had become American and international standards, but the neat arithmetic relationship among the "standard" sizes did not translate into demand by shippers or ship lines. Not a single ship was using 30-foot containers. Only a handful of 10-foot containers had been purchased, and the main carrier using them soon concluded that it would not buy any more. As for 20-foot containers, land carriers hated them.[25]

Conflicts over standards in logistics and software systems define the terrain of translation in more recent years. Once the logistical problem of container standardization had been resolved, logistical operations shifted attention to the problem of data standards. Although present in a rudimentary form in the 1960s with earlier incarnations in World War II, the computerization of transport industries did not really take off until the 1980s following the standardization of shipping containers and the advent of just-in-time production.[26]

Effectively integrating and simulating the logic of containerization in order to produce enhanced efficiencies, the information architecture of code can also be understood as a container or silo formation.[27] Again, the drive toward interoperability across different software systems is an example of translation as homolingual address or equivalence.[28] Software technologies are key devices in the translation of labor and the mobility of things as actionable, visible, and subject to control and instrumental consolidation. Once registered within the database logic of informatized sovereignty, electronic waste and its modalities of labor and social life become governable within the economy of real-time. Such an idiom of translation is one of co-figuration and equivalence, to draw on the formulation of Sakai. Yet logistics software consists of multiple standards whose disparities in code produce conflict and competition in the effort to determine systems commensurate with the demand for intermodal freight transportation, pervasive labor management, and economic hegemony. Such tensions over standardization give rise to the hetero-lingual dimension of translation—its social practices of "differential inclusion," struggle, and multiplication—that confers a non-governable potential to electronic waste.[29]

While I am in no way idealizing such practices—as noted earlier, there is enor-mous social, environmental, and individual damage that attends the toxic life of electronic waste—I wish to stress that once captured within the instrumental world of logistics that economizes labor, life, and space according to efficiencies in time, the work of translation becomes automated and effectively annulled. And it is precisely at this moment of informatization coupled with logistics that the region becomes constituted within the sovereign space of the database. Once code is king the variable capacity of labor, life, and things finds itself subject to an inten-sive form of territorial and proprietary control that formal settings such as ASEAN, APEC, and NAFTA can only gesture toward.[30] But no matter how much com-munication regimes may be indifferent to noise, contingency, feedback, and indeed life itself, the difference necessary for the work of translation is never entirely eradicated by techno-scientific systems.[31] More likely certain modes of labor and life simply migrate off the radar and subsist instead in a world of non-governance, by which I mean idioms of expression, practice, and economy external to the state-corporate nexus that defines contemporary sovereign power.[32]

The Limits of Translation

With its indifference to matter, substance, or qualities and concern instead with the management of mobilities and efficiencies of action, logistics dispenses with borders that distinguish labor, life, and milieu.[33] In doing so, the constitutive differences that make possible the translation of relations between labor, discourses, social-technical practices, economies, and geocultural formations are surrendered to the world of ubiquitous homologies.[34] What I am calling "ubiquitous homologies" stems from the political economy of globalizing design industries (where architecture begins to resemble a sports shoe, toothbrush, motorbike, office chair, computer monitor, etc.), and shares something with what Sakai terms "co-figuration," "linguistic equiva-lence," and "homolingual address"—all of which are homogenizing operations of translation that make up the sovereign power of the nation-state.[35]

This is the limit of translation, and hence the scene of the political. With bor-ders (limits) comes struggle. It may seem a contradiction is at work in this formula-tion: The subtraction within logistics of constitutive differences does not immediately lend itself to the idea of the political as the struggle with borders. Nor does such a formulation of logistics as a system of techno-social and economic practices of indifference to borders correspond with the concept of translation, which both assumes and requires difference as a condition of operation. How, then, to address the political and conceptual challenges that attend the rise of new indifferent forms of communication and governance? The erasure of constitutive differences through the biopolitical power of logistics defines the limits of translation. But the occlusion of difference should not be taken as some kind of finitude since the coding of indifference in itself multiplies the fields of distinction through the force of relations. The indifference of logistics to borders is only internal to its technics of operation—a kind of generic predisposition—and does not hold a determining force in any totalizing sense or "last instance." With reference to Randy Martin's *An Empire of Indifference*, Brett Neilson suggests that at work here is perhaps not "an indifference to borders so much as a process of commensuration across borders."[36] Certainly such an understanding corresponds with the much-vaunted ambition on the part of computer engineers and their policy advocates (to say nothing of academic devotees such as Henry Jenkins and advertising gurus) to arrive at a state of "convergence culture" (or, more simply, economic globalization in its social-technical form). While this may indeed be the case, I am also wishing to invoke this dynamic of communicative—and thus spatial—indifference in terms of the social and economic dimensions of electronic waste as an assertion of refusal, irrespective of whether or not such a practice is fused with political content. The key question here is: What expressive capacity might non-governable subjects and spaces consist of? There are and always will be relations. In this process new border struggles are comprised and the work of translation is remodulated in ways coextensive with the production of subjectivity.

The analysis of electronic waste flows serves to cleave the interrelations of software, labor, and logistics in order to identify how the indifference of communication special to logistics technology points to the limits of translation, which holds implications for biopolitical regimes of governance. The heterolingual address of translation is the analytical method that makes visible the possibility of escape from biopolitical technologies of control at work in the global logistics industry. Or, rather, the non-governable dimension of social and economic life within the electronic waste industries asserts a singular indifference to the regulatory control of logistics. This is the practice of refusal. The extent to which labor and life can withstand the encroaching predisposition of logistics as a control system *par excellence* is—in part—a matter of time, capital, and the sovereign demand that populations comply with technologies of governance.

A study of the economies and socialities of electronic waste in China helps illuminate the political status and potential of non-governable subjects and spaces. The earlier discussion of labor and the circuits of exchange in Ningbo's electronic waste industries are a case in point. As forms of social relation, the labor and economy in Ningbo's e-waste industries operate outside the scope of state-corporate regimes of governance supported by logistics technologies of control. Of relevance here is the constitution of regions and the politics of translation in order to address an emerging tension of scale that extends more broadly to the global management of labor and life at play in the logistics industry. Such an analytical strategy indicates how the problems of non-governable spaces and subjects—for better and worse—reside beyond the informational sovereignty that imbues the biopolitical power of logistics. The social practice of translation (re)constitutes regions as they figure around the economy of electronic waste. Translation here is not so much a conscious act on the part of workers in electronic waste industries—at least not in any way that I am capable of discerning—as a social-technical relation of exteriority that arises through structural conditions and the techno-social operations of logistics software managing the movement of labor, commodities, resources, and finance. What I am calling a social-technical relation of exteriority extends to the challenge of method and analysis: There is always the subject that resides beyond comprehension, that refuses to be known as such—something Gayatri Spivak carefully analyzed as the politics of the subaltern condition.[37]

Insofar as that which is perceived or manifests as non-governable—the labor and economy of electronic waste, in the case of this chapter—some final points can be proffered. The spatialities of non-governable subjects and objects constitute regions in ways that do not readily correspond with more hegemonic regional formations. Translation thus becomes a form of inventing new circuits of movement. Within such a context, regions become contested geocultural and political spaces, bringing into question the dominant understanding of regions as defined within the political-economic discourses of trade agreements, innovation and knowledge transfer, and statist formations of geopolitical equivalence such as ASEAN and its expansion into ASEAN+3 (China, Japan, South Korea) and ASEAN+6 (Australia, New Zealand, India). Regions, when understood as conflictual constitutions underscored by the movements and frequently informal practices of language, culture, and labor, comprise geocultural formations that seriously question the power of border technologies such as trade formations, migration and labor regimes, state alliances, and global logistics. Moreover, the analytical method of translation as social practice and heterolingual address initiates a critique of sovereign power by elaborating the tensions embedded within the informal and formal dynamics of geocultural configurations. Sovereign border regimes, in other words, are brought into question with the rise of non-governable subjects and spaces associated with the social-economic life of electronic waste.

Informal circuits of exchange comprise the multiplication of economies that attend the movement of electronic waste. Such configurations may be territorial in terms of the distribution of waste, as seen, for example, in the intranational or transregional economies of electronic waste. Within this complex of relations there is a sense in which the non-governable aspects of labor, waste, and economy reside outside the biopolitical power of logistics technologies. While this chapter has concentrated on the very localized case of electronic waste in Ningbo, there are always multi-scalar dimensions and circuits that both manifest in the local and connect the local to the trans-territorial whose specificities reconfigure how the regional comes to be understood. As long as the movement and treatment of electronic waste evades the sovereign power of informatized logistics, then the

90 Economies of Waste

connection of waste with regions remains open to the possibility of multiple configurations. There is also the lingering problem of method—something this book is continually in search of. Practices of "dirt research" offer an ensemble of techniques that assist in infrastructural analysis and the politics and economy of waste.

Dirt Research

Data consists of materials, details, inscriptions, and symbols in motion. We gather or capture data and in so doing render it temporarily static to produce information and knowledge about the world. The digital coding of data within the grammar of algorithms shares with the analog technology of archives the logic of governance, of ordering, of method. How to move between the digital and the analog is a question of translation across time and space. Some relevant analytical methods within media research include the political economy of "supply chain capitalism" (Tsing) as a way of identifying the production, distribution, and labor of electronic waste. Another consists of media archaeologies that bring medium theory stemming from Innis together with cybernetics, German media theory, and software studies to register the transformation of bodies and institutions technologically situated within communication systems. These sorts of interests in the materiality of communication can be considered as contemporary extensions of dirt research.

The phrase "dirt research" described the "direct" method by which Canadian political economist and communications theorist Harold A. Innis (1894–1952) collected material for his research on economic history in Canada. The result of extensive travels across Canada, where he gathered oral testimonies on the staples industries (fur trade, cod fisheries) and transport systems (rivers, railways) combined with exhaustive archival research, Innis's method of dirt research sought to establish a "general organizing principle" by which patterns of economic and social development could be understood "beyond the basic data."[38]

Innis's method of dirt research during his staples work was later combined in his communications work with a form of data mining from his "idea file"—an index of file cards consisting of telegraphic notes, ideas, and quotations derived from his expansive reading across Canadian economic history, ancient history, and philosophy.[39] The resulting texts comprised a pre-digital form of recombination—or what John Watson calls "textual scrambling"—to the extent that some might consider them partial works of plagiarism. Innis, on the other hand, was refining a method that enabled him to sketch vast historical relations in an effort to crystallize his thesis on the correspondence between civilization and culture and the spatial and temporal power of communication media and transport technologies.

Dirt research might be understood as both *a priori* and *a posteriori* metadata organizing a research process. Architect-designers Born, Furján, and Jencks suggest that "Dirt is designed. It is uniquely composed, site specific, and innately intelligent. . . . Dirt is a design tool. Collecting and composing dirty matter is a fruitful foundation for the creation of spaces, artifacts, and atmospheres."[40] As architects and designers are often wont to do, there is a tendency here of valorizing an aestheticization of that which, in the case of depletion design, is also a political practice addressing the proliferation of data. Nevertheless, we get a sense that dirt research is at once shaped by the model or program of investigation (design) while feeding back into the organizing principle itself as a result of the material and affective properties or qualities of the object of research (data).

Dirt research within the current conjuncture investigates how circuits of capital connect with the constituent force of labor, life, and things, shaping the production of time, space, and economy in variational ways. The capacity for change does not assume some form of conscious will. Such a faculty is beyond the reckoning of objects and code and assumes an articulated agency only occasionally displayed in the case of subjects more inclined toward the unconscious routines of habit. As noise, it is enough for entities to resonate as material and immaterial perturbations. Yet the paradox of noise is the unforeseen gift offered to technologies of control: As contingency, noise is the prompt for biopower to remodel its parameters and in so doing bolster the fortunes of control and its technologies of extraction. A story of origins within Italian *operaismo* consists of the *refusal of work* as the catalyst for capitalist restructuring and the transformation of labor processes. The shift from Fordist to post-Fordist modes of production and the governance of labor-power was not a result of management of their own volition refining structures of capital. Rather, the refusal of work in the form of factory strikes, infrastructural sabotage, and willful acts of laziness cajoled capital into adjusting its mode of production in ways that could accommodate more flexible, mobile, and contingent modes of work and capital accumulation.

Within the economy of networks the extension of this logic is taken to its extreme, with the rise of "free labor" as a norm through which productivity is registered in the online action of users. Content is not so relevant here as the proliferation and aggregation of data, which media proprietors endlessly recombine to mine users' tastes and habits in the packaging of profiles to be sold to third parties. Data is the myth of a new empirics, of abstraction made concrete. Where does this leave a politics of refusal if not as withdrawal made anew in the social production of value, where life itself is put to work? What new forms of capital restructuring are precipitated by informatized labor? Mental and social fatigue within the ecology of networks eventually leads to the depletion of refusal. Politics as a practice of conflictual constitution is left empty-handed.

Depletion design is also a practice of organization. This includes tracking the distribution of electronic trash following the stages of manufacture and consumption to investigate how electronic devices "become the means for possible infrastructures of reuse."[41] And it consists of generating rumors as a tactical intervention into fluctuating contours of markets, corporate practices, and government agendas. As Keller Easterling proposes, "Design also vividly anticipates and materializes change, using tools found in many forms of cultural persuasion."[42] The use of pictograms and design databases as techniques of cartographic analysis in projects by Bureau d'études and Josh On's *They Rule* are indicative of how design engages in the production of counter-imaginaries of corporate capitalism.[43] Dirt research of global infrastructures and logistical operations special to supply chain capitalism would do well to design counter-depletion into its repertoire of methods.

The recent revival of media archaeology is one idiom of analysis that registers within media theory the practice of dirt research. Jussi Parikka notes how "practices of reuse (zombie media), alternative design, an attention to components and materials used, are all tapping into the entanglement of intensity of non-human matter (dust), and the matter of abstract political economy of work and production."[44] Intensity and political economy. Affect and power. To diagram the relations of such agencies is to design the operation of depletion and generation, of subtraction and multiplication. At this point the material condition of dust with its often imperceptible force shifts to the level of program, or dirt research.

As a method, dirt research brings institutional borders, disciplinary limits, and expertise into question. First and foremost, dirt research challenges what Innis termed "monopolies of knowledge" shaped by the spatiotemporal bias of communication media in conjunction with institutional forms. In the case of electronic waste, it is clear the academy is well behind other actors in understanding the economic operation, environmental impact, and conditions of work associated with this industry. Dirt research entails, then, a certain intermingling of bodies and brains, institutional settings, and disciplinary practices. As a transversal mode of knowledge production it necessarily encounters conflict of various kinds: geocultural, social, political, and epistemological. How dirt research organizes itself across a diagram of coordinates and forces cannot be programmed but must instead engage the social-technical practice of translation. The seriality of disruption, dissipation, and undulations of intensity and attention will then define the transnational organization of dirt research.

Notes

1. http://transitlabour.asia.
2. Jussi Parikka, "New Materialism of Dust," *Artnodes: E-Journal on Art, Science and Technology* 12 (2012), http://artnodes.uoc.edu/index.php/artnodes/article/view/n12-parikka. See also Jussi Parikka, "Dust and Exhaustion: The Labor of Media Materialism," *CTheory* (2013), http://www.ctheory.net/articles.aspx?id=726. These pieces have been developed and revised in Jussi Parikka, *A Geology of Media* (Minneapolis: University of Minnesota Press, 2015).
3. A parallel can be found here with Schumpeter's logic of "creative destruction," where failure becomes the source of renewal in the reproduction of capital. The prospects for a politics of refusal within such a system become extremely depressing in so far as it is unlikely to do much more than reinforce the power of the hegemon. Such a scenario returns us, yet again, to the core question: What *is* politics?

Economies of Waste **93**

4. Georges Canguilhem, *Knowledge of Life*, trans. Stefanos Geroulanos and Daniela Ginsburg (New York: Fordham University Press, 2008), 103.

5. Sean Cubitt, "Telecommunication Networks: Economy, Ecology, Rule," *Theory, Culture & Society* 31, nos. 7–8 (2014): 193.

6. On translation as social practice, see Jon Solomon, "Re: A Hierarchy of Networks?; or, Geo-Culturally Differentiated Networks and the Limits of Collaboration," posting to edu-factory mailing list, January 23, 2008, http://www.edu-factory.org.

7. A wonderful recent study of electronic waste can be found in Jennifer Gabrys, *Digital Rubbish: A Natural History of Electronics* (Ann Arbor: University of Michigan Press, 2011). See also Matthias Feilhauer and Soenke Zehle, eds., "Special Issue: Ethics of Waste in the Information Society," *International Review of Information Ethics (IRIE)* 11 (2009), http://www.i-r-i-e.net/issue11.htm. Other key work in this emergent field includes Richard Maxwell and Toby Miller, *Greening the Media* (Oxford and New York: Oxford University Press, 2010) and Cubitt, "Telecommunication Networks."

8. See Richard Maxwell and Toby Miller, "Creative Industries or Wasteful Ones?," *Urban China* 33 (2008): 28–9, 122, http://orgnets.net/urban_china/maxwell_miller.

9. For a comprehensive analysis of the inside workings of the e-waste industry in China, see Adam Minter, *Junkyard Planet: Travels in the Billion-Dollar Trash Trade* (New York and London: Bloomsbury, 2013), 182–211. See also Minter's Shanghai Scrap blog at http://shanghaiscrap.com/.

10. Special thanks to students enrolled in an MA International Communications module I coordinated at the University of Nottingham, Ningbo, in 2009 and 2010. Their collaboration in fieldwork helped me enormously in gaining some understanding of these economies. Documentation by students can be found at Urban-Media Networks: Anthropologies of Urban Transformation, http://orgnets.cn/.

11. Sandro Mezzadra and Brett Neilson, "Border as Method, or, the Multiplication of Labor," *Transversal* (March, 2008), http://eipcp.net/transversal/0608/mezzadraneilson/en. See also Sandro Mezzadra and Brett Neilson, *Border as Method, or, the Multiplication of Labor* (Durham: Duke University Press, 2013).

12. http://transitlabour.asia/concepts/.

13. See Steve Hess, "The Ethnic Explosion at Shaoguan: Weighing In on the Labor Export Programs of Southwest Xinjiang," *China Elections and Governance*, September 8, 2009, http://en.chinaelections.org/newsinfo.asp?newsid=20996. See also China Labor Watch, "Labor Violations Exacerbate Ethnic Tensions in South China," July 6, 2009, http://www.chinalaborwatch.org/20090706uyghur.htm#.

14. For an analysis that offers more specific detail of e-waste in Ningbo, see Meng Xing, "An Investigation of the Situation of E-Waste Recycling: Concerning the Recycling Industry in Ningbo," May 29, 2009, http://orgnets.cn/?p=708.

15. Mezzadra and Neilson, "Border as Method, or, the Multiplication of Labor."

16. Brett Neilson, "The World Seen from a Taxi: Students-Migrants-Workers in the Global Multiplication of Labour," *Subjectivity* 29 (2009): 425–44.

17. See also Jenny Chan, "Meaningful Progress or Illusory Reform? Analyzing China's Labor Contract Law," *New Labor Forum* 18, no. 2 (2009): 43–51.

18. See Jenny Chan and Charles Ho, *Dark Side of Cyberspace: Inside the Sweatshops of China's Computer Hardware Production* (Berlin: World Economy, Ecology and Development (WEED) 2008), http://procureitfair.org/news-en/201cthe-dark-side-of-cyberspace 201d-2/.

19. Chan, "Meaningful Progress or Illusory Reform?," 46.

20. For maps and a short overview of e-waste flows in the East and South Asian regions, see UNEP, "The Great E-Waste Recycling Debate," http://www.grid.unep.ch/waste/html_file/36–37_ewaste.html.
21. See Naoki Sakai, "Translation," *Theory, Culture & Society* 23, nos. 2–3 (2006): 71–86; and Naoki Sakai, *Translation and Subjectivity: On "Japan" and Cultural Nationalism* (Minneapolis: University of Minnesota Press, 1997).
22. Thanks to Brett Neilson for highlighting this formulation.
23. See Marc Levinson, *The Box: How the Shipping Container Made the World Smaller and the World Economy Bigger* (Princeton: Princeton University Press, 2006), 127–49.
24. Deborah Cowen, "A Geography of Logistics: Market Authority and the Security of Supply Chains," *Annals of the Association of American Geographers* 100 (2010): 612.
25. Levinson, *The Box*, 144.
26. See Brian Holmes, "Do Containers Dream of Electric People: The Social Form of Just-in-Time Production," *Open* 21 (2011): 30–44. See also Brian Ashton, "Logistics and the Factory without Walls," *Mute Magazine*, September 14, 2006, http://www.metamute.org/editorial/articles/logistics-and-factory-without-walls.
27. Thanks to Julian Kücklich for bringing this point to my attention.
28. There is a strong case to be made here for understanding the network structure that defines contemporary relations of communication and economy in terms of the principle of "notworking." For an elaboration of this concept and condition, see Geert Lovink, *The Principle of Notworking: Concepts in Critical Internet Culture* (Amsterdam: Hogeschool van Amsterdam, 2005), http://www.hva.nl/lectoraten/documenten/ol09–050224-lovink.pdf.
29. On the concept of "differential inclusion," see Neilson, "The World Seen from a Taxi."
30. Association of Southeast Asian Nations (Indonesia, Malaysia, Philippines, Singapore, and Thailand), http://www.aseansec.org; Asia-Pacific Economic Cooperation (21 members), http://www.apec.org/; North American Free Trade Agreement (Canada, Mexico, United States), http://www.nafta-sec-alena.org/.
31. The indifference of communication is equivalent to self-referentiality, which is another way of saying that such systems are high on redundancy. This said, it would be a strategic mistake to think that such operations are without material effects.
32. I understand this relation not in terms of some kind of absolute exteriority—a position increasingly untenable in a capitalist and techno-social system of immanence and the Anthropocene—but rather in terms of a "constitutive outside." For an elaboration of this concept as it operates within network societies and information economies, see Ned Rossiter, *Organized Networks: Media Theory, Creative Labour, New Institutions* (Rotterdam: NAi Publishers, 2006).
33. While some of the key voices of Italian political philosophy—notably Virno, Lazzarato, and Negri—maintain that the borders of language, political action, labor, and life have become indistinct with the advent of post-Fordism, my interest in this chapter is to maintain a conceptual separation between categories of this sort in order to suggest how the control society instantiated by the global system of logistics and its use of software to manage labor practices amplifies even further the increasing indistinctions between labor, life, and the possibility of a politics of refusal.
34. See Sakai, "Translation" and *Translation and Subjectivity*. See also Rada Ivekovic, "Trans-border Translation," *Eurozine* (January, 2005), http://www.eurozine.com/articles/2005–01–14-ivekovic-en.html.
35. The work of "heterolingual address," by contrast, engages the antagonism of incommensurability within cultural difference, thus providing a basis from which to critique—among other things—the geopolitics of sovereign power.

36. Brett Neilson, email correspondence, September 7, 2009. See also Randy Martin, *An Empire of Indifference: American War and the Financial Logic of Risk Management* (Durham and London: Duke University Press, 2007).

37. Gayatri Chakravorty Spivak, "Can the Subaltern Speak?," in Nelson Cary and Lawrence Grossberg, eds., *Marxism and the Interpretation of Culture* (Urbana and Chicago: University of Illinois Press, 1988), 280–1.

38. John Watson, *Marginal Man: The Dark Vision of Harold Innis* (Toronto: University of Toronto Press, 2008), 123.

39. Ibid., 267.

40. Megan Born, Helene Furján Lily Jencks, and Phillip M. Crosby, eds., *Dirt* (Philadelphia and Cambridge, MA: PennDesign and MIT Press, 2012), 9.

41. Ibid., 152.

42. Keller Easterling, "Rumor," in Furján Born and Lily Jencks, eds., *Dirt*, 31.

43. http://bureaudetudes.org and http://theyrule.net/.

44. Jussi Parikka, "Dust Matters," in Carolin Wiedemann and Soenke Zehle, eds., *Depletion Design: A Glossary of Network Ecologies* (Amsterdam: XMLab and the Institute for Network Cultures, 2012), 62.

5

NEW REGIMES OF KNOWLEDGE PRODUCTION

With the rise of ubiquitous computing and the informatization of labor and life, it is clear that the current conjuncture is defined by the networked condition. No matter what social milieu, geocultural situation, or mode of production, the individual today is always connected to circuits of capital. This is no more evident than in the banality of users logged on to the Internet with their mobile phones and laptops. Always clicking, moving from one site to the next, the distracted mind of the user multiplies the money for the monopoly providers of idle curiosity. Google, Facebook, Bebo, MySpace, Tudou, YouTube, Twitter. Such engines of entry into the "experience economy" of social networks can certainly be diagnosed with a political economy of data mining and the aggregation of taste. But one wonders what the implications are here for the production of knowledge when users engage in the social production of value and network corporations devise new business models for the extraction of rent from the work of the common.[1] What sort of effects does this networked condition have on institutional settings associated with knowledge production? And what kind of social-technical relations emerge to comprise new diagrams of the political? This chapter addresses these questions with reference to the intersection between global logistics industries and knowledge production.

Complex problems (human rights violations, climate change, border disputes, migration control, labor management, informatization of knowledge) hold the capacity to produce trans-institutional relations that move across geocultural scales, and this often results in conflicts around the status of knowledge and legitimacy of expression. A key reason for such conflicts has to do with the spatiotemporal dynamics special to sites—both institutional and noninstitutional—of knowledge production. Depending on the geocultural scale of distribution and temporality of production, knowledge will be coded with specific social-technical protocols that give rise to the problem of translation across the milieu of knowledge. This is not a question of some kind of impasse in the form of disciplinary borders, but a conflict that is protocological. For media theorist Alexander Galloway, "Protocol refers to the technology of organization and control operating in distributed networks."[2] The name we give dominant systems of organization and control is logistics.

Logistics knows its subjects. The software applications special to logistics visualize and manage the mobility of people, capital, and things, producing knowledge about the world in transit. As discussed earlier in this book, logistics is an extension of the "organizational paradigm" of cybernetics. Both belong to the "machine stream ensemble" of neoliberal economics as it emerged following World War II.[3] Common to neoliberal economics, cybernetics, and logistics is the calculation of risk. And to manage the domain of risk, a system capable of reflexive analysis and governance is required. This is the task of logistics.

This chapter explores the complex of problems set out above with reference to the global logistics industry—an emergent regime of protocological control that already shapes the conditions of labor and life for many, and increasingly affects how knowledge production is governed and undertaken now and in the future. This chapter, and indeed much of this book, is a response to the making logistical of universities and their operations, where the work of knowledge production is increasingly subject to processes of financialization orchestrated through algorithmic architectures and data economies. In the interest of clarity, a distinction between knowledge production and epistemological transformation is required.[4] The latter is deadlocked for reasons associated with the crisis of the university in a "knowledge economy," but the former is proliferating as new assemblages are produced through the galvanizing force of global capitalism.

Nowhere is this more explicit than in the struggle and mutually constitutive relations between the informal and formal sectors of a range of economic and social activities associated with global logistics industries and supply chain management. A case in point can be found in electronic waste industries in China or scrap metal economies surrounding the port of Piraeus, as discussed in previous chapters. Even though one may struggle with the idea that informal economies and their attendant labor practices might be considered as sites of knowledge production, such examples nonetheless highlight the ways in which a kind of situation awareness—be that in the form of technical adaptation of hardware and software systems or labor strikes and infrastructural sabotage—of logistical operations holds a shaping force that alters how logistics knows its subjects.

Logistics, Standards, Protocols

One of the key ways in which logistics undertakes the work of governance is through the application of technologies of measure, the database and spreadsheet being two of the most common instruments of managerial practice. In the case of cognitive labor, the political-economic architecture of intellectual property regimes (IPRs) has prevailed as the definitive instrument of regulation and served as the

98 New Regimes of Knowledge Production

standard upon which the productivity of intellectual labor is understood. This is especially the case within the sciences and increasingly within the creative industries, which in Australia, Europe, and the United Kingdom have replaced arts and humanities faculties at many universities.

There are, however, emergent technologies of both labor management and economic generation that mark a substantial departure from the rapidly fading power of IPRs, which are predicated on state systems enforcing the WTO's TRIPS Agreement—something that doesn't function terribly well in places like China with its superb economies of piracy or in many countries in Africa where generic drugs are subtracting profits from the pharmaceutical industry and its patent economy.[5] Intellectual property regimes are no longer the site of real struggle for informational labor, although they continue to play a determining role in academic research and publishing when connected to systems of measure, such as global university and journal rankings, "quality assurance" audits of "teaching performance," numbers of international students, and so forth. In the age of cognitive capitalism, new sites of struggle are emerging around standards and protocols associated with information mobility and population management in the logistics industries. Significant here, is the return of materiality to computational and informatized life.

Standards are everywhere. Their capacity to interlock with one another and adapt to change over time and circumstance are key to their power as non-state agents of governance in culture, society, and the economy.[6] Standards require a combination of consensus and institutional interconnection (or hegemony) in order to be implemented through the rule of protocols.[7] In this way, one can speak of environmental standards, health and safety standards, computational standards, and manufacturing standards whose interinstitutional or technical status is made possible through the work of protocols. The capacity for standards to hold traction depends upon protocological control, which is a governing system whose technics of organization shape how value is extracted and divorced from those engaged in variational modes of production.

Central to this chapter and the next is the extent to which knowledge production becomes subsumed within logistical operations of measure. If logistical software systems were to fully migrate and become integrated within the academy, at what point or over what issues would research inquiry register as an activity of risk or signal something like dangerous thought? Certainly, an investigation of logistics may illuminate such emergent conditions, but my interest here is to turn logistics back upon the question of method and the spatial formation of social relations as found within informal labor sectors.

The Logistical University

Over the past ten or so years the proliferation of non-university institutions such as NGOs, think tanks, and activist media and cultural organizations engaged in the production of knowledge signals less an "epistemological revolution" and more a political challenge to the university and its monopoly of knowledge. Such a shift is further amplified by the increasing tendency for Anglophone universities to rely on a casual labor force to undertake a raft of teaching, administrative, and occasional research duties. Coupled with the industrialization and commercialization of knowledge,[8] the rise of the university as a teaching machine polices the practice of research as the preserve of tenured senior faculty who manage projects. Critical research is prompted to migrate beyond the territory of the university.[9] Arguably, conditions are in place for a substantive epistemological transformation predicated on institutional and technological cultures—something along the lines of Kuhn's paradigm shift or Foucault's epistemic rupture. Given the modern constitutive relationship between epistemology and disciplinarity, it is unlikely such a change will be generated from within the borders of the university. Today, the conditions for epistemological change are no longer tied in any exclusive manner to the contours of disciplines within university settings. While one might consider the challenge of method and practice of concept production as things that disciplines within the humanities, at least, are largely inclined to avoid given their conservative predilection, it would be a gross oversight to suggest that inventive methods and wild concept production have stalled in society at large.[10]

The critical question for academics and university-based scholars is to discern how they might adjust their own knowledge practices with reference to knowledge production undertaken in non-university settings. It would be a mistake, however, to overlook the politically sharp lines of division and institutional dispute that distinguish the forms of knowledge production across non-university settings. The agenda of consultancy firms and think tanks supplying clients (both governmental and non-governmental) with commissioned policy reports is vastly different from the sort of policy work undertaken by activist organizations engaging in, say, cultural or environmental policy critique. The basic genre of expression may hold some similarities, but the social-political constituencies, technics of organization, aesthetics of presentation, and funding alliances are more likely to sever any possible correspondence between the two.

The transformation of knowledge practices is also a question of method as much as politics, and for the vast majority of academics such a question will never be entertained. There is neither the desire to engage in the work of a reflexive critique of practice, no matter the frequent lip service given to such an idea, nor is there the structural compulsion to do so when the bovine gaze of the academic persona is fixated on the command chain, beholden to managerial and government directives setting out the latest calibration of audit regimes. As such, the problematic of complexity and the work of transdisciplinarity are largely shunted to the side, if at all acknowledged, by those in the academy.

While the institutional time of the university is not, as yet, beholden to the real-time assessment of labor performativity,[11] commodity production, and the efficient movement of people and things special to the logistical worlds of transport and communication industries, the managerial grammar of logistics is nonetheless encroaching upon the academy. Witness, for instance, the place of KPIs as a managerial tool enlisted to determine annual workloads and associated protocols for career advancement within the university. Note that the content of such work does not matter; it is all about outputs that register the activity of knowledge work. Even though the period of assessment is typically comprised of intervals spread over the course of a year, and therefore does not hold the intensity of real-time assessment and decision making as found in many logistics industries, it is evident that knowledge production within the university has become quantifiable and assessable through recourse to logistical tools. As the time of the university speeds up and further incorporates logistical technologies of governance, the modalities and techniques of knowledge production will similarly undergo transformation. Meanwhile, the institutional and technological terrain of knowledge production will increasingly be difficult to distinguish from corporate sectors well advanced in their management of staff productivity with the aid of logistical software.

Indeed, the university in which I currently work has recently implemented a new staff travel and expense management system (TEMS), which is a module within Concur, which was acquired by SAP in December 2014. This runs alongside Cornerstone OnDemand, which is a not too demanding management system that licenses the Compass system to handle staff performance and training, and this, at least at Western Sydney University, is bolted on to Talent2, which deals with staff payroll and human resource management. The Cornerstone system now integrates Concur's TEMS. So while Cornerstone is for the time being independent of the big logistical software developers IBM, SAP, and Oracle—which in recent years acquired Cornerstone's market rivals, Kenexa, SuccessFactors, and Taleo—this doesn't mean that organizations cannot *de facto* extend the platform imperialism of these dominant tech companies. But such platform combination is far from smooth in terms of interoperability. The jumble of modules within different systems to some extent shields academic labor from the perfect "real-time" machine of logistical media. Of course the logical "solution" would involve ditching Cornerstone and opting for Fieldglass, "a cloud-based Vendor Management System (VMS) to manage contingent workforce and services procurement programs."[12] Acquired by SAP in May 2014, Fieldglass is designed to govern contingent labor, which makes up around 50 percent of academic workers in the sector in Australia (with levels much higher in some faculties and universities).[13] With Fieldglass combined with the Concur travel ledger system, the fantasy of real-time platform interoperability could start to become a reality within the logistical university. Or a nightmare.

The political-economic technologies of measure are key to the division of labor in and across university settings. The rise of temp work in the university is a well-known feature across much of the United States and United Kingdom. In his book *Nice Work if You Can Get It*, Andrew Ross opens the final chapter, "The Rise of the Global University," with the following assessment: "Higher education has not been immune to the impact of economic globalization. Indeed, its institutions are now on the brink of channeling some of the most dynamic, and therefore destabilizing, tendencies of neoliberal marketization."[14] Arguably, one of the central reasons higher education embodies the intensity of transformations wrought by neoliberalism has to do with ways in which post-Fordist labor is "multiplied and divided."[15]

A quick listing of examples is sufficient to get an idea of what I am talking about here: Systems of ranking institutions of higher education within a global frame serve to distinguish universities and the labor within them along national and geocultural lines of division; this in turn shapes the global mobility of students and thus the logic of capital accumulation, again dividing universities, labor, and disciplines in terms of market competition and geocultural segmentation. The construction of special economic zones for higher education, which is most notable across the Asian, Middle Eastern, and African regions, functions to divide national markets internally and externally along the lines of domestic and global spatialities that have implications for income generation derived from teaching and research activities in terms of the scope of student catchment and institutional sources for research funding.

The political-economic architecture of intellectual property regimes is another state supported device through which lines of division are constructed between what McKenzie Wark has termed the "vectoral class" (those who proprietize and thus enclose the productive efforts of biopolitical labor) and the "hacker class" (those engaged in the collaborative work of co-production and creation of the common).[16] Universities and corporations have sought to further establish systems of measure from such labor through the global rankings of journals and citation indices. Such rankings overwhelmingly favor journals that are part of Anglo-American publishing consortia that over the past twenty years have set out to aggressively take over the few remaining independent journals that support research and intellectual debate in national and regional settings.[17] The effect of this has been to consolidate the hegemony of global English and erode the connection between the production of knowledge and its frequently local social-political conditions of possibility. This, notwithstanding the fact that the very notion of the local has become enormously complicated with the consolidation of economic and cultural globalization coupled with the rise of the network society.

Additional lines of division operate in terms of what Andrew Ross calls the "new geography of work," and what I am wishing to frame in this chapter as the uneven distribution of expertise. Incorporated into the uneven distribution of expertise is the racialization of labor, both of which connect back to the construction of special economic zones for global universities. It is on this basis that this chapter concludes that the twenty-first-century logistical university in its global manifestations is in many ways disturbingly similar to programs of institution formation and the management of populations undertaken by nineteenth-century colonial powers. I will develop these aspects of my argument shortly, but first

102 New Regimes of Knowledge Production

I wish to say a few more things about the multiplication of labor and how this dynamic and condition relates to the rise of the logistical university.

The Informatization of Knowledge and the Production of the Common

In his book *How the University Works*, Marc Bousquet's crucial insight is that the flexibilization of labor is at the center of the informatization of the university as it embraces the force of neoliberal regimes.[18] This orientation of labor around processes of informatization draws on work undertaken by various researchers associated with Italian post-*operaismo* thought. One of the key analytical and political precepts developed out of such work, as summarized by Tiziana Terranova, makes the distinction between the social production of value and the model of classical political economy, which measures the time and cost of labor in determining the production of commodity value.[19]

Michael Hardt and Antonio Negri note that traditional models of measure (e.g., intellectual property regimes, university and journal ranking systems, citation indicators, etc., all of which operate within the contemporary logistical university), and thus the law of value, are in crisis today due to profound contradictions within the force of economic globalization and the multiple antagonisms between the cooperative logic of biopolitical labor and capitalism's mechanisms of expropriating the wealth of the common as it is produced by the creativity of biopolitical labor.[20] In his dialogue with Negri, Cesare Casarino reiterates this point, noting how the common provides "the locus of surplus value" for capital, whose apparatuses of capture—or regimes of measure—expropriate the wealth of the common.[21]

A distinction needs to be made here between the concept of *the common* and that of *the commons*. The latter is associated with processes of enclosure and proprietary control of that which was previously collectively owned and managed. In a neoliberal paradigm, such a process has been marked by the shift of public goods to private ownership. The key point here is that the commons—whether they are understood in terms of ecology, culture, or relationships—are predicated on the dual logic of scarcity and ownership, and are thus assumed to be resources in need of protection. Within liberal democracies, the state is frequently bestowed with such a role. The commons is thus ascribed a representational quality vis-à-vis the structural logic of the state. There is also a tendency in debates on the commons to inscribe and contain public resources within novel legal regimes such as the creative commons. The juridical, in other ways, assumes a primacy as a border technology in terms of how the commons is made intelligible and governed.

The common, by contrast, cannot be owned or managed, most especially by statist formations that assume the identity of the people or the public. The common does not operate within the logic of representation, in other words, and instead is a force mobilized through nonrepresentational relations and the multiplication of biopolitical labor. Nor is the common a resource underscored by the logic of scarcity. And while the common holds an economic potential—something that is made clear in the moment of expropriation—its "wealth" is not inherently economic. As I have written elsewhere with Soenke Zehle:

> If we understand *the commons* to refer both to the material context and the consequence of practices of peer-production, *the common* is the political potential immanent in such practices. Such an understanding of the common situates it conceptually as the latest iteration of the political; just as there exists an "excess of the political over politics," the affirmation of the common is offered as a condition of possibility for collaborative constitution; for the sharing of affects of love, solidarity and wrath; and for the translation of such affects and experiences across the "irreducible idiomaticity" of ethico-political practices and the production of subjectivity.[22]

At stake here is how both the political potential of the common and the materiality of the commons as distributed forms of collective practice become enmeshed with biopolitical practices of governmentality and economy that extract value from social relations of production.

Casarino makes the "important qualification" that there is always a remainder of the common that is not appropriated by capital. There is the suggestion that this "outside" or "externality" provides the point of separation between capital and the common, which otherwise risk becoming indistinguishable. The precise content of this common is left without elaboration by Casarino. My sense is that asymmetrical institutional-social temporalities between capital and the common are key here. Where the university is often accused of being "out of time" or "too slow" by those who heavily identify with the business sector and industry, perhaps one could also suggest that the time of the common and living labor holds a special complexity that refuses absorption into capital's apparatuses of capture and regimes of measure, which are always circumscribed in a way that living labor is not. I can only note such speculations in passing—the empirical-conceptual content here is the material of future research.

When transferred to the setting of the university and its transformation under conditions of economic globalization, questions such as the following emerge: How does the social production of value (brand desire, affect, subjectivity, online social networking, etc.) shape the commodity value of the university degree? What relation does this have with the globalization of higher education? And how does the logistical university—defined increasingly by privatization (as distinct from being a public good), labor flexibility, and informational management—relate to the social production of value?

Let me outline in concrete fashion how the social production of value shapes the commodity value of the university degree. Anyone who is astute to the conditions of cognitive labor within universities will not have trouble making the connection between diminishing numbers of full-time faculty, increasing casualization of teaching staff, the massive expansion in administrative labor and the viral-like proliferation of managerial personas, the structural reproduction of adolescent research subjectivities through short-term contracts for junior researchers on cross-university projects, and what I would term the incapacity of the disciplines to invent new conceptual and methodological idioms of practice.

It is a well-known if rarely articulated strategy of refusal for coordinators of course modules to reissue the same material for students year in and year out. Admittedly this is a practice that has gone on for years in universities, but it takes on substantially different hues with the shift from the public-state university to the pseudo-corporate and increasingly logistical university. Whereas the academic of the public university who trotted out the same module outline every year was justifiably accused of intellectual and pedagogical laziness, these days it is more a matter of survival as academics struggle to manage an enormous increase in managerial and administrative workloads that accompany the ever-expanding mechanisms that undergird the madness of audit cultures (another feature that defines the logistical university). Come the start of a new semester, it is not uncommon for academics who have spent whatever recess from teaching duties by writing grants, undertaking marking of student assignments, fulfilling administrative duties, meeting with dissertation students, and maybe, if lucky, engaging in some research, to then find themselves having no time to redevelop old course materials (forget about producing new materials), and thus resort out of desperation and self-survival to repeat whatever it was that they taught the previous year.

The result of such practice—which I would expect to be widespread across the sector—is that disciplines become impoverished. You might counter this charge by telling me it is the job of research to provide the material of innovation for the disciplines. To do so falls into the trap of privileging research and thus dividing the important and mutually informing relationship between research and teaching. Moreover, it assumes that research activity is actually doing the job of disciplinary reinvention. I would suggest that, to the contrary, the vast majority of national and supranational funded research—especially in the humanities—is funded on the grounds that it reproduces the orthodoxies of the disciplines, in which case very little is gained by way of disciplinary innovation.

This brings me to the social production of value. When academics no longer have the time and perhaps intellectual stamina let alone curiosity to test the borders of their disciplines, what do they do? Well, in similar fashion to capital—and indeed, precisely because they are subjects of the corporate, logistical university—they look to appropriating the creativity of the common. In my own field of digital media studies, it has become very clear over the past ten to fifteen years that academics have contributed very little by way of conceptual and methodological invention. Such work has been undertaken outside and on the margins of the academy by artists, activists, computer geeks, and designers.

How is such work undertaken? It is undertaken through practices of collaborative constitution and the multiplication of labor made possible by the mode of information and the media of digital communication.[23] The key social-technical features here of flexibility, adaptation, distributive co-production, data recombination, open/free content and code, and modulating axes of organization (both horizontal and vertical) all define the culture and labor of networks. And as the generative content of the common is absorbed by and more often enclosed within non-generative proprietary regimes that function to shore up the borders of the corporate university, there is also an informational dimension of open and generative network cultures that is carried over and interpenetrates the institutional dynamic of the university.

Actually, an increasing number of universities are recognizing the value of adopting open-content practices—MIT's OpenCourseWare being one of the more widely known examples.[24] The reason for this has to do with the fact that there is very little "product differentiation" across degree programs from one university to the next, and universities are slowly but surely understanding that economic leverage for higher education comes not from the sale of prepackaged, static material (although this is still the dominant economic model). Rather, they see their business as that of awarding degrees (that is, granting an institutional/symbolic legitimacy upon a learning experience, which is the basis of determining tuition fees) and service delivery. This is a model that effectively duplicates the business model of open source software providers who understand that users (including educational institutions, corporations, small businesses, and organizations) expect to download content (operating systems and office software, for example) for free, but are then willing to pay for labor that customizes the software to specific institutional needs, with follow-up service as required. Only the high-end logistical software companies such as SAP and Oracle are able to charge for both ends of the software spectrum—product and servicing.

The Uneven Distribution of Expertise

What is the relation between the logistical university and the uneven distribution of expertise across the higher-education landscape? Indeed, what is expertise and who is an expert? And what are the geocultural configurations upon which such relations might be mapped out? With the rise of Web 2.0 and its attendant self-publishing and promotion platforms such as blogs, wikis, Twitter, and YouTube, everyone these days is an expert. In some respects this seeming democratization of knowledge production is a structural phenomenon brought about by the outsourcing of labor and content production in the media industries. These days, even the corporations want everything for free. And with the social production of value, which in the case of news media comes in the form of citizen journalism that willingly supplies content for free, the cost of labor is effectively removed from the balance sheet.

106 New Regimes of Knowledge Production

How, though, does this Cult of the Amateur impact upon the distribution of expertise within the university? With the rise of mass education and user-pay systems, many academics nowadays complain of the "dumbing down" of curricula. Academic departments have become in most cases almost entirely dependent on income derived from student fees, with international students making up a substantial portion of annual budgets. This is especially pronounced in universities in Australia where, after more than two decades of partial deregulation and massive cuts in government expenditure on education, it has become a routine practice for academics to slide students over the ever-diminishing hurdles of assessment. If they didn't, then the security of their own jobs would be at stake.

Not only has the dependency relationship on student fees had substantive impacts on the design and content of curricula, it has also exacted a toll on the capacity for academics to keep abreast with—let alone make contributions to—advances in their field. Increasingly, the insistence by students and administration for entertainment-on-demand styles of not so much teaching but "course delivery" has resulted in more academic time expended on maintaining online administration and content management systems such as the notorious WebCT and Blackboard. (Although for reasons I fail to understand, such systems are embraced with an at times dogged enthusiasm by some colleagues I have worked with at various universities over the years.)

Similar practices are the norm in British and North American universities, no matter what the "quality assurance" reports might say to the contrary. Such systems of measure long ago lost any relationship with their referent and function in a very similar way to the production of public opinion, which does not exist according to Bourdieu's compelling thesis.[25] What does exist is the ever-increasing extension of self-referential reporting measures into the time of academic work. The tyranny of audit cultures inscribes academic subjects into auto-generative discursive practices of accountability and conditions the overproduction of administrative functionaries, whose job is to keep track of the bureaucratic madness that such systems guarantee. As Andrew Murphie argues, the technics of audit "not only restructures value, relations of production, subjectivity and more in the present; it also provides passage to the social relations of the future."[26]

Within conditions such as these, which again are typical of the logistical university, it would seem the very notion of expertise is in crisis. And arguably it is. But there are also ways in which expertise is upheld, since once it can be quantified as a measure a crucial symbolic value can then be accrued that can then be transferred as brand value for individual academics and their institutions. This in turn results in a capacity to charge higher student fees and attract the much vaunted external research funds, whose boards of assessors place great emphasis on so-called esteem indicators provided by journal ranking systems and citation indices that hold their own geocultural and political economic bias that reinforces what Harold Innis termed "monopolies of knowledge."[27] Such measures supposedly confer upon the body of academic research a quality assurance that effectively removes from the assessor the task of critical assessment, which is now designed to be as automated and therefore as time efficient as possible. Again, these are some of the key features that characterize a logistical mode of knowledge management. Though it remains to be said, the calibration of such systems of automation are deeply ideological and underscored by cabals of self-interested academic groups and individuals who set out to game the systems of large multinational bibliometric companies such as Thompson Reuters who control the key citation databases used by universities to verify impact and govern academic labor.[28]

This brief survey of teaching and research practices within the logistical university comprise the "new geography work." A far-from-uniform informational geography of intellectual property regimes, content management systems, database economies, flexible labor, and open content production becomes integrated with a geocultural system that valorizes the reproduction of Western knowledge traditions and hegemony of global English.[29] There are further implications here for disciplinary innovation and the production of subjectivity. With the rise of the global university, local knowledge traditions and expertise have very weak purchase within an educational machine that demands modes of flexible, just-in-time delivery provided by staff in contract positions whose structural and ontological insecurity is offset by largely generic course modules whose uniformity ensures a familiar point of entry for the next short-term academic hired by the global university.

Protecting Logistical Populations

Part of the flexibility of what Stefano Harney and Fred Moten term the "algorithmic institution" tasked with the management of "logistical populations" is immanent to the technical operation of enterprise databases such as Oracle and IBM, which are prone to bugs, hardware malfunctions, software glitches, and the like.[30] Yet the logistical fantasy of a smooth world of seamless interoperability is not disturbed by technical malfunctions alone. As Harney and Moten write, "Every attempt by logistics to dispel strategy, to banish human time, to connect without going through the subject, to subject without handling things, resists something that is already resisting it, namely the resistance that founds modern logistics."[31] Logistics is always troubled by that which it cannot obtain, by the indeterminate temporal and spatial horizons and hidden reserves of human subjectivity that forever entice the technocratic tendency with the promise of enhanced measures of efficiency, yet which by definition remain beyond the calibrating optic of logistics. This is why so much cognitive attention and so many financial resources are expended upon designing more complex computational infrastructures. The combined efforts of engineers and capital probe the territory of the technical in an attempt to graft increased processing speed and operational performance upon the transit of people and things. That the rationality of logistics is circumscribed by the technical does not especially diminish its force to penetrate labor and life,

108 New Regimes of Knowledge Production

extracting value and remaking a world subordinate to processes of capital accumulation.

Structurally oblivious to their function in the reproduction of value within an economy of data, the human has entered a new period of machinic arrangement whose operation is abstracted into the realm of semiotic capitalism.[32] An imaginary world of cooperation, sharing, and participation provides a powerful narrative for the entrepreneurial self whose capacity to organize collective forms of refusal is consistently undermined by the disaggregating effects of value extraction derived from the computational logic of recombination hidden within the vaults of algorithmic architectures.[33] In effect, this means the architecture is never questioned. Any plea for change or deeper level access is met with resounding indifference by the proprietors of control. The function of the client is to submit to service. Such a technique of capture provides the basis for scalar expansion. One may choose to migrate to other providers, but the time and cost associated with adapting organizational processes and activities to slightly reconfigured architectures is significant. So no matter how much a client may wish to flee service-oriented systems, the operational indebtedness to a particular architecture more often exceeds the will to escape.

Knowledge rubs up against the politics of parameters. New uses of data became a constant in the social life of institutional settings, laden with a politics that remains for the most part implicit as it is pervasive.[34] Implied here is a system operating in "protected mode," a form of prophylactic for organizers of the data as well as for those "future users" at risk of going crazy.[35] As Friedrich Kittler observes, the power of the protected mode is "derived . . . from the efficacy of silence."[36] Unable to intervene in the operating system of the machine, the user is locked out from issuing commands that alter the architecture and addressable memory special to the "Real Mode" of Intel's x86 central processing unit (CPU) introduced in 1978. Intel's 80286 16-bit microprocessor, released in 1982, distinguished between "Real Mode" and "Protected Mode," a CPU designed for multitasking applications operating in real-time secured by increased operating system control.[37] Modern operating systems such as Windows, MacOS, and Linux continue to use this mode to protect us from our machines, in some sense, even today.

The widespread adoption of Protected Mode systems impacts upon the economy of expression, practice, subjectivity, and knowledge. In one of his rare moments of invoking a concept of power, Kittler suggests that the Foucauldian analysis be reoriented around an investigation of how protected modes specific to technological systems and their "privileges" provide the key to reconstructing the transformation of bureaucracies. While not renowned for political statements, Kittler considers the issue of access rights as, in effect, the new front of a geopolitical war against the hegemony of the United States and the imperial extension of its IT industry across global economy and society.

One might reasonably assert that open source software (OSS) offers such an alternative. But for the most part OSS mimics, if not aspires to, the aesthetic regime of the hugely dominant operating systems. DIY hardware assembly might offer a more deviant alternative, though even more so than OSS it is unable to scale up to pose any real challenge to the IT behemoths. The DIY hardware movement is increasingly tied to "maker culture," which as the long tail of "artisan-alternatives" is not prepared to admit how the valorization of localism frequently depends on global supply chains. Virtuous acts of rarefied consumption coupled with the satisfaction of self-assembly fulfill a hipster imaginary of distinction.[38]

The Racialization of Labor

In which cases might a racialization of labor underscore the logistical university? In short, what are the labor inequalities that shape the market of higher education on a global scale and how are new (or, as the case may be, neocolonial) class subjectivities being reproduced? There are multiple hues of labor differentiation across universities at a global level. To make the claim of differentiation along the lines of race is to suggest a reproduction of the nineteenth-century biological category of race as the basis upon which division is operating. The official positioning of universities across the world would be most defiant in maintaining this is certainly not the case, and indeed may be inclined to issue legal writs against anyone making such a charge, if it was perceived that brand damage was a stake.

Over two decades ago Étienne Balibar and Immanuel Wallerstein observed that "in traditional or new forms (the derivation of which is, however, recognizable), *racism is not receding, but progressing* in the contemporary world."[39] Arguably, this is no less the case today, and one of the sites in which racism is reproduced, albeit in new guises, is that of the logistical university. The category of race, as Balibar and Wallerstein go on to analyze, is one of the key modalities enlisted in the construction of the "people," or what Foucault analyzed in terms of the biopolitical production of territory, populations, security, and subjectivity.[40] Other social-political devices through which populations are constituted include the nation, class, ethnicity, gender, and broadcast media of communication. How the category of race intersects with these technologies of governance that define the rise of the nation-state and industrial modernity has been a matter of considerable research, which is in no way exhausted yet. It may seem a surprise to many that the seemingly archaic category of race should figure within the time and space of logistical modernities. But, as I go to show, forms of institutional racism are central to the problem of labor within the global university, which operates in logistical ways.

The operation of what Balibar terms "racism without races" is registered in the division of labor and uneven distribution of expertise operating at global universities present in China. How to situate the differences between labor regimes in the global university and those of nineteenth-century colonialism? In form they are similar. In both cases domestic functionaries are enlisted to provide the linguistic and cultural interface between the imperial institution and local populations, which include government officials and industry representatives. But one key difference is that relatively high-ranking officials in the nineteenth century could freely have lavished all the racist epithets on the lower ranking colonials. Today, however, the globally mobile (white) academic has to be careful about how the discourse on race is handled since it can endanger their position, to say nothing of the offence its enunciation may provoke. There is a difference here with the twenty-first-century variants of differential racism that needs to be analyzed. And the concept of "racism without races" helps such analysis part of the way. Racism without race is predicated on modes of division that, while not invoking the biological category of race, are nonetheless reproducing the logic of racism—namely, to divide and exclude on the basis of race—through other means but which at their heart are racist in orientation, no matter how unconscious or unintentional that may be.[41]

A notable feature across global universities operating in China today is the substantial presence of domestic Chinese in the administrative ranks, with considerably fewer Chinese working as academic faculty. This is not the case with universities in Hong Kong, Taiwan, or Singapore. While smaller scale operations may combine academic and administrative roles and have those carried out by foreigners on casual contracts familiar with the "culture" of the national system within which they are working, the larger universities employ local Chinese for administrative work on an almost exclusive basis. These staff often hold an undergraduate degree from a U.S., British, or Australian university, and many will also have postgraduate qualifications from an overseas university. In many cases their degrees will have been awarded from their current employer, which again ensures familiarity with the culture and administration of their particular institution.

In principle, the Chinese administrators working within global universities in China are not there because they are Chinese but because they have met the job selection criteria—relevant degree or diploma, competency in English language, good interpersonal skills, relevant experience, and so forth. The official positioning is thus definitely not about race in its classic nineteenth-century articulations. On the other hand, if these administrative staff were not Chinese, then they most likely would not be working in these universities. Why, then, are there so few and in enough cases no non-Chinese staff among the administrative ranks at these global universities?

If it was just a matter of holding the appropriate qualifications and skills, then there could be people from any number of racial and ethnic backgrounds working as administrators in China based international universities. As noted earlier, while the primary administrative and teaching language of these universities is English, there is a need for at least some administrative staff to have a high proficiency in *Putonghua* in order to interface at linguistic and cultural levels with local, provincial, and national government departments and businesses. But there is no obvious reason or need for all administrative staff to be of Chinese origin. It would seem that there is an important subjective desire at work for Chinese administrative staff with largely Anglophone qualifications to find work back home. What emerges from this phenomenon is a dual-language system where intra-institutional and transnational administration and engagement with academic staff is conducted in English, whereas the informal socialization among administrative staff and their interaction, to some extent, with Chinese students is conducted in *Putonghua* or local dialects.

To not be Chinese, in other words, means to not be participating in those institutional and social circuits conducted exclusively in Chinese. This enlisting of the (middle-class) elite "locals" in administrative positions strikes me as very similar to the colonial strategy of engaging indigenous elites to administer colonial institutions (British India being the classic example) and in doing so reproduce and reinforce (or in some cases produce) a local class system. My understanding of such operations is that racial distinctions determined the institutional positions and conditions of the laboring subject. Institutions of globalized higher education provide the institutional settings and organizational cultures through which the logic of differential racism is played out today.

Moving to the question of academic faculty and the international staff that compose its ranks, the opposite display of racialized labor becomes notable: namely, the tendency for Chinese to not be among those holding academic positions, though this is shifting in more recent years. Perhaps this is even more remarkable than the case of the Chinese majority within administrative positions. The opportunity for movement within administration from a U.S. or British university to a global university operating in China, or some other country for that matter, is less likely than in the case of academics, who tend to be much more mobile within both national and global settings. Why, then, do so few Chinese academics comprise the ranks of faculty within global universities in China? One reason has to do with remuneration. Local Chinese are paid substantially less than their international colleagues, and in this respect the economy of labor in global universities reproduces that of most other businesses in China. Unlike other business sectors, however, the global universities do not—at least not yet—fill their academic ranks with local Chinese in order to save on labor costs. Key to the brand value of the global universities is the assurance these institutions make to students that they are receiving a product and experience that essentially reproduces what they could expect if they were enrolled at the "home" institution in the United Kingdom or United States. An important part of that assurance thus rests on a significant portion of academic staff who are either on secondment from or at least familiar with the workings of the home institution. There are also administrative practicalities for this practice associated with the running of equivalent programs, submission and moderation of grades, establishment of academic and administrative committees, and so on and so forth.

From the perspective of the Chinese academic who may give thought to shifting from a Chinese university to one of the increasing number of global universities setting up shop in China, a number of practicalities need to be considered. The linguistic barrier presented by the necessity to have a working command of

112 New Regimes of Knowledge Production

English is just one of various factors to take into account. While the low pay may be equivalent between Chinese and global universities, the Chinese academic will have to forego the frequently informal ways in which income is supplemented within the Chinese system. The household items and food parcels supplied by the national teachers' union, for example, would not be part of academic life in a global university. Moreover, they will have to suffer the knowledge that for effectively the same labor they are being paid a fraction of the amount received by their international colleagues. It must be said that such differentiation of remuneration levels is not based on whether one is Chinese or not. The same applies for those international teachers who have entered the global university from within China, and thus are structurally positioned as part of a domestic labor force (though without many of the benefits received by local Chinese, many of whom are Party members). Nonetheless, the material effect of these multiple forces results in an academic body that is largely absent of Chinese staff.

While the differentiation of work across the spectrum of academic and administrative life points to standard divisions of labor in universities around the world, often enough both the individual worker and collective experience will embody these distinctions in singular ways and thus become subjects that multiply rather than divide the borders of labor. This process, whereby the borders of labor become multiplied, is made clear in the relationship between cognitive labor and the social production of value, as described earlier in this chapter. The racialization of labor, on the other hand, serves as a technology of division in the case of global universities currently operating in China.

Both the multiplication and division of labor are features of the logistical university and its expropriation of the social production of value. Cognitive labor includes modes of peer-to-peer production that make available resources in the form of an informational *commons*. While more immediately understandable as a technology of division, the racialization of labor also feeds into the symbolic production of a commons in terms of the image repertoire and affective registers that are communicated about the global university as a site for international experience and certification. When situated within China, such an imaginary is reproduced in material ways in terms of the domination of mainland Chinese in administrative ranks coupled with the general absence of Chinese academics from faculty programs.

The relationship between the multiplication and division of cognitive and racialized labor, however, is substantially different in terms of how they connect with the social production of *the common*, which can be understood as the political potential that subsists within and conditions the possibility of the commons. The point of connection between such immediately distinct modes of labor lies precisely within the ways they shape the brand value and thus economy of the global university. While there is unlikely to be political affiliation between transnational cognitive labor and Chinese administrators in global universities operating in China (the geocultural disparities being largely insurmountable), there is potential for relations to be forged between workers who experience the informatization of labor as it manifests in both global and national academies. It is at the point of shared experience borne out of struggle that the possibility arises for differential inclusion in the social invention of the common. Both the racialization of labor and the uneven distribution of expertise hold the capacity to be a part of such a process.

As the hegemony of the Chinese state unfolds and exerts its power across the geocultural terrain of global institutions, it should come as no surprise that labor within those institutions becomes increasingly comprised of mainland Chinese workers whose skills, expertise, and symbolic value is no longer perceived as second tier. Such a transformation will occasion new lines of struggle in the globalization of higher education. The challenge for biopolitical labor will be to assert the autonomy of the common from emergent apparatuses of capture. A key part of this struggle will involve inventing new social forms from within logistical technologies of measure.

The Organization of New Institutional Forms

With the expansion of institutional forms comes a distribution of expertise, whether or not one group of experts recognizes or attributes legitimacy to the expressions of another. There is a strong cultural and technical tendency toward ghettoization with the rise of network society—registered most clearly with the move toward "cloud computing" and "national webs." Along with infrastructural issues, cloud computing presents problems of political economy and protocological disjunctures. And in the case of national webs, access to online information is limited according to national borders defined by "IP-range, domains, registering and hosting."[42] With the rise of cloud computing and data-mining economies, it is no longer a question of distinguishing cognitive labor in terms of the content it produces. Instead, we are faced with an emergent techno-system whereby the simple act of clicking and storing data on server farms—whose protocols are designed to prevent easy transfer across "clouds"—entrusts the security of data to corporations and governments with little regard for user's privacy or desire to move across technical infrastructures.

The implications for knowledge production are multiple: Because data is the basic unit of economic profitability (the cost of storage coupled with the economy of data mining), knowledge produced by informatized labor becomes secondary. Everyone, in short, has the capacity to be produced as cognitive labor, since the measure of economic value shifts from a logic of scarcity (IPRs) to one of aggregation, recombination, and storage that corresponds to the materiality of digital information and social production of value.[43] Not only do issues of privacy, security, data transferability, capital accumulation, and surveillance become important within such a paradigm, so too do questions of borders and regions, as cloud providers such as Google divide the world according to state demands (as in the

114 New Regimes of Knowledge Production

case of China), local and regional customization of software, and pricing regimes based on market interests.

Many have identified how the borders between work, life, and politics have become more porous if not collapsed. And while this may be the case in any number of empirical and conceptual instances, new borders are always produced. Borders are also multiplied if we understand the border as a space and time of singular intensity whose forces hold the power of conflictual constitution. How, then, to think the work of organization and new institutional forms when the field of tensions that comprise the border operates in both perceptible and imperceptible ways for different agents situated in a complex of relations? Perhaps this is a question also of governance. There is the option to do nothing, which is always something (not nothing) anyway: The act of withdrawal or indecision of course shapes the organization and activity of life and things. To address tensions and affinities in contexts where labor is not a central galvanizing force requires an act of reflexivity, or maybe just requires one to be conscious of or sensitive to the situation at hand. There is no standard protocol or method to enlist in such instances. Instead, a process of invention is required. And invention emerges at the scene of the border, which registers "the 'non-democratic' element of democracy," as elaborated by Balibar.[44] Here, the mode of address for organization is nonrepresentational and shaped to a high degree by conflict, failure, contingency, passions, and affect. There can only be situated, transversal methods for dealing with such conditions. And here we see another point of conflict with the often global or abstract view of logistics.

How to proceed with an analysis of the networks through and within which collective knowledge production occurs? Maybe start with a diagram of relations. For sure the concept and politics of labor need to be expanded beyond a kind of narcissistic joy of self-recognition. This is the danger of affirmation, unless we see affirmation as a registration of difference, conflict, and the constitutive outside. Think of the diagram of labor within the IT industries in Kolkata, as discussed in chapter 2. Without the violent act of primitive accumulation by the corporate-state, where the land of peasants is expropriated through the legal mechanisms of the state in the interests of property development, there is no IT industry and no cognitive labor to address as a potential political constituency.[45] In other words, the diagram of the outside of IT labor is precisely the scene of the political. With the dispossession of farming land, the subjectivity of the peasant is effectively programmed into the subject of care work as domestic labor, security, construction, and service labor. The so-called skilled labor of the IT worker does not exist without this relation. How to develop a mode of organization and analysis shaped by these variabilities is a key challenge.

Networks and their transversal relations to a range of institutional settings suggest one possible source for sustaining desire and the production of knowledge, which may take the form of refusal, dispute, sabotage, and the like. Modes of outsourcing knowledge production are becoming intensified in ways that don't reduce the power of the state so much as register its ongoing transformation. If this results in external forces that give rise to new institutional forms and alternative modes of knowledge production, then that is no bad thing.

Notes

1. See, respectively, Tiziana Terranova, "Another Life: The Nature of Political Economy in Foucault's Genealogy of Biopolitics," *Theory, Culture & Society* 26, no. 6 (2009): 234–62; and Matteo Pasquinelli, "Google's PageRank Algorithm: A Diagram of the Cognitive Capitalism and the Rentier of the Common Intellect," in Konrad Becker and Felix Stalder, eds., *Deep Search* (London: Transaction Publishers, 2009), 152–62.

2. Alexander Galloway, "Protocol," *Theory, Culture & Society* 23, nos. 2–3 (2006): 317. See also Alexander R. Galloway, *Protocol: How Control Exists after Decentralization* (Cambridge, MA: MIT Press, 2004).

3. Michel Foucault, *The Birth of Biopolitics: Lectures at the Collège de France, 1978–1979*, Michel Senellart, ed., trans. Graham Burchell (Basingstoke: Palgrave Macmillan, 2008), 225.

4. This chapter is developed from a paper responding in part to these two terms, which framed Construction des savoirs en mondialisation: Changement de paradigmes cognitifs. Une révolution épistémologique?, Collège International de Philosophie, Paris, November 7–8, 2011.

5. See the fascinating work of Melinda Cooper, who has been studying the economy and geopolitics of clinical labor trials within the pharmaceutical industries—the rise of which can partly be seen as a way of offsetting profits lost from the diminishing returns availed through IPRs as a result of the increasing availability of generic drugs, which in turn can be understood as a sort of pirate economy that even intersects with aspects of open source cultures. Melinda Cooper, "Experimental Labour-Offshoring Clinical Trials to China," *EASTS East Asian Science, Technology and Society: An International Journal* 2, no. 1 (March, 2008): 73–92. See also Melinda Cooper and Catherine Waldby, *Clinical Labor: Tissue Donors and Research Subjects in the Global Bioeconomy* (Durham: Duke University Press, 2014).

6. See Martha Lampland and Susan Leigh Star, eds., *Standards and Their Stories: How Quantifying, Classifying and Formalizing Practices Shape Everyday Life* (Ithaca: Cornell University Press, 2009).

7. But there can also be standards for protocols. The TCP/IP model for Internet communications, for example, is a protocol that has become a technical standard for Internet-based communications. Christopher Kelty notes the following on the relation between protocols, implementation, and standards for computational processes: "The distinction between a protocol, an implementation and a standard is important: *Protocols* are descriptions of the precise terms by which two computers can communicate (i.e., a dictionary and a handbook for communicating). An *implementation* is the creation of software that uses a protocol (i.e., actually does the communicating; thus two implementations using the same protocol should be able to share data). A *standard* defines which protocol should be used by which computers, for what purposes. It may or may not define the protocol, but will set limits on changes to that protocol." Christopher M. Kelty, *Two Bits: The Cultural Significance of Free Software* (Durham: Duke University Press, 2008), 330n28, http://twobits.net.

8. Again the rough time frame here is ten to fifteen years, though in the case of the sciences this history is much longer, dating back to post-World War II years. See Jean-François

Lyotard, *The Postmodern Condition: A Report on Knowledge*, trans. Geoff Bennington and Brian Massumi (Minneapolis: University of Minnesota Press, 1984).

9. Brian Holmes summarizes this situation with his usual analytical succinctness. Responding to a debate on Nettime regarding open versus closed, proprietary-driven models of publishing, he writes: "The fact that this is an autonomous, self-organized seminar betrays my conviction that the university lacks an outside, or to put it another way, that critical thinking needs to articulate itself beyond the nexus of professional obligations that Lisa describes. But this proposal is not simply antagonistic. The point of (re)establishing an external locus of critique is to help transform the inside, to build both pressure and desire for new forms of education and intellectual activity. Institutional change is fundamentally necessary. Only a critical university system could provide the capacities to steer the knowledge society, or what's more aptly called cognitive capitalism." Brian Holmes, "Re: some more nuanced thoughts on publishing, editing, reading, using," posting to Nettime mailing list, July 30, 2011, http://nettime.org.

10. See Geert Lovink and Ned Rossiter, "In Praise of Concept Production: Formats, Schools and Non-representational Media Studies," in Kelly Gates, ed., *Media Studies Futures, The International Encyclopedia of Media Studies, Vol. 5* (Cambridge and Malden, MA: Wiley-Blackwell, 2013), 61–75.

11. Needless to say, the time of knowledge production is not without its constitutive power in shaping new class subjects. As Bernard Stiegler observes of Lazzarato's *Les Gouvernements des inégalités, Critique de l'insécurité néolibéralé* (Paris: Éditions Amsterdam, 2008): "Maurizio Lazzarato shows very well how this *elimination of the time of knowledge* constitutes the very heart of the project of a government of inequalities in which neoliberalism essentially consists, and it does so at the very moment when an ideology abounds which would have us believe that the very cognitive capitalism responsible for proletarianizing the 'knowers' ['*sachants*'], as Jean-François Lyotard called them, could in fact be made to pass for a 'knowledge society.'" Italics in original. Bernard Stiegler, *For a New Critique of Political Economy*, trans. Daniel Ross (Cambridge: Polity, 2010), 134–35n1.

12. http://www.fieldglass.com/.

13. See Raewyn Connell, "Why Australia Needs a New Model for Universities," *The Conversation*, November 21, 2015, https://theconversation.com/why-australia-needs-a-new-model-for-universities-43696. See also Toby Miller, "Humanities Top to Bottom: The Cognitariat and Publishing," *Ctrl-Z: New Media Philosophy* 5 (2015), http://www.ctrl-z.net.au/journal/?slug=issue-5.

14. Andrew Ross, *Nice Work if You Can Get It: Life and Labor in Precarious Times* (New York: New York University Press, 2009), 189.

15. See Sandro Mezzadra and Brett Neilson, "Border as Method, or, the Multiplication of Labor," *Transversal* (2008), http://eipcp.net/transversal/0608/mezzadraneilson/en.

16. McKenzie Wark, *A Hacker Manifesto* (Cambridge, MA: Harvard University Press, 2004).

17. See Paolo Do, "L'università: un laboratorio per la informetrics society?," *ROARS (Return on Academic ReSearch)*, June 6, 2015, http://www.roars.it/online/luniversita-un-laboratorio-per-la-informetrics-society/.

18. Marc Bousquet, *How the University Works: Higher-Education and the Low-Wage Nation* (New York: New York University Press, 2008), 55–89.

19. See Tiziana Terranova, "The Internet as Playground and Factory: Prelude," The New School, New York, 2009, http://vimeo.com/6882379. See also Terranova, "Another Life."

20. Michael Hardt and Antonio Negri, *Commonwealth* (Cambridge, MA: Harvard University Press, 2009), 314–6.

New Regimes of Knowledge Production **117**

21. Cesare Casarino, "Surplus Common: A Preface," in Cesare Casarino and Antonio Negri, eds., *In Praise of the Common: A Conversation on Philosophy and Politics* (Minneapolis: University of Minnesota Press, 2008), 20.

22. Ned Rossiter and Soenke Zehle, "Acts of Translation: Organizing Networks as Algorithmic Technologies of the Common," in Trebor Scholz, ed., *Digital Labor: The Internet as Playground and Factory* (London and New York: Routledge, 2013), 226. Oddly enough, Michael Hardt seems to confuse the common with the commons in one of his preparatory texts leading up to the publication of *Commonwealth*. See Michael Hardt, "Politics of the Common," *Z-Net*, 2009, http://www.zmag.org/znet/viewArticle/21899.

23. That such invention is undertaken through practices immanent to media of communication would suggest that it is a mistake to assume that informational modes of communication and practice result in outcomes such as the logistical university. Clearly, such a position is one that holds a technologically determinist viewpoint, which is undermined by the fact that social-technical practices of collaboration constitution facilitate the production of the common.

24. For a discussion of the implications of initiatives on cultural and disciplinary formations, see Ross, *Nice Work if You Can Get It*, 202.

25. Pierre Bourdieu, "Public Opinion Does Not Exist" (1973), in Armand Mattelart and Seth Siegelaub, eds., trans. Mary C. Axtmann, *Communication and Class Struggle, Vol. 1: Capitalism, Imperialism* (New York: International General, 1979), 124–30.

26. Andrew Murphie, "Auditland," *PORTAL Journal of Multidisciplinary Studies* 11, no. 2 (2014), https://epress.lib.uts.edu.au/journals/index.php/portal/article/view/3407.

27. Harold A. Innis, *The Bias of Communication* (Toronto: University of Toronto Press, 1951).

28. See Do, "L'università: un laboratorio per la informetrics society?"

29. See Ross, *Nice Work if You Can Get It*, 202.

30. Stefano Harney, "Istituzioni algoritmiche e capitalismo logistico" ("Algorithmic Institutions and Logistical Capitalism"), in Matteo Pasquinelli, ed., *Gli algoritmi del capitale. Accelerazionismo, macchine della conoscenza e autonomia del comune* (Verona: Ombre Corte, 2014), 116–29; and Stefano Harney and Fred Moten, *The Undercommons: Fugitive Planning & Black Study* (New York: Minor Compositions, 2013), 90–91.

31. Harney and Moten, *The Undercommons*, 91–92.

32. See Maurizio Lazzarato, *Signs and Machines: Capitalism and the Production of Subjectivity*, trans. Joshua David Jordan (Los Angeles: Semiotext(e), 2014).

33. See, for instance, Tiziana Terranova, "Red Stack Attack! Algorithms, Capital and the Automation of the Common," Quaderni di San Precario, February 14, 2014, http://quaderni.sanprecario.info/2014/02/red-stack-attack-algorithms-capital-and-the-automation-of-the-common-di-tiziana-terranova/.; and Trebor Scholz, "Platform Cooperativism vs. the Sharing Economy," *Medium*, December 5, 2014, https://medium.com/@trebors/platform-cooperativism-vs-the-sharing-economy-2ea737f1b5ad.

34. Liam Magee and Ned Rossiter, "Service Orientations: Data, Institutions, Labour," in Irina Kaldrack and Martina Leeker, eds., *There Is No Software, There Are Just Services* (Lüneburg: Meson Press, 2015), 73–89, http://meson.press/books/there-is-no-software-there-are-just-services/.

35. See Friedrich A. Kittler, "Protected Mode," in *The Truth of the Technological World: Essays on the Genealogy of Presence*, trans. Erik Butler (Stanford, CA: Stanford University Press, 2013), 210.

36. Ibid., 213.

37. Kittler's object of critique is the 80386 32-bit microprocessor released in 1985, which improved upon the protected mode of the 80286 by allowing mode switching. The

118 New Regimes of Knowledge Production

80386 also had greater market penetration and was widely adopted across a range of institutional settings.

38. For a critique of maker culture, see McKenzie Wark, "A More Lovingly Made World," *Cultural Studies Review* 19, no. 1 (2013): 296–304, http://epress.lib.uts.edu.au/journals/index.php/csrj/article/view/3170/3454. See also Alexander R. Galloway and Garnet Hertz, "Conversations in Critical Making," *CTheory* 21C008e, July 15, 2015, http://ctheory.net/articles.aspx?id=757.

39. Étienne Balibar and Immanuel Wallerstein, *Race, Nation, Class: Ambiguous Identities* (London: Verso, 1990), 9.

40. See Foucault, *The Birth of Biopolitics*. See also Michel Foucault, *Society Must Be Defended: Lectures at the Collège de France, 1975–76*, trans. David Macey (London: Allen Lane, 2003); and Michel Foucault, *Security, Territory, Population: Lectures at the Collège de France, 1977–1978*, trans. Graham Burchell (Basingstoke: Palgrave Macmillan, 2007).

41. Balibar offers the following definition of "racism without races": "It is a racism whose dominant theme is not biological heredity but the insurmountability of cultural differences, a racisms which, at first sight, does not postulate the superiority of certain groups or peoples in relation to others but 'only' the harmfulness of abolishing frontiers, the incompatibility of life-styles and traditions; in short, it is what P. A. Taguieff has rightly called a *differentialist racism*." See Étienne Balibar, "Is There a 'Neo-Racism'?," in Balibar and Wallerstein, *Race, Nation, Class*, 21.

42. https://wiki.digitalmethods.net/Dmi/NationalWebConditionDiagnostics.

43. Terranova, "Another Life."

44. Étienne Balibar, *Les frontières de la démocratie* (Paris: La Découverte, 1992). See also Manuela Bojadzijev and Isabelle Saint-Saëns, "Borders, Citizenship, War, Class: A Discussion with Étienne Balibar and Sandro Mezzadra," *New Formations* 58 (2006): 22–4.

45. Further analysis of the development of Rajarhat New Town on the northeast periphery of Kolkata can be found in Brett Neilson and Ned Rossiter, "The Logistical City," Transit Labour: Circuits, Regions, Borders, July 30, 2011, http://transitlabour.asia/blogs/logisticity. See also the more empirically detailed texts by Ishita Dey, Suhit Sen, and Ranabir Samaddar on the Transit Labour site and especially in their book, *Beyond Kolkata: Rajarhat and the Dystopia of Urban Imagination* (New Delhi: Routledge, 2013).

6
CODED VANILLA

Finance capital, supply chain operations, and labor-power define three key staples of contemporary globalization abstracted by algorithmic architectures and software systems. The expenditure of labor-power special to capitalist societies is, since Marx, the less novel of these three dynamics. But labor has been transformed in distinct ways with the onset of algorithmic capitalism, and is crucial to the emergence and dominance of finance capital and supply chain management as world-making forces. Finance capital and supply chain operations intersect with labor-power through logistical technologies that measure productivity and calculate value using real-time computational procedures. Logistical technologies derive their power to govern as a result of standardization across industry sectors coupled with algorithmic architectures designed to orchestrate protocological equivalence and thus connection between software applications and workplace routines.

The story of the standardization of shipping containers since the late 1960s is relatively well known.[1] More obscure is the extent to which enterprise resource planning (ERP), customer relationship management (CRM), and supply chain management (SCM) systems for managing administrative and financial tasks have penetrated a diverse range of institutional settings and industry sectors. These include the global logistics industries, which span shipping, road and rail transportation, warehousing and procurement, along with medical and health services, education providers, mining, and energy. In cases where ERPs have moved across from private to public sectors, "the systems often carried with them large amounts of 'accumulated functionality.'"[2] Neil Pollock and Robin Williams note how "this 'history' had important implications for the reshaping of adopting organisations (public organisations and specifically universities)."[3] ERP and CRM systems are promoted as real-time digital platforms that bring the diversity of organizational practices into a single operation. Their implementation is motivated by a managerial desire to obtain "a clear and unobstructed view of overall financial operations."[4] Interoperability is valorized across a range of packages or modules. In the case of ERP and CRM systems, an organization might choose to implement functional and technical modules that deal with financial management, logistics, sales and distribution, human resources, procurement, materials management, workflow planning, and so forth. Upon implementation, these modules enable operational oversight of both internal and external events as well as activities determined as relevant to an organization. The determination of relevance is an automated process choreographed by the algorithmic parameters of particular modules and their capacity to communicate with other modules.

This chapter sets out to explore the production of a seamless, standardized world as both fantasy and material condition. Central to such an account is the implementation and use of ERP systems, but also their economy within organizations that find supplementary lines of income generation through the mining of data. The distinction between implementation and economy registers in both organizational techniques and methods of analysis. The study of implementation lends itself to ethnographies of organizational cultures, and this has largely been the case in research on ERPs in university settings. A study of the economy of ERP systems, for the purpose of the argument I develop here, is more interested in how the technical parameters of software determine organizational practices and financial transactions within a logistical paradigm. While not exclusive of issues around implementation, the term economy marks a difference of method from ethnographic approaches, which analyze the implementation of ERP systems in institutions from the perspective of users and stakeholders. A study of the economy of enterprise systems points instead to the programming of measure, calculation, and decision that, due to the constraints of parameters, determines the production of subjectivity and circuits of movement.

This is not to say that subjectivity is overdetermined in the Althusserian sense, in which multiple forces coalesce in the production of singular events or entities. My interest is more specific and concrete than the theoretical inflection Althusser brought to bear in his collective study of the relation between subjectivity and structural forces. For Althusser, the ideological state apparatuses effectively invite subjects to occupy particular positions and personas through the process of interpellation. I am suggesting that ERP software takes a step further at the level of design and intention: Participation within the economy of logistical life requires acquiescence and submission. The power of algorithmic architectures and pervasive computing is such that there is no other option, whether one is aware of it or not. This does not mean that there is no resistance to ERP systems in workplace settings, nor does it mean that enterprise software is immune from computational errors or problems associated with implementation. It rather points to the indifference of enterprise systems and algorithmic architectures more broadly: Operating below the threshold of perception, we have no idea of the time and force of algorithmic action.

Software coupled with infrastructure determines our situation. And while both are heavily engineered and seemingly constrain, even repress, any possibility for action outside of parameters, they nonetheless present new sites of struggle against practices of extraction. A politics of alternatives remains possible despite the seeming impossibility and futility of such work. Less clear is whether alternative politics correspond with a life free of algorithmic determination. To develop this line of argument, the chapter presents a series of vignettes that register the operation and transformative affect of enterprise software systems on the economy of data and governance of labor. The chapter tracks the inception and governance of ERP systems within universities, then moves to finance capitalism and gamification to extend the analysis of logistical software and infrastructure as key apparatuses that govern culture, society, and economy within the historical present.

Debt and the Enterprise University

In the last chapter I examined how the rise of the "global university" as an institution characterized by highly mobile students and locally adjusted pay rates for faculty is an instantiation of the offshoring of what have become known as educational services. As a service, education provision is organized around economic factors much like any other operation. As Andrew Ross observes, "it is not at all easy to distinguish some of the new offshore academic centers from free trade industrial zones where outsourcing corporations are welcomed with a lavish package of tax holidays, virtually free land, and duty-free privileges."[5] Ross goes on to suggest that the global university is not a simple case of corporate culture migrating to the academy, although these features do figure substantively in the composition of higher education institutions over the past twenty years or so. Ross rather proposes that the university is also a key point of reference for post-Fordist management culture across the knowledge industry more broadly, where workers are not required to clock in their hours on the time sheet but are afforded a flexibility in time and the spaces of work similar to those experienced by the informatized academic.[6] Within the cultural industries, much of this work is analyzed in the name of precarity, the condition of which sees the at times liberating aspects of individual self-determination underscored by economic struggle and existential insecurity.[7]

A further point of indistinction between the higher education sector and other organizations can be found when ERP and CRM systems occupy the center of analysis. Indeed, I would go so far as to suggest that the correspondence between the academy and the corporate world may best be understood not from the traffic in managerial culture and labor practices across institutional settings, though there is no doubt such movements are key at the level of what Ross terms institutional "coevolution." One sees such coevolution not only in the management discourse that dominates institutional life, but also the mobility of labor between corporate and university settings along with the numerous examples of collaborative research projects between industry and academia. Rather than posit a constitutive force between discourses, subjects, and institutions, I would instead propose that attention to enterprise software systems may help explain the emulation of conduct between otherwise diverse institutional forms and organizational cultures.

Outside of business and management studies, computer science, and accounting, critical research on ERP implementation and use has often adopted Science and Technology Studies (STS) and Actor-Network Theory (ANT) approaches in the analysis of organizational cultures and identification of key "stakeholders."[8] A consistent finding across this literature concludes that ERP systems function to centralize administrative and managerial power in conjunction with a further displacement of academic staff and students already isolated from arenas of decision making. Writing from a quite different perspective and drawing on his experiences in the academic labor movement, Marc Bousquet analyzes how the "informationalization of labor" is a managerial undertaking that "manipulate[s] objects *as if* they were data."[9] Irrespective of whether they are car parts, novels, military armories or, for that matter, knowledge workers, all can be made available according to "an informatic logic: on demand, just in time, and fully catalogued."[10]

In Britain, Europe, and Australia, ERP systems are coincident with neoliberal policies geared toward the corporate turn within universities characterized by a decline in government funding for higher education and a subsequent commercialization of knowledge and introduction of fee paying models for student tuition. As Erica L. Wagner and Sue Newell explain, "The trend toward ERP 'business solutions' reflects the 'marketisation' of universities where institutional governance is now the domain of professional managers who aim to mitigate risks while remaining competitive in an increasingly complex global higher education marketplace."[11] Moreover, ERP systems have a leveling effect on institutions, making universities much like any other organization.[12] When ERP systems are taken as the object of study, the extent to which new modes of governance special to higher education institutions extend to other sectors of industry and society begins to appear as less a case of universities setting policy agendas vis-à-vis institutional reform or, vice versa, universities being subject to the external force of corporatization wrought by neoliberal policies and the commercialization of daily life. Instead, the university becomes one of many institutional settings whose economy increasingly comprises data extracted from routine practices managed through digital interfaces, databases, and software systems. The enormous costs of ERP consultancy, implementation, customization, and maintenance—running into the tens and often hundreds of millions of dollars—is offset by the promise of future cost savings through leaner, more efficient operations following the restructuring of organizations brought about by enterprise systems. The reality is somewhat different, with organizations having to wait years before seeing economic returns on their ERP investment, and running the risk of financially crippling themselves in the intervening years.

Unless organizations have finances to meet the considerable costs associated with customization, they will be forced to adjust their practices to parameters embedded in generic software packages.[13] As historian of technology Rosalind Williams notes, "Since the cost of adaptation is high, the bias is toward standardization."[14] A further risk is therefore born with modifying the default settings of ERP systems. The more localized customization becomes, the greater the chance of conflicts in the standards and protocols that enable updates from software suppliers and communication between organizations and operations.[15] The implications here for coordinating the movement of people, things, and finance along global supply chains are not hard to imagine. Without real-time interconnection logistical operations become exercises in inefficiency. Customization becomes the culprit of protocological conflict. It is in this sense that software determines organizational change.

A few words need to be said on how the technological force of determinism is invoked in this chapter's analysis of logistical media. Countless textbooks and introductory works crowding the field of media and communication attribute a moral depravity to those perceived as sliding into techno-determinist positions.[16] Certainly, on the face of it there seems something sensible in pointing out the clear limitations of the classic sender-message-receiver model of communication. Let your kid watch too many violent cartoons or load up on aggressive video games and they will flip into a rampant psycho. That sort of thing. Aside from the often hysterical claims of an evil media, the critique of linearity here usually overlooks the more nuanced model of cybernetics proposed by Norbert Wiener, which was interested in processes of nonlinearity, random noise, and feedback.[17] Within models of second-order cybernetics, complexity, and variation are subsumed within a dynamic system. Determinism does not dispense with contingency. Pairing German media theorist Friedrich Kittler with the economic writings of Marx and Engels, Geoffrey Winthrop-Young quotes the following correspondence between Engels and Joseph Bloch in 1890:

> According to the materialist conception of history, the ultimately determining element in history is the production and reproduction of real life. Other than this neither Marx nor I have ever asserted anything else. Hence if somebody twists this into saying that the economic element is the only determining one, he transforms that proposition into a meaningless, abstract, senseless phrase.[18]

By Winthrop-Young's account, a Kittlerian approach can replay this proposition as the media-technological determination of "the production and reproduction of data" and discourse as a force underscored by contingency.[19] Similarly, ERP software is not the only determining element in the transformation of organizational cultures and economies. Budget cuts, policy directives, labor composition, geographic location, and currency exchange rates are among the key elements that shape organizational change. But, very specifically, enterprise software coordinates activity in a wide range of material settings (ports, warehouses, transport, university activities, military operations, etc.) through predefined and, for the most part, fixed parameters. That ERP systems function through computational processes that require certain personnel in an organization to be allocated role X as distinct from others being assigned access to area Y, or to be granted permission to undertake task Z demonstrates the relation between ERP systems and security as it pertains to those working within an organization, which I take here as an instance of subjectivization determined by code.

In the case of enterprise software, the tendency is for organizations to accept the supplier's template in order to minimize immediate costs associated with implementation and future costs resulting from ongoing maintenance. The sum effect makes for diminished organizational and cultural variation within and between industrial sectors and institutional practices. The now widespread adoption of ERP systems across the higher education sector registers the rise of the enterprise university as an institution whose component parts function as interoperable units able to respond to external contingencies as they arise. Fluctuations in currency exchange rates and visa regulations that affect international student enrollments can be offset in the marketing office by adjusting ERP modules that inform a policy directive issued across the university to target domestic students and increase local enrollments in degree programs. As Williams recollects following the implementation of SAP's R/3 client-server enterprise system and relational database at the Massachusetts Institute of Technology in the mid-1990s as part of its Reengineering Project: "Once work is reconfigured in technological terms . . . it is profoundly shaped by the logic of the supporting technology. The rules that govern the technology start to govern everything else."[20] Simon Head considers the impact of ERP implementation on labor as a reiteration of Taylorist techniques of labor management, in which workplace routines "are the assembly lines of the digital age, complete with their own new digital proletariat."[21]

As soon as informal and contingent elements such as infrastructural sabotage, economies off the grid, software glitches, labor strikes, and financial crashes are introduced into the logistical scenario then parallel worlds come into being. This means not that the "failed" determinism of the technical system enters the realm of the fantastic but rather that the constraints of the system prompted unforeseen action. While economies off the grid would seem to be outside of logistical technical systems, and therefore immune to technical determinism, they nonetheless hold a relation to such systems either because they are excluded or as a consequence of their force. Moreover, if one were to experience a guided tour of informal economies off the grid, there would in all likelihood be encounters with material objects whose presence was made possible precisely because of systems of production and distribution enabled by the grid. So the invocation here of economies off the grid needs to be read as condition that is only even partial, outside perhaps the more extreme off-the-grid lifestyles entirely absent of goods obtained through supply chain networks.

Even if contingency can't formally be incorporated into the parameters of logistical operations defined by software architectures and strategic interests, it doesn't mean that it is outside the universe of logistics *per se*. Instead, another manifestation or extension of logistics emerges, when understood as an operation underscored by the problem of movement: financial transaction, labor migration, military deployment, administrative routine, and so forth. Logistics, in other words, is not only an adaptive technology able to accommodate contingency. It is also a technology of penetration, seeping into reserves of life that exist beyond the world of supply chains. As Stefano Harney and Fred Moten ascertain, "Logistics is no longer content with diagrams or with flows, with calculations or with predictions. It wants to live in the concrete itself, in space at once, time at once, form at once."[22] For now, the economy and design of enterprise software does not have that kind of traction, though it is worth noting how social media technologies instantiate the moment of "lifestream logistics" in which our relations of touch, perception, and response are captured by gesture-based interfaces whose user experience design is framed within a juridical regime that sees life as the object of patent law.[23]

It would be negligent of critique to overlook the politics of parameters in a study of how ERP and CRM systems shape organizational practices and economies of extraction. How might the rules and parameters of enterprise systems govern the economy of data accumulated through routine organizational practices? What sorts of data are gathered and where do they go? What are we to make of provocations by university CEOs who declare with zeal that their organization's finances can be expanded substantially through the sale of data amassed through ERP systems to interested third-party clients? Is this just part of a logistical lifestream moving from social media data-mining economies to the higher education sector in dire need of new models of revenue generation? No doubt that is part of the sales logic coming out of the IT sector. But it is not one that is widely advertised or discussed within university settings, since issues around privacy and data security are understandably highly sensitive and do not augur well for placating the already nervous state of a frazzled faculty.

Who really needs a manager when decisions become computational calculations? The world increasingly becomes coded vanilla.[24] Decision is democratized to include the grammar of code, at least for those invested in the object-oriented ontology (OOO) paradigm. But it is no longer a two-way street between the world of subjects and objects when engineers design the defaults of software that then decide how organizations will operate. As Alexander Galloway puts it, "object-oriented infrastructure skims off unpaid surplus-value from living networks."[25] Such operations special to technologies of post-Fordist capitalism apply just as much to how universities search for new ways to extract value from the work of experience manifested as data within ERP systems.

With the financial models on income returns stemming from student debt repayments looking to fall considerably short of expectation, universities may become emboldened—if they are not so already—to explore alternative options for supplementing their operating budgets through the trade in data.[26] As one business report on higher education management put it in 2007, "Highered

126 Coded Vanilla

institutions across the globe are rethinking their ERP and CRM investments with a new goal in mind: total financial management coupled with total student relationship management from recruitment and enrollment, through retention, graduation, and even alumni giving."[27] The sale of data to third parties in search of new market demographics is an extension of the logic of financialization of debt by the university sector.

By Maurizio Lazzarato's reckoning, "Debt acts as a 'capture,' 'predation,' and 'extraction' machine on the whole of society, as an instrument for macroeconomic prescription and management, and as a mechanism for income redistribution. It also functions as mechanism for the production and 'government' of collective and individual subjectivities."[28] Following the tech-wreck of 2000–2002 and then financial crash in 2008 triggered by the trade in derivatives associated with subprime mortgages and the housing bubble, the financialization of student debt has become one of the new grazing grounds for capital, registering the "transfer of fiscal responsibility from the state to the individual."[29] The economy of debt through student loans is now firmly entrenched in the repertoire of university techniques in fund-raising. It has resulted in many students shackled with debts in the tens of thousands of dollars and often higher, particularly those graduating from Anglophone academies where policies of privatization tend to be more deeply entrenched than elsewhere in the world. Andrew Ross notes how in the U.S. context student loans could not be discharged through bankruptcy, making them "among the most lucrative sectors of the financial industry."[30]

Collective analysis of student debt by New York based participants in the Strike Debt assembly, an offshoot from the Occupy movement, resulted in the Rolling Jubilee project that raised funds in order "to purchase distressed debt for pennies on the dollar."[31] While such interventions will in all likelihood be limited in scale due to problems in sustaining and enlarging social-political movements, they nonetheless highlight the financialization of the education sector—something largely unknown by many working within higher education to say nothing of broader publics. My interest is in how data derived from ERP operations within but not limited to higher education institutions constitute a new form of finance capital in logistical economies.

Financialization and Algorithmic Extraction

Since the mid-1990s high-frequency trading has involved an algorithmically engineered world of automated securities trades (stocks, bonds, derivatives, options, futures) that execute mathematical calculations, crunching data and performing trades that frequently exceed the capacity of the human brain to compute.[32] In a Twitter post on April 20, 2014, media theorist Geert Lovink wrote, "The topic of High-Frequency-Trading quickly dissolves into a smorgasbord of mnemonics and technical terms."[33] But what if instead of examining finance software, we considered algorithmic operations adjacent to finance capital and in so doing identified dynamics, conditions, and processes that might open new lines of critique of finance capital? Central to such an inquiry is the relation between finance capital, algorithms, and labor. Again, ERP systems provide a point of entry here.

First, however, it is helpful to set out some of the defining features of financialization. Christian Marazzi: "it is necessary to analyze financialization as the other side of a process of the value *production* affirmed since the crisis of the Fordist model, i.e., since the incapacity to suck surplus-value from immediate living labor, the wage labor of the factory."[34] Marazzi deviates from conventional critiques of financial capitalism, arguing that *"financialization is not an unproductive/parasitic deviation of growing quotas of surplus-value and collective saving, but rather a new process of value production."*[35] In assessing this process which has seen massive social and economic transformations over the past thirty years, with a hugely disproportionate shift from the so-called real economy of manufacturing to the new generator of surplus-value in financial capitalism, Marazzi observes the following: "There has been a transformation of valorization processes that witness the extraction of value no longer circumscribed in the places dedicated to the production of goods and services, but, so to speak, extending beyond factory gates, in the sense that it enters directly into the sphere of *circulation* of capital, that is, in the sphere of the exchanges of goods and services."[36]

Algorithmic architectures are central to the organization of communication systems that make possible the circulation of capital. According to Tiziana Terranova, "an algorithm is an abstraction."[37] Their power is to "modulate our relationship with data, digital devices and each other." Algorithms reorganize production, distribution, and consumption, constituting new modes of value creation. If one leading software developer's declaration that "63% of the world's transaction revenue touches an SAP system" is anywhere near accurate, then a considerable portion of this activity is of a logistical kind.[38] Algorithms hold value as a means of production upon converting what Terranova calls the social knowledge "abstracted from that elaborated by mathematicians, programmers, but also users' activities . . . into exchange value (monetization) and its (exponentially increasing) accumulation (the titanic quasi-monopolies of the social Internet)." Terranova is careful to point out that while capital—and more orthodox variations of Marxism—view algorithms as forms of "fixed capital" or "instrumental rationality" in the pursuit of capture and control, "it seems important to remember how for Marx, the evolution of machinery also indexes a level of development of productive powers that are unleashed but never totally contained by the capitalist economy."[39] Translated to the work of code, this means that algorithms cannot be reduced to homogeneous rules, functions, instructions, and infallible executions.

In *The New Ruthless Economy: Work and Power in the Digital Age*, Simon Head identifies a series of connections between the rise of ERP systems in U.S. corporations, the stagnation of wages throughout the "golden years" of the 1990s, and mass layoffs despite increases in workers' productivity. In Head's narrative, ERP systems control labor in ways that amount to a continuation of the model of the Fordist assembly line and the Taylorist science of managing labor. In her study of financialization and global management consultancy in China, Kimberly Chong gently contests Head's view that ERP systems mark a continuity of Fordism, and recounts how "ERP systems started to be installed en masse in the 1980s—around the same time that the predominant model of capitalism, which has its roots in the United States, shifted away from the welfare capitalism that characterised Fordism."[40] Chong notes instead how this period coincided with the role of stock markets as a determinant force in the "allocation of resources" coupled with the rise of "shareholder value," or, in a more extensive sense, what Randy Martin terms "the financialization of daily life."[41] The "new economy" of the dot-com era was soon to follow, then crash, only to be reborn as subprime mortgages, which, following the 2008 financial crisis, migrated in part to the financialization of student debt. The consultancy culture and business of ERP implementation have largely managed to ride through the past thirty years remarkably unscathed; indeed, it has been a period of exceptional growth in the enterprise software market. One key reason for the success of ERP systems rests with their allure for corporations as "a representation of modernity and vector of value."[42] They become a measure within both corporate and nonprofit sectors of best practice and a standard for organizational reform geared toward greater productivity, efficiency, and profit generation.

Chong places labor as the centerpiece of management consultancy: "the crucial work of management consulting is to establish the practice of managing labour *as* financial capital."[43] And the chief device for managing labor is through ERP systems: "ERP systems are a means of automating and disseminating the fundamental practices of financialisation."[44] Building on the ethnographic research of Anna Tsing and Marilyn Strathern, and the STS/ANT work of Annemarie Mol and John Law, Chong considers ERP systems as constructing labor as a "financialised subject" to be governed within an array of an organization's financial assets.[45] Labor is reduced to the status of data, able to be managed and shuffled about within the algorithmic environment of ERP systems. Moreover, ERP systems are perfectly suited to the logic of neoliberalism vis-à-vis the organization of production and management of labor: "ERP systems both institute the economic rationale for, and provide the technical means of, contracting-out."[46]

How, though, do ERP systems extract value from the dual uncertainty of both living labor and algorithmic architectures? ERP modules in finance, payroll, and human resource management calculate wages, deductions, overtime, annual leave, financial risk, market growth, and the like. These modules do not extract value so much as manage its allocation. Designed to automate basic financial and administrative of operations within and across organizations, these particular ERP modules make labor accountable and measurable, albeit in fairly limited ways. As extraction machines, ERP systems are realized once the data accumulated through routine organizational practices is aggregated and packaged as tradable commodities to third-party clients. By mining ERP data, organizations are able to develop new revenue streams usually associated with the economy of social media corporations such as Facebook and Twitter. In the case of ERP systems within universities if not other organizations, the economy of data mining is easily undertaken without the consent, let alone awareness, of academic employees, prospective students, or even high-level management who may then find themselves targets of marketing campaigns based on demographic data supplied. Such is the abstract operation of algorithmic architectures, where computational processes whir along in the background of daily institutional practices.

Despite the seemingly totalizing force of ERP systems, Luciana Parisi insists that there is an incomputable ontology intrinsic to algorithmic architectures. Receptive to uncertainty and randomness, incomputable algorithms are, for Parisi, "instances of postcybernetic control" able to prehend (anticipate) and preempt change and transformation immanent in the present.[47] If we are to take ERP systems as a technology of control in which labor is constituted as a financial subject to be made accountable within a temporal regime that coincides with the extraction of value, what sort of design flaws within algorithmic architectures corresponding with ERP systems occasion the possibility of refusal or subtraction from the logistics of control?

The backend security of ERP systems such as those provided by SAP is known to have glitches and software vulnerabilities, and intentionally so: As with most software developers, ERP providers require an automated traffic in data on software performance as part of the system testing, development, and updating process. However, this access to an organization's data opens the potential for ERP companies or their subsidiaries to have advance insight into a client's market strategies and financial transactions. Such a practice effectively transfers the power of what ERP providers like to promote to clients as "real-time business intelligence" enabled through data analytics that make possible the prediction of market trends and management of organizational operations.

To suppose that ERP providers are engaged in some form of insider trading based on the capacity to access critical business data can be passed off as a form of paranoid speculation. More alarming for organizations is the vulnerability of ERP systems to unauthorized access to data. The prevalence of security flaws within ERP systems is detailed in a report from a Russian consultancy firm specializing in security monitoring of SAP: "According to the statistics of vulnerabilities found in business applications, there were more than 100 vulnerabilities patched in SAP products in 2009, while it grew to more than 500 in 2010. By the August of 2013, there are more than 2700 SAP Security notes about vulnerabilities in various SAP components."[48] The substantial increase in security flaws may be related to the launch in 2012 of SAP HANA (High-Performance Analytic Appliance), an in-memory relational database management system with cloud services promoted in 2013. The migration of an ERP system to cloud computing increases the likelihood of security vulnerabilities associated with Internet communications.[49]

130 Coded Vanilla

The design of computational exploits to hack into ERP systems should not be seen as the stuff of organized crime alone. In October 2012 the hactivist network Anonymous claims to have breached the SAP ERP system of Greece's Ministry of Finance in the lead up to another round of economic austerity measures to be voted on by the government. Earlier in 2012 Anonymous had taken down the website of Greece's Ministry of Justice. Mobilizing under the Twitter hashtag #OpGreece, Anonymous called on Greek citizens to revolt, and claims to have "gained full access to the Greek Ministry of Finance" were followed by a list of username and password details for numerous leaked documents.[50] Before signing off with a passing critique of Greek citizens' financing of European banks and international hedge funds, the announcement makes clear the weakness of the Ministry of Finance's ERP systems: "Those funky IBM servers don't look so safe now, do they . . . We have new guns in our arsenal. A sweet 0day SAP exploit is in our hands and oh boy we're gonna sploit the hell out of it."[51] While the hack by Anonymous was not acknowledged by SAP, it is worth noting in as much as it signals a political awareness on the part of social-political movements of the power of ERP systems and the need to focus critical attention on logistical media and financial infrastructure. Key to the power of logistical media such as ERP systems is the capacity to govern labor in real-time. The temporal regime of ERPs thus marks an obvious target for techno-political attack.

Refusing Gamification

Amazon's automated marketplace, Amazon Mechanical Turk (AMT), is one example that suggests how labor circumvents algorithmic control. Launched in 2005, Mechanical Turk is a crowdsourcing platform that allocates microtasks involving basic data entry—tagging objects in photographs, writing short product descriptions, transcribing insurance claims, commenting on blog posts, maintaining Twitter profiles, etc. Payment varies from pennies to dollars depending on the task and is adjusted according to country of origin with "turkers" from poorer countries paid less than those from wealthier countries. The assumption underlying AMT is that humans can be organized to do low-level routine tasks more efficiently and reliably than machines.[52] That is, humans can be trained to work like machines. There is nothing especially novel about such an assumption. It was one that defined the industrial age with weaving technologies such as the spinning jenny and the assembly lines of Henry Ford's car manufacturing plants. The only problem is that humans also cheat systems. Paid a few dollars per hour and without any form of job security, bonuses, or benefits, and a requirement for those residing in the United States to report earnings to Mturk.com as taxable income for the Internal Revenue Service (IRS), it is no wonder that workers in the virtual sweatshop of AMT might be inclined to enter false data for HITs (Human Intelligence Tasks) accepted.[53] Better to break the rules than become the unexpected recipient of fraudulent billing, identify theft, scams, and spams.[54]

Breaking the rules can manifest as a form of subtracting value from Amazon's profits. Whether it is writing cheat scripts that autocomplete HITs, promoting the websites of other businesses, or faking your ethnic identity to fill in market research questionnaires, Amazon is not immune to meting out reprisals on those identified as violating the Turk Participation Agreement. Vincent Mosco notes how in January 2013, "Amazon stopped accepting new applications from international Turkers because of what the company deemed unacceptable levels of fraud and poor worker performance."[55] In tandem with the legal obligation of turkers to report earnings to the IRS, this policy change on Amazon's part produces a subtraction of another kind—namely, the exclusion of international labor from the nationally protected low-pay service economy of AMT.

In an attempt to reassert the power of control over the all-too-human tendency to shirk from the task at hand, the managerial class has been on the lookout for strategies and techniques that bring labor back into the fold of efficiency and increased productivity. Gameplay is now seen as one key "solution" to recapture the distracted soul of workers. Gamification techniques designed for organizational reform are increasingly implemented across a range of institutions in an effort to further enhance productivity levels from labor and organizational activities through the logic of play. According to ex-SAP employee and gamification consultant, Mario Herger: "Gamification generates a tremendous amount of data on your employees' skill levels . . . . If you gamified every system and every interaction in your corporation, you'd know exactly what each person does and at what level of skill."[56] Gamification brings game design and the logic of play into nonentertainment settings. A key goal is to change social behavior, forging closer links between companies, employees, and their customers by generating data for computational analysis. Workplace performance, for example, is tracked through gamification applications. At IT firm Accenture, "collaboration scores are included in their annual performance reviews."[57] In various games designed in conjunction with ERP systems, employees "earn" points for inputting data, teams are assigned "goals" and "challenges," performances are evaluated, and "desired behaviors" are modulated through user experiences of play. The coupling of play and labor— what game theorist Julian Kücklich coins as "playbor"—registers the current level of managerial discourse and software engineering that casts the worker as a subject optimized for efficiency.[58] The next step for capital's cycle of replenishment would be to make the realm of the unconscious a site of "primitive accumulation" from which economic value can be extracted through computational means.[59]

According to Gartner analyst Brian Burke, gamification is also "leveraged for change management" in organizational settings. And as Imran Sayeed, chief technology officer (CTO) of NTT Data Inc., explains: "The nice thing about a game is that it collects incredible analytics, and so every manager can see the progress of their team members through the game—where they did well and where they are having issues—so they can offer to help them offline."[60] This centrality of management within the seat of control is one that resonates across sectors. *Virtual U* is a

132 Coded Vanilla

computer simulation and serious game of university management training released in 2000 and designed by Stanford University education and business administrator, William Massy. As Massy and his colleagues explain: "While Virtual U is necessarily a simulation of real academic life, it is grounded in authentic data and provides serious lessons in higher education. Toward these ends, Virtual U draws on data from 1,200 colleges and universities in the United States."[61] Bousquet describes how players of *Virtual U* have but one option: to occupy the seat of power as president of a university.[62] In producing the subjectivity of the manager in control, *PR Newswire* reports that *"Virtual U* players strive for continuous improvement by setting, monitoring, and modifying a variety of institutional parameters and policies. Players are challenged to manage and improve their institution of higher education through techniques such as creative resource allocation, minority enrollment policies, and tenure parameters, among others."[63]

While *Virtual U* has now become an obscure artifact in the history of digital games for workplace settings, countless others have taken its place. The logic of play within *Virtual U* is duplicated over a decade later in *Lead In One*, a game concept developed within the SAP Community Network for an iPad application in which players assume the role of a sales manager. Business leads are received, duties are assigned to members of a sales team, and market prospects are analyzed based on data from previous sales, Twitter, and social media feeds. The infant world of play made computational increasingly intersects with ERP systems within institutional settings seeking to extract greater value from data generated by their workforces.

As much as ERP systems are designed with the intention to control worlds, their reach will remain highly circumscribed, at least for the foreseeable future. Labor refuses, parameters by definition have limits, and the extraction of value by capital's machines can only subsume that which is named. Anonymity becomes a strategy of subtraction. The anonymity that attends the culture of improper names has historically been a resource for political work seeking to refuse the logic of identity and its susceptibility to apparatuses of capture. As detailed by Marco Deseriis, a genealogy of improper names includes acts of collective struggle perhaps best exemplified by Ned Ludd, "the eponymous leader invented by the English Luddites to resist the introduction of labor-saving machines during the Industrial Revolution."[64] Other examples of improper names central to Deseriis's study include North American mail artists in the 1980s adopting the alias of Monty Cantsin, the collective pseudonym of Alan Smithee assumed by Hollywood film directors since the late 1960s who wished to dissociate themselves from films meddled with by Hollywood studios without their consent, and activists in Italy gathering from the mid-1990s around Luther Blissett as "a figure of immaterial labor." More recently, anonymity is often associated with the pranks, hacks, and collective actions organized in the name of Anonymous, an improper name spawned on the image-based Internet bulletin board of 4chan.[65]

Anonymity may seem a strategy of collective withdrawal not feasible in the case of enterprise planning systems whose real-time monitoring of movement and calculation of labor productivity require people, finance, and things to register within databases and screen interfaces as objects to manage in the interests of efficiency. Yet while we all need our user accounts to sign into platforms of work and play, these devices require a subject to activate a new file of data generation and compilation. At least this is the case for tasks not fully automated. At this point, the political limits of object-orientated ontology become clearly apparent. For as long as there are subjects that are more than just an addition to the expansive agency of objects, there is also scope for a political imaginary not reducible to, or able to be readily replaced by, the ontology of objects. The strategies of subtraction offered by techniques of anonymity may not combat the economy of data generation and its subsequent exploitation within economies of exchange, but they can shield against the often assumed correspondence between data and the empirical thing in itself. For as much as we know in the post-Snowden world of the NSA that our data are never secret, at least for now our dreams remain free as sources of the imaginary beyond the actionable.

Notes

1. See Marc Levinson, *The Box: How the Shipping Container Made the World Smaller and the World Economy Bigger* (Princeton: Princeton University Press, 2006). See also chapters 1 and 4.
2. Neil Pollock and Robin Williams, *Software and Organisations: The Biography of the Enterprise-Wide System, or, How SAP Conquered the World* (Oxon and New York: Routledge, 2009), 11.
3. Ibid.
4. Rosalind Williams, "Technology and Business," in *Retooling: A Historian Confronts Technological Change* (Cambridge, MA: MIT Press, 2002), 118.
5. Andrew Ross, "The Rise of the Global University," in *Nice Work if You Can Get It: Life and Labor in Precarious Times* (New York and London: New York University Press, 2009), 201.
6. Ibid., 204.
7. See Rosalind Gill and Andy Pratt, eds., "Themed Section: Precarity and Social Work," *Theory, Culture & Society* 25, nos. 7–8 (2008). See also Brett Neilson and Ned Rossiter, "Precarity as a Political Concept, or, Fordism as Exception," *Theory, Culture & Society* 25, nos. 7–8 (2008): 51–72; and Brett Neilson and Ned Rossiter, "From Precarity to Precariousness and Back Again: Labour, Life and Unstable Networks," *Fibreculture Journal* 5, http://journal.fibreculture.org/issue5/neilson_rossiter.html.
8. See, for example, Pollock and Williams, *Software and Organisations*. See also Paolo Quattrone and Trevor Hopper, "What is IT? SAP, Accounting and Visibility in a Multinational Organisation," *Information and Organization* 16 (2006): 212–50; and Kimberly Chong, "The Work of Financialisation: An Ethnography of a Global Management Consultancy in Post-Mao China," PhD Dissertation, Department of Anthropology, London School of Economics and Political Science, 2012.
9. Marc Bousquet, *How the University Works: Higher-Education and the Low-Wage Nation* (New York: New York University Press, 2008), 60–61.

134 Coded Vanilla

10. Ibid., 61.
11. Erica L. Wagner and Sue Newell, "'Best' for Whom?: The Tension between 'Best Practice' ERP Packages and Diverse Epistemic Cultures in a University Context," *Journal of Strategic Information Systems* 13 (2004): 307.
12. See Neil Pollock and James Cornford, "ERP Systems and the University as a 'Unique' Organisation," *Information, Technology & People* 17, no. 1 (2004): 31–52.
13. Ibid., 33.
14. Williams, *Retooling*, 119.
15. Pollock and Cornford, "ERP Systems and the University as a 'Unique' Organisation," 34–35.
16. As Geoffrey Winthrop-Young so delightfully phrases this predicament: "To label someone a technodeterminist is a bit like saying that he enjoys strangling cute puppies." Geoffrey Winthrop-Young, *Kittler and the Media* (Cambridge: Polity, 2011), 121.
17. Norbert Wiener, *Cybernetics: or Control and Communication in the Animal and the Machine*, 2nd edition (Cambridge, MA: MIT Press, 1961). See also the extensive documentation of the Macy conferences on cybernetics in Claus Pias, ed., *Cybernetic–Kybernetik: The Macy Conferences, 1946–1953, Vol. 1* (Zürich-Berlin: Diaphanes, 2003).
18. Karl Marx and Friedrich Engels, *Selected Correspondence* (Moscow: Progress Publishers, 1975). Quoted in Winthrop-Young, 123.
19. Winthrop-Young, *Kittler and the Media*, 123–24.
20. Williams, *Retooling*, 116. As discussed in chapter 3, SAP is a German based software developer specializing in ERP and CRM systems. One recent report placed SAP as holding 25 percent of the worldwide market share in ERP revenue. SAP's closest competitor, Oracle, held 13 percent of market share. See Louis Columbia, "2013 ERP Market Share Update: SAP Solidifies Market Leadership," *Forbes*, May 12, 2013, http://www.forbes.com/sites/louiscolumbus/2013/05/12/2013-erp-market-share-update-sap-solidifies-market-leadership/.
21. Simon Head, *The New Ruthless Economy: Work and Power in the Digital Age* (New York: Oxford University Press, 2003), 8.
22. Stefano Harney and Fred Moten, *The Undercommons: Fugitive Planning & Black Study* (New York: Minor Compositions, 2013), 88, http://www.minorcompositions.info/wp-content/uploads/2013/04/undercommons-web.pdf.
23. As Soenke Zehle notes, "On 25 October 2011, computer and mobile gadget maker Apple was assigned patent 8,046,721 by the US Patent Office, granting the life-style corporation additional rights over the 'slide-to-unlock' gesture of its touch-based devices" (342). Soenke Zehle, "The Autonomy of Gesture: Of Lifestream Logistics and Playful Profanations," *Distinktion: Scandinavian Journal of Social Theory* 13, no. 3 (2012): 341–54.
24. Wagner and Newell note that "Organizations adopting ERP software need to configure the software to meet their local needs but are encouraged to adopt the 'vanilla system' (that is without modifications) since the 'best' industry practices are supposedly embedded in this standard configuration." Wagner and Newell, "'Best' for Whom?," 306. See also Jessica Davis, "Scooping Up Vanilla ERP: Off-the-Shelf versus Customised Software," *InfoWorld* 20, no. 47 (1998): 1–4. Citing a Forrester Research industry survey presumably made in the U.S. in the mid-90s, Davis makes the point that "only 5% of companies buy an application with the intention of modifying it to match their business processes" (1).
25. Alexander R. Galloway, "The Poverty of Philosophy: Realism and Post-Fordism," *Critical Inquiry* 39, no. 2 (Winter, 2013): 363.

26. On the budget implications for universities in the U.K. not accurately factoring in the default rate on student loans, see Rowena Mason and Shiv Malik, "Unpaid student loans 'a fiscal time bomb for universities,'" *The Guardian*, March 21, 2014, http://www.theguardian.com/education/2014/mar/21/student-loans-unpaid-debt-problem-universities-adrian-bailey.

27. Joseph C. Panettieri, "The New Face of ERP," *University Business: Solutions for Higher Education Management*, June 2007, http://www.universitybusiness.com/article/new-face-erp.

28. Maurizio Lazzarato, *The Making of Indebted Man*, trans. Joshua David Jordan (Los Angeles: Semiotext(e), 2012), 29.

29. Andrew Ross, "Democracy and Debt," *Social Text: Periscope*, "Special Issue: Is This What Democracy Looks Like?," 2013, http://what-democracy-looks-like.com/democracy-and-debt/.

30. Ibid.

31. Andrew Ross, "Dossier from Strike Debt," *The South Atlantic Quarterly* 112, no. 4 (2013): 783. See also "Strike Debt / Occupy Wall Street," *The Debt Resistors' Operations Manual*, September 2012, http://strikedebt.org/drom/.; and Andrew Ross, *Creditocracy and the Case for Debt Refusal* (New York and London: OR Books, 2013).

32. See David Golumbia, "High-Frequency Trading: Networks of Wealth and the Concentration of Power," *Social Semiotics* 23, no. 2 (2013): 278–99.

33. Tweet by @geertlovink, April 20, 2014.

34. Christian Marazzi, *The Violence of Financial Capitalism*, trans. Kristina Lebedeva (Los Angeles: Semiotext(e), 2010), 49.

35. Ibid. Italics in original.

36. Ibid., 49–50.

37. Tiziana Terranova, "Red Stack Attack! Algorithms, Capital and the Automation of the Common," Quaderni di San Precario, February 14, 2014, http://quaderni.sanprecario.info/2014/02/red-stack-attack-algorithms-capital-and-the-automation-of-the-common-di-tiziana-terranova/. Quotations of Terranova hereafter are from this reference.

38. SAP, *Helping the World Run Better*, 2012 Annual Report, 4. A presentation for the U.S.-based University Alliances Program in 2009 claims that 80–85 percent of all business transactions are through ERP systems of one kind of another, http://www.sdn.sap.com/irj/uac/go/portal/prtroot/docs/library/uuid/f08809dc-c6b2–2c10–1c98–ad9e37224973?overridelayout=true.

39. The rise of crypto currencies such as Bitcoin would appear to offer one such alternative to what David Harvey and others refer to as the state-finance nexus. Due to limits of space and the need to contain an argument, I will not pursue this line of investigation here. For a critical overview of Bitcoin and the Institute of Network Cultures' event on MoneyLab: Coining Alternatives in Amsterdam, 2014, see Jerome Roos, "In Each Other We Trust: Coining Alternatives to Capitalism," *ROAR Magazine*, March 31, 2014, http://roarmag.org/2014/03/moneylab-conference-alternative-currencies/. See also David Harvey, *The Enigma of Capital and the Crises of Capitalism* (New York: Oxford University Press, 2010). An important critical engagement with Bitcoin, alternative currencies and the question of value can be read in Nathaniel Tkacz, Nicolas Mendoza, and Francesca Musiani, eds., "Special Issue: Value and Currency," *Journal of Peer Production* 4 (January, 2014), http://peerproduction.net/issues/issue-4-value-and-currency/.

40. Ibid. See also Head, *The New Ruthless Economy*. Interestingly, Chong argues that Head's "description of ERP systems as a kind of Taylorist machinery is accurate but the contextualisation of his argument is misplaced. The relevance of ERP systems, for an analysis

136 Coded Vanilla

of how capitalism operates, derives not from their capacity to automate managerial techniques that resemble older practices of management, but the capacity in which these objects are deployed, which is based on accounting and more importantly on a new regime of value" (21). Head extends his thesis on the relation between Taylorism and computer business systems in *Mindless: Why Smarter Machines Are Making Dumber Humans* (New York: Basic Books, 2014).

41. Chong, "The Work of Financialisation," 18. See also Randy Martin, *Financialization of Daily Life* (Philadelphia: Temple University Press, 2002).

42. Chong, "The Work of Financialisation," 21.

43. Ibid., 11.

44. Ibid., 26.

45. See ibid., 37–40, 49.

46. Ibid., 25.

47. Luciana Parisi, *Contagious Architecture: Computation, Aesthetics, and Space* (Cambridge, MA: MIT Press, 2013), 81.

48. Alexander Polyakov and Alexey Tyurin, *12 Years of SAP Security in Figures: A Global Survey, 2001–2013*, ERPScan, October 2013, http://scn.sap.com/docs/DOC-55421.

49. See Vincent Mosco, *To the Cloud: Big Data in a Turbulent World* (Boulder: Paradigm Publishers, 2014), 144–47.

50. Anonymous, "#OpGreece GREEK MINISTRY OF FINANCE CREDENTIALS," Pastebin, October 29, 2012, http://pastebin.com/hwLDmEmH. See also Polyakov and Tyurin, *12 Years of SAP Security in Figures*, 40; and "Anonymous Hacks Greek Ministry of Finance," *Infosecurity*, October 30, 2012, http://www.infosecurity-magazine.com/view/29043/anonymous-hacks-greek-ministry-of-finance/.

51. Ibid.

52. See Brittany Paris, "Speed, Sensation, Crisis: Constructing the Individual in Web 2.0," MA Thesis, Department of Culture and Media, The New School, New York, 2013. See also Jonathan Zittrain, "Ubiquitous Human Computing," *Philosophical Transactions of the Royal Society* 366 (2008): 3813–21, http://iis-db.stanford.edu/evnts/5812/Zittrain_Paper.pdf.

53. See Katharine Mieszkowski, "'I Make $1.45 a Week and I Love It'," *Salon*, June 24, 2006, http://www.salon.com/2006/07/24/turks_3/. See also Jason Huff, "Serf Boards," *The New Inquiry*, May 5, 2014, http://thenewinquiry.com/essays/serf-boards/.

54. See ★★★ IMPORTANT READ: HITs You Should NOT Do! ★★★, http://turkernation. com.

55. Mosco, *To the Cloud*, 171. See also Ayhan Aytes, "Return of the Crowds: Mechanical Turk and Neoliberal States of Exception," in Trebor Scholz, ed., *Digital Labor: The Internet as Playground and Factory* (New York: Routledge, 2012), 79–97.

56. Quoted in Tam Harbert, "Case Study: 3 Heavyweights Give Gamification a Go," *Computerworld*, September 18, 2013, http://www.computerworld.com/s/article/9242418/Case_study_3_heavyweights_give_gamification_a_go?pageNumber=2.

57. Ibid.

58. For critical analyses of the combinatory logic and condition of "playbor," see Julian Kücklich, "Precarious Playbour: Modders and the Digital Games Industry," *Fibreculture Journal* 5 (2005), http://five.fibreculturejournal.org/fcj-025-precarious-playbour-modders-and-the-digital-games-industry/. See also Scholz, *Digital Labor*, 2013.

59. For a harrowing account of the exploitation of sleep by capitalism, see Jonathan Crary, *24/7: Late Capitalism and the Ends of Sleep* (London and New York: Verso, 2013).

60. Quoted in Harbert, "Case Study: 3 Heavyweights Give Gamification a Go," 2013.
61. Terese Rainwater, Neil Salkind, Ben Sawyer, and William Massy, "Virtual U 1.0 Strategy Guide," http://www.virtual-u.org/downloads/vu-strategy-guide.pdf.
62. Bousquet, *How the University Works*, 73.
63. "Virtual U Released; University Management Goes High Tech Computer Simulation Tackles the Management Challenges of Higher Education," *PR Newswire*, June 27, 2000, http://www.thefreelibrary.com/Virtual+U+Released%3B+University+Management+Goes+High+Tech+Computer . . . -a062987647.
64. Marco Deseriis, *Improper Names: Collective Pseudonyms from the Luddites to Anonymous* (Minneapolis: University of Minnesota Press, 2015), 2.
65. See Gabriella Coleman, *Hacker, Hoaxer, Whistleblower, Spy: The Many Faces of Anonymous* (London and New York: Verso, 2014).

7

IMPERIAL INFRASTRUCTURES

Like much of the infrastructure that supports our daily life and global economies, the topic of data centers is one that is largely surrounded in mystery. The very banality of communication rarely compels our imagination to take the step into making the concrete abstraction of infrastructure something we might know and address. Ushered in with the proliferation of digital media throughout social life, and made operational on a planetary scale in the transition from mainframe computing to facilities able to accommodate multiple servers that support the digital economy of software-as-a-service (SaaS), the rise of data centers integrates society with an economy whose technical infrastructure is defined by storage, processing, and transmission. Think cloud computing or the low-latency networks required for high-frequency trading followed by other sectors further down the food chain of speed (military-industrial complexes, medical services, urban systems, and entertainment industries). But also consider the way institutional differentiation is increasingly hard to identify as a result of the limited backend options for organizations to combine and configure off-the-shelf software services.[1] So no matter that institutions potted across the world are indeed different, the computational architecture of their operations is increasingly the same, varying only according to the minimal options offered by parameterized systems—from logging, billing, visualization, data authentication, predictive analytics, business intelligence, search, conversion, publication, and backup. Situated within the new universality of computational regimes, the calibration of subjectivity and routines of organizational culture have become standardized.[2] It is no wonder, then, that we so frequently feel logged into another groundhog day. This is a defining feature of logistical media: Low-level demands prompted by minimal parametric variation are what make the world of supply chain capitalism turn around. Again and again. Such is the weird ambience of our logistical nightmares.

How to operate outside such constraints and invent new systems of organization and cultures of expression comprises a parametric politics of the present.[3] As discussed in the previous chapter, parameters have a determining force in the production of subjectivity and the organization of practices and systems. A parametric politics, therefore, is a politics of design. It seeks to test the points at which systems fail to comprehend the disruption to legacy rule sets. Regardless of whether this takes the form and force of contingency or a more targeted intervention that makes visible and intelligible the operational logic of the machine as a site of struggle and agency, the effects will be similar. Rules are changed, even if only as a temporary rupture awaiting the attention of a remote systems operator who can think of any number of better things to do with their day. As much as theorists of affect may suppose that the induction of intimate atmospheres constitutes a more preferable world, the brute materiality of infrastructure designed for communication, economy, and political control are primary in compositing the world within which we subsist as a set of interchangeable modules. At least this is the perspective I suggest we assume of logistical media.

The formatting of infrastructure becomes central to the task of a politics that has not yet relinquished the relation between structure, economy, and subjectivity. A motivating undercurrent running throughout this book has been the question of how to collectively design strategies of intervention that identify increasingly obscure and often invisible systems of control. When algorithmic architectures modulate and pattern how we encounter the world what, seriously, can one do other that submit and click accept? Escaping offline is not an option. But there are alternatives. As architectural theorist Keller Easterling proposes: "Exposing evidence of the infrastructural operating system is as important as acquiring some special skills to hack into it."[4] In the case of the software and infrastructure that comprise logistical media, the object of intervention is at once distant as infrastructure may just as likely be located thousand of miles from where we may live—though often in the case of data centers, it may also be located just around the corner. Such infrastructure is also highly securitized. And yet the object of communications infrastructure is also highly integrated into our daily lives as software and technological devices.

This paradox of remote intimacy has long been a feature of communications media. It just becomes amplified with digital logistical media that coordinate global supply chains and govern work routines. The prospect of submitting entirely to regimes of control is just too depressing. Paranoia as method, however, does lend itself to a form of diagnosis, disclosing something about the infrastructural conditions of our present. Remember the pre-Snowden era. Many had a hunch that something on the scale of the United States' National Security Agency's (NSA) PRISM machine was entirely possible. Some even had a deep technical knowledge that confirmed such surveillance operations were underway. Paranoia as method, in this instance, served as a preemptive strategy of our post-Snowden present. But did it have any substantive effect in terms of shifting our online

140 Imperial Infrastructures

practices and behavior? Hardly at all. Fortune 500 companies are ramping up their encryption systems, but most of us carry on as usual, comfortably indifferent with the sense that resisting against online spaces of obfuscation and control can also only achieve so much before the surveillance machine regains its authority to interrupt and inspect without consent.[5]

The key point this chapter takes from the case of NSA's PRISM program is that it inaugurated a new regime of territorial power based upon the aggregation and analysis of data in real-time. Territory is understood here as spatial and temporal regimes specific to the operation of data. Territory is thus not limited or reducible to the geographic and political borders of the nation-state. The geoeconomic and political geographic transformation of spatial calculation is, as Deborah Cowen argues, central to "the work of logistics [which] is concerned precisely with the production of space beyond territory."[6] Framed within a technics of territory, the Snowden revelations also suggest a new kind of empire and machinic imperialism in terms of the use of communications infrastructure for data sharing and surveillance as systems of logistical control.[7] As Internet entrepreneur Kim Dotcom notes, the "Five Eyes Alliance" between intelligence agencies in the United States, Canada, Australia, New Zealand, and the United Kingdom "effectively permits those governments to circumvent the prohibition against gathering data on their own citizens by sharing information across the Five Eyes intelligence community."[8] The data and information shared on an NSA operated spy cloud shows how these intelligence agencies are working together to overcome legal and geographic limitations of the nation in their own state-based democratic contexts. Along with the tech companies in collusion with NSA (Facebook, Google, Microsoft, Yahoo, Apple, and Dropbox), we can assume other aligned countries might act or be acting already in similar ways. The capacity of the PRISM program to exploit vulnerabilities in real-time at the level of communication links between data centers further extends this book's general definition of logistical media.[9] Moreover, it points us in the direction of communications infrastructure as it relates to the production of territory.

In setting out an account in this chapter of the relation between territory and telegraphy, I wish to establish a parallel with contemporary digital infrastructures such as data centers.[10] Focusing on the combinatory force of logistics and infrastructure between the 1800 and 2000 communication systems of cable, I argue that the logistical operation of imperial infrastructures produces territory in ways that skew and structure the relation between states and empire. This periodization is less motivated by identifying the operation of prevailing "discourse networks" or inscription machines, as Kittler and his protégés would have it, and rather more about a variation of geomedial power, as developed by media archaeologist Jussi Parikka,[11] in which the materiality of communication media conditions infrastructural power as a territorial program. Indeed, my argument in this chapter is that the logistical infrastructure of cable is compelled toward territorial expansion. It may seem that the geopolitical is primary here. Certainly there is a geopolitical interest that runs throughout this chapter and indeed much of this book. Whether there is a "deep time" (Zielinksi) component to logistical media at the mineral level, which consists, for example, in the rare earths used in the manufacturing of microchips, hard drives, computer screens, and fiber-optic cables with secondary economies in the electronic waste industries (chapter 4), is not something this book addresses.[12] But I am suggesting that in conjoining the geopolitical with logistical media, one identifies the operative dimension of geomedial power.

Think of string. It might be purchased as a ball, but if it is to have a life beyond the storage cupboard its tendency is to unravel into chaos across the kitchen floor. This potential is amplified when the ball of string makes contact with the hands of a child, the fumbling fingers of an adult, or curious paws of a cat. The cat, child, fingers, string, and floor coupled with the physical-cognitive capacities and properties of each are combined as a device or apparatus. The social and physical struggles that may ensue from this chaos instantiate a form of geopolitics played out across the surface of the floor.

The concept of logistical media invoked throughout this book is not much different, though there is one key distinction: Chaos is far less a part of the organizing logic than the multiple technical, economic, geopolitical, and material parameters that drive logistical media as a system of coordination, communication, and control. Logistical media are activated as orientation systems in the instance of the arrangement between software, infrastructure, and labor. This chapter examines how the territoriality of power manifests through communications infrastructure such as telegraphic cables and data centers to produce a new sovereign entity that I term *the logistical state*.

The Territory and Territoriality of Power

How does infrastructure constitute the state? In setting up the foundations for a theory of the state, Max Weber follows Leon D. Trotksy: "Every state is founded on force." This classical definition of the state is often translated and interpreted as the state's monopoly on violence and has informed much theorization of the state throughout the twentieth and twenty-first centuries.[13] Weber makes the important additional qualification that brings population—or what he prefers to term "community"—and territory into the orbit of state power: "The state is the human community that, within a defined territory—and the key word here is 'territory'—(successfully) claims the *monopoly of legitimate force* for itself."[14] What might it mean to think the state, territory, and population as they intersect with processes of informatization and, more specifically, the geography of data centers? If territory consists of the organization of power across spatial scales and technical systems, then what are the implications of infrastructure for a theory of the state?[15] And how might we think the temporal properties special to the optimization of speed (low-latency) within data centers? Such questions begin to alter the baseline Weberian model of the state that has informed so much theorizing of the state, whether in radical or conservative veins. Approaching the question and constitution of the state in such a way involves foregrounding the production of territory through infrastructure—rather than a monopoly on violence or exertion of force—and thus contributes a media-theoretical perspective to scholarship on state formation. A focus on infrastructure as it bears upon the composition and territorial scope of the state unshackles state formation from classical varieties of political thought and social imaginaries that assume territory and state as tied to the geographic borders of the nation. I am not suggesting an infrastructural approach eclipses the extensive and diverse theorization of the state so much as further complicates the organizational logic of power attributed to the state as an entity of transformation.

For centuries territory has been synonymous with the contest of power. Conventionally understood as a bounded space of varying scales, Stuart Elden, in his book *The Birth of Territory*, argues for a more critical appraisal of territory as it bears upon the authority of the state. Elden proposes an investigation of historical dimensions and conditions of possibility not typically featuring in studies of the state as a "bordered power-container" (Giddens).[16] But as Elden notes of John Agnew's identification of the "territorial trap," the spatiality of power need not be reduced to the territory of the state. The territory of data centers includes not just the geography of cables that span its operations; it might also be understood in a more diagrammatic sense as consisting of elements or entities and their capacities brought into relation. Such a notion of territory also suggests a more flexible comprehension of time and space that can be termed *territoriality*. One could inquire, for example, not only into the temporality of low-latency networks special to high-frequency trading, but also into the labor regimes that construct data centers, assemble its hardware, undertake technical maintenance, and administer platform operations. The temporal rhythm and spatial circumstance of each of these jobs is not independent of the spatial configuration and temporal propensity of data centers. The 24/7 maintenance of servers, for instance, may combine onsite technicians with remote network operators residing in different time zones. Such examples illustrate the ways in which the territory and territoriality of data centers is both enabled and defined by multiple spatial layers in conjunction with variable circuits of time. Part of the scalar dimension of data centers is not territorial in the geographic sense but is rather derived from amassing colossal amounts of data that enable the centralization of analytic and economic power. "For the data-driven world," as Gary Hall notes, "is one in which the data *centre* dominates."[17] The capacity of data centers to operate as sovereign entities instantiates infrastructural imperialism in the form of logistical empires.

There is thus both a territory and territoriality to logistical media and infrastructural power from which geopolitical implications and media-theoretical propositions emerge. As a political technology of containment, logistical media produce new forms of territory that govern the movement and economy of data tied to labor, finance, and things. Territoriality, by contrast, consists of the production of space and time beyond the constraints of bounded space specific to the borders of the nation-state. The movement of data, operation of software, and design of infrastructure is enforced through juridical regimes that encode the territoriality of logistical media with legal protocols bringing logistical operations in relation to institutional settings of both state and suprastate legal apparatuses.[18] The policy, technical, and legal architecture of intellectual property regimes (copyright, patents, trademarks) generates economy, culture, and even subjectivity underscored by multiple fronts of dispute within geopolitical and geocultural spaces of connection and disconnection.

Territoriality, in other words, involves the work of producing complex arrangements and systems of transmission and exchange that operate both on spatial scales and temporal horizons. Importantly, territoriality also consists of spatiotemporal practices not reducible to the sovereign authority of states. An example of this consists of forms of territoriality produced through reappropriating infrastructural technologies such as radio telescopes, which I discuss in this book's concluding chapter to foreground how infrastructure of communication forge sonic geographies generated from the acoustic soundwaves retrieved from outer space. Elden suggests that rather than understanding territoriality as "the condition or status of territory," it can also be analyzed as "a mode of operating toward that territory."[19] If territoriality is about operational practices that stem from and, in turn, produce territory as new spatialities, then logistical media provide an empirico-analytical device that give insight into such processes.

In sum, then, I will proceed with the following hypothesis: Territoriality consists of operational practices specific to infrastructural systems and technical devices, the effect of which produce territory as spatial arrangements and temporal dynamics that may contest or conflict with state-based claims to control over the bounded space of the nation and its sovereign extensions. Such a proposition opens the possibility for a theory of sovereign media, which I elaborate in the concluding chapter to this book. In establishing a point of reference for these concluding reflections on media and logistics, I first focus in this chapter on the territory and territoriality of state formation wrought by imperial infrastructures of logistical media.

While this chapter explores how infrastructure constitutes the territory of state and empire, I conclude in the next chapter that the imperial tendency of infrastructure is best understood in terms of "sovereign media"—a term that first emerged in the nineties during the heydays of net-cultural theory and one worth reviving to describe what Eva Horn calls the "medial a priori."[20] This Kittlerian precept is reiterated by Stefan Heidenreich as the "technical a priori" that foregrounds how the material properties of media technologies define the situation of their transformation.[21] Yet for Heidenreich the technical *a priori* also comprises a "gap" between the discursive practices of technological and cultural research. Attending this line of division are disciplinary, institutional, and economic forces, which operate as "incentives" underscoring the invention of media technologies.

144 Imperial Infrastructures

Understanding media in such a way involves a shift away from an ontological concept of technology that focuses exclusively on technical properties as the drivers of change and instead casts such considerations within a broader constellation of processes that include cultural practices, epistemic objects, and institutional routines.[22] The geotechnical arrangements of infrastructural imperialism in an age of fiber-optic cables, data centers, and low-latency computing lend logistical media its pervasive quality. Such infrastructure not only conditions the possibility of a logistical world gone awry, its technical properties are coupled with a computational force and political economy of data analytics and integrated technologies that saturate every surface and substrate of organic life and inorganic matter.[23]

When communications infrastructure is not synonymous with the state, nor even exclusive to the private sector (since throughout the history of communication technologies there are frequent examples of public-private partnerships to fund the construction of infrastructure), we might shift the unit of analysis from political or commercial form—which is an analysis of institutional apparatuses and political economy—and instead focus on what Easterling calls the "disposition" or "propensity" of infrastructure space and what medium theorists tend to call the properties of technological forms.[24] This becomes a question of ontology derived from the activity of organization. Daniel Gethmann and Florian Sprenger frame this nicely with regard to telegraphic cables: "The cable supplies the world with an idea of its connectivity."[25] Here, the ontological dimension of cable infrastructure is integrated with or immanent to its substrate, the territoriality of the planet. Arguably, the ontology of cable at both material and conceptual levels conditions the possibility for the world to know itself through relations. The move from technological propensity to planetary knowledge registers the difficulty of teasing out the distinction between ontology and epistemology.

The refrain of this chapter asks what is special about communications infrastructure such as telegraphy and data centers that lends itself to a territorial propensity? And can this tendency be considered a form of infrastructural imperialism beyond or autonomous from both the state and corporation? Moreover, does territory precede infrastructure—the planet as substrate to the propensity of cables—or does infrastructure produce the world as territory? As John Durham Peters deduces, "infrastructural media are media that stand under."[26] If technological properties are ontologically prior to the state and corporation, questions of state formation and global economy can be approached from the perspective of logistical media and the infrastructure of its operations. But they do not sit in isolation from the environments with which they are enmeshed.[27]

Another political motivation drives my choice in fabricating an analytical device that parallels the 1800s with our 2000s, woefully ignoring the passage of the long twentieth century. In "exposing the evidence of the infrastructural operating system," we can also speculate on the ruins of infrastructure. Whether it is decommissioned cables and data centers made obsolete, or earlier communications infrastructure such as destroyed satellite antennae, or even the hacking of algorithmic architectures that orchestrate the financial transactions of high-frequency trading, the infrastructure of power are surpassed by the march of history. Such a view shares something with Parikka's summary of the legacy of twentieth-century philosophical thought: "only once things fail, *then* you start to see their complexity."[28] This is also an axiom at the core of cybernetic systems that are engineered as logistical media. To think of the ruins of logistical infrastructure is a form of immanent critique. This is particularly the case with artistic practices that collectively repurpose infrastructure for projects never programmed into the blueprints of their initial conception.

The question of how knowledge is organized and, subsequently, how labor is managed is also part of this story. In developing a critique of data-driven capitalism, what can we learn from the ways in which knowledge is produced and organized within a technical apparatus? How central is infrastructure to such developments, and how might the ruins of a logistical future be reappropriated from the slumber of disregard as a resource with which to imagine and practice counter-systems that are not beholden to technologies of capture that define the current conjuncture? These are questions I address more directly in the next chapter. First, it is necessary to establish how infrastructures of communication as technologies of power are involved in the production and organization of territory. In foregrounding the relation between infrastructure and organization, the case of the telegraph provides another point of entry into the production of technical knowledge as a foundation of infrastructural power. As the Invisible Committee observe in their analysis of political insurrection and logistics, "*power no longer resides in the institutions . . . power now resides in the infrastructures of this world.*"[29]

Arranging Infrastructures of Circulation

While Brian Larkin defines infrastructures as the physical forms that "comprise the architecture for circulation," Keller Easterling is keen to emphasize that the "dispositional" activity of infrastructure is "not reliant on movement but rather on unfolding relationships inherent in its arrangement."[30] For Easterling, "Designing infrastructure is designing action." There is an interesting determinate quality to Easterling's proposition here, even if she prefers to bridge her thought with Latour's thesis on the performative action of humans and nonhumans as "indeterminate" or "dislocated."[31] As Easterling notes in an earlier short text in Mark Shepard's collection on the sentient city, "many infrastructures are the urban formula, the very parameters of global urbanism."[32] It is this aspect of parameters as the formula to how infrastructure makes worlds that has captured my imagination in writing a theory of logistical media. More precisely, the politics of parameters comprise the political beyond the imagination of the state. The political, understood as practices of struggle, manifests in logistical infrastructure and software that at once constitutes populations as labor-power and exploits subjectivity through the extraction of value generated by digital life. The question of how logistics imagines the state,

146 Imperial Infrastructures

and how its political-economic imaginary refigures the distribution of statehood and the organization of its sovereign operations, takes us to the center of a tussle between sovereign media and the ways in which modern sovereign entities such as the state have become dependent on nonpublic infrastructures in order to maintain and exert control.[33] Residing within a media theory of logistics, therefore, is also an implicit critique of the fanciful versions of digital politics as seen in the celebration of Twitterism as a tool for democracy, or the heat around social media inspired revolutions and the advocacy of inclusion-through-consumption.

When infrastructure is defined in relation to systems of communication and the logistics of global supply chains, it is hard not to retain a sense of movement in conjunction with Easterling's "unfolding" arrangements of infrastructure. As Peters reminds us, like Harold Innis before him, "the notion of communication as the transfer of psychical entities such as ideas, thoughts, or meanings" is something we might hold on to.[34] How might the parameters of IT infrastructures shape the production of knowledge and the constitution of subjectivity? Can a relation even be established between the content of data and the economic interests that frame decisions on investment in IT infrastructure? And do the technical requirements that distinguish different types of data storage have a bearing on the production of its hardware?

In probing the question of logistical media—of the political geography of infrastructures and the material force of their situation—we might ask where the data centers are located and whether this has any bearing on the design of business imaginaries of cloud-based economies. The static mass of data centers is lodged in dirt and concrete and seemingly without an object of acceleration required to meet Newton's second law of motion. There would seem, therefore, to be no obvious material force generated from their situation. Yet the speed with which data moves along the cables extending from data centers across oceanic and continental territories does, by contrast, rely on post-Newtonian and nonmechanical physics. Herein lies the paradoxical force of the situation of data centers: They are static in terms of infrastructural location, but at the operational level they are mobile in terms of the acceleration and transmission of data.

At another register, situation here also refers both to the setting within which we find ourselves, and the predicament that attends such placement. This is the force of determination. It offers a refuge for those in need of identity (and allocates one to you whether you like it or not), and it imposes terrible constraints upon our desire for freedom. But as Heidenreich astutely observes, "Materiality of media does not need to consist in solid objects only. *Whatever transfers a force through space or time should be considered.*"[35] As is so often the case with data centers and cloud computing, "The fundamental material layer often goes unnoticed, even though it sets some basic conditions for all communication based upon it." For Heidenreich, critical attention should be turned toward the impact of standards and protocols and the ways in which they "enforce material-independent constraints."[36] This takes us to the politics and economy of enterprise software systems, as discussed in previous chapters. But it also allows us to think of how data centers exert change and transformation upon economies through the velocity of data as a result of their processing operations and the materiality of cables. And perhaps also the more immaterial force they exert through their material presence as objects in prompting responses to issues of security, surrounding economies, laboring subjectivities, and so forth.

Indeed, what sort of data traffics through different data centers distributed in strategic locations throughout the world? Are there juridical regimes specific to different types of data? How is the provenance of data complicated in legal ways by the location of its storage? What sort of protocols of hardware and storage are required for, say, financial data as distinct from the data collected by the state or military apparatus, or produced from what Soenke Zehle terms the "logistical lifestreams" that define our social media worlds?[37] And to what extent do the technical operations, geography of location, and political economy specific to different data centers determine the types of businesses and organizational practices dependent on hosting services? These are questions that also go some way toward designing a media theory of data centers, which are a key communication infrastructure for the logistical processes of contemporary capitalism and global supply chains. But there are no definitive one-size-fits-all answers here. Sometimes *difference makes a difference*. And sometimes it doesn't.

The data center as communications infrastructure extends from bricks and mortar of the building, the specific cabling, monitoring, security, and fire safety mechanisms of its internal operations; the training regimes (e.g. Cisco networking certification) required of its human operators; the kinds of specific computing devices engineered to optimize rack space and save costs (e.g., 1RU servers); the "hardened" software operating systems (usually Linux or other UNIX variants); the software utilities used to monitor, route, load balance, and optimize bandwidth and network traffic; the algorithms that ensure security, redundancy, and optimization in the writing of data to disc—the list could go on. Many of these are necessarily standardized and the pathways from military to financial to broader commercial application and back again are often complex, circuitous, and seemingly ad hoc (but for the strong geographic concentrations of these various industries in parts of the United States and elsewhere). A media theory of data centers would, therefore, need to accommodate the apparently paradoxical situation of both differentiation (by technical operation, geography, and political economy) and standardization.[38]

Telegraphy, Territory, Empire

Frequently hidden from view until it breaks down, the geography of communications infrastructure that drives global economies also defines new territories of power. As Matthew Tiesen explains in his account of high-frequency trading (HFT) and the spaces of finance capital, "In light of HFT's appetite for unlimited speeds and unlimited financial-arbitrage opportunities, the central nodes of the global finance network—London, New York, Chicago, Tokyo, etc.—are becoming its peripheries insofar as these days it's the spaces in between the exchanges where the real action occurs—or has the potential to occur."[39] And as Michael Lewis makes clear in *Flash Boys: A Wall Street Revolt* (a book whose peculiar genre fuses straightforward reporting with the anxious pace of a conspiratorial thriller), the relation between the geography of fiber-optic cable and algorithmic capitalism is determinate in the economy of high-frequency trading.[40] The "colocation" of exchange servers with the computers of high-frequency trading firms function to minimize the journey of data, resulting in a form of insider trading that always outpaces the efforts of brokers, hedge-fund managers, and ordinary traders. While there is nothing especially new about the impact of finance driven capitalism on labor—Rudolf Hilferding, John Hobson, and later Vladimir Lenin identified how over a century ago the structural force of financialization and imperialism is the basis of "organized capitalism"[41]—I would nonetheless suggest that data centers register an intensification of such processes. Bringing critical attention to the coupling of algorithmic capitalism with data centers instantiates a materiality that helps demystify the abstraction often associated with processes of capital accumulation. Although such a move also invites further mystification: how to study the inaccessibility of data centers as an infrastructural object? And how to even begin analyzing the algorithmic architectures specific to HFT and other computational operations of capital?

Vincent Mosco notes that 40 percent of data centers are located in the United States,[42] with Scandinavian countries and Canada attractive options due to their cool climate and abundance of water supplies, which along with "their bandwidth Internet connections, political stability and financial incentives" are key to offsetting energy costs associated with air-conditioning used to cool racks of servers.[43] Yet the growth over the past ten years or so in the construction of data centers around the world, particularly within the Asian region, signals a historic and paradigmatic shift from the extraction of surplus value from labor as a core structural dynamic of the capitalist mode of production to an arguably novel form of surplus data within an economy of algorithmic capitalism that at first appears less dependent on the subject of labor. This is especially the case with high-frequency trading, where the nano-speed of trade operates beyond the threshold of perception and with minimal human oversight or intervention.

When deontologized at the conceptual level as a technical object, the infrastructure of data centers starts to make clear that labor remains not only as a condition of possibility, but also a necessary supplement to the algorithm, filling in the gaps for processes not yet automated by the machine. Amazon's Mechanical Turk (AMT) is one chief example here, where Human Intelligence Tasks (HITs) are enlisted for low-value services of microwork not yet accommodated by algorithms.[44] This microwork can only be practically facilitated by the new infrastructure of data centers—it is instructive that one of the largest operators of such centers in the world has taken it upon itself to help coordinate the alignment of suppliers and customers of such labor. But AMT should not be taken as exceptional here. The sites of labor coordinated through the auspices of the data center are many and varied and only increasing. Other less apparently novel examples would include the algorithmic monitoring of labor within logistical infrastructure such as ports and warehouses, as discussed in earlier chapters. When the efficiency and performativity of labor is scrutinized in real-time by enterprise software in such settings, the case of AMT positions labor quite literally as if it were an algorithm designed to direct particular functions that result in a known outcome. This is the internal logic of AMT, which is premised on an indifference to variation. Yet as various critics have pointed out, this does not entirely close the possibility of disruption and inconsistency on the part of labor.[45] Scripts can be written to automate the click and enter routine of AMT tasks involving basic data entry such as tag clouds for photographic collections. Workers also reproduce such operations manually. But in doing so, labor effectively becomes the algorithmic machine, which functions on the basis of parameters and need not be flustered about whether or not the data is incorrect so long as it is submitted. Until, that is, quality assurance regimes are imposed to ensure a standard of service.

If the future of work is stupidity, what lines of the political might be staged against infrastructures that precipitate the obsolescence of labor and not, simply, its transformation into new jobs, as narratives of industrial modernity would have it?[46] This question invites a revisiting of theories of the state as a sovereign entity that prepares the ground for the construction and commercial viability of data centers. In his study of the English East-India Company, Philip Stern examines the ways in which a colonial commercial entity was organized and functioned in ways similar to a sovereign state.[47] Indeed, Stern maintains that the East India Company should not be envisioned as state-like or semi-sovereign, but rather through its regulation of territory, law, populations, economic and civic life, diplomacy, trade, taxation, war, and the like as a governing form he terms the "company-state." Such a thesis is novel for the way it pits claims for sovereign authority within a period of modern empire and state formation across a range of institutional actors. The rise of organizations with constitutional powers to decide and govern is not peculiar or limited to colonial economies. Nonetheless, a model for producing sovereign entities beyond the state emerged in part from the corridors of trade and commerce facilitated by juridical systems and technical apparatuses of the modern colonial era of capitalism.[48]

Later in this chapter I discuss how infrastructure bears upon the state and empire as logistical formations. For now, I turn to the ways in which electric telegraphy in the nineteenth century can be understood as setting the foundation for infrastructural power on an imperial scale. The telegraph precipitated the rise of two key components of global logistics and infrastructural power that arc across the epochs of 1800 and 2000 as instantiations of infrastructural imperialism: scientific management and the industrial research laboratory. As Paul Israel writes in his fascinating history of telegraphy and American mechanical invention, "Both the telegraph operating room and the telegraph manufacturing shop provided informal technical schools and experimental laboratories similar to those found in other industries."[49] Telegraphy not only lends the imperial imaginary of empire with an infrastructural architecture that conjoins land with sea, it also precipitates an organizational form for the production of knowledge. From the mid-twentieth century, and especially following the advent in the 1990s of computational forms of production and distribution, laboratories are most often settings in which knowledge becomes enclosed within intellectual property regimes that inscribe a logic of scarcity upon goods, services, and ideas for the purpose of commodity exchange. The struggle or, as the case may be, affirmation of closed knowledge systems has been around for centuries in the form of guilds, religion, and customary tribal knowledges. Both telegraphy and fiber-optic networks clearly offer potential for opening as well as enclosing knowledge. The tendency, however, has been toward the latter.

Related to the geography of data centers are the imperial and colonial histories of communications infrastructure—the submarine telegraph cables that first established the corridors of trade, connecting the territory of empire to the speed of communication.[50] The expansive infrastructural programs undertaken by colonial powers in a large part produced the territorial imaginary of empire and economic system of imperialism. The nineteenth-century projects of transcontinental and submarine telegraphy, and the railroads along which telegraphic lines tracked, serve as the classic examples of how infrastructure secures and indeed constitutes the space and time of empire as at once unified and "networked" while retaining a political-economic geography predicated on the logic of cores and peripheries. No matter if this imaginary with material underpinnings was far less coherent and functional in reality as a system of control, its force of infrastructural power nonetheless made substantive impacts upon colonial economies, subjectivity, institutions, and social life. Bernhard Siegert's account of how the speed and geography of telegraphy intersected with new forms of knowledge, governance, and subjectivity provides a nice description of what I would call the protoform of logistical media:

> With telegraphy, a new form of police knowledge based on photography and anthropometry became effective for the first time: from now on, the knowledge identifying an individual and conveying him to himself could be made available anywhere in the world. That such knowledge of things and people could be sent infinitely more quickly than things and people themselves not only enabled worldwide manipulations of the commodities exchange, but also a new conception of the individual that did not depend on location.[51]

The arrival of telegraphy, then, ushered into existence the affective experience and technical condition of logistical life that brought continuity and connection between colonial centers and margins. An accelerated life at once concrete and abstract, a life of immediacy and simultaneity in which movement and transportation is measurable, accountable, and interchangeable with objects and things rendered as data. But it is the question of how infrastructural operations as a form of sovereign media constitute and govern territory, which in turn bears upon state formation, that is of interest here. As historian Jürgen Osterhammel summarizes in his monumental *The Transformation of the World*, "the *twentieth* century was the great epoch of the nation-state. In the nineteenth century world, empire remained the dominant territorial form of the organization of power."[52] While empire is not the precondition for state formation, one can nonetheless make note of the overlap in the territory of infrastructure across these two political organizations of power. This pertains especially in the case of the geography of telegraphic cables, which provided the cartographic coordinates and geomedial framework for rolling out the network of fiber-optic cable necessary for the operation of data centers in the twenty-first century and the rise of the logistical state as an emergent form through which transcontinental power is organized. I discuss this in more detail later in this chapter.

The range of commercial and governmental entities involved in the laying of telegraphic cables was quite diverse, with companies being founded seemingly on the hop as commercial opportunities presented themselves to a consortia of investors. Frequently the state or colonial administration would step in to finance costs associated with the laying of cable. This underwriting of commercial interests could extend for years, even decades, into the future. Early on, then, prototypical forms of public-private partnership preceded what has become a standard feature of neoliberal structural arrangements. Daniel R. Headrick notes the political motivation for government support of commercial interests: "The cables around Africa, in the West Indies, and across the Pacific were subsidized by various governments for imperial reasons."[53]

Like the various forms of state subsidization (tax incentives, cheap land leases, zoning, etc.) to fund the construction of data centers over the past decade or so, accounts of government subsidies to cable companies run throughout the history of telegraphy. A consideration of telegraphy in Australia in particular serves as a case that registers the imperial dimension of communications infrastructure. The history of telegraphy in Australia illustrates this chapter's interest in how the territoriality of infrastructure is key to processes of state formation. Telegraphic communications also brings Australia as a networked, infrastructural node into the geopolitical territory referred to in news media and discourses on global trade as the Asian region, which I suggest is undergoing a process of consolidation with the gravity of the world's data centers shifting to Asia.[54] As Mosco notes, China is investing heavily in the development of cloud computing and data center construction, and by 2016 "the Asia region is expected to lead the world cloud traffic and workload."[55] As an outpost of empire, Australia becomes tied to the old and new worlds through infrastructure, starting with telegraphic submarine cables.

152 Imperial Infrastructures

In Australia, where the colonial administrations paid considerable sums to cable companies for a reduction in the "exorbitant charges—almost £10 for a twenty-word cable message to Britain," the uncertainty of communication was not necessarily overcome by subsidies from the state.[56] Whether through sabotage of lines, cable breakdowns resulting from natural causes, or human fallibility in the decoding of Morse signals, the unreliability in telegraphic transmissions was a persistent problem motivating the push for alternative cable routes.[57] Such moves attempted to offset the tendency toward monopoly players and their pricing regimes, although a government monopoly of telecommunications post-Federation (1901) defined most of the twentieth century in Australia. Security issues were another concern when much of the world's telegraphic communications trafficked through British controlled infrastructure.

Despite the frequent interruptions that typified for many the experience of cable services, the age of telegraphy—or what Tom Standage defines as "the Victorian Internet"—was not, in many ways, so different from the pervasive exuberance of the dot-com years in the 1990s and, arguably, continues today with innumerable companies launched as start-ups into the world of app economies and data services.[58] A score of companies oversaw the laying of submarine and overland cables. Many were cobbled together or established as subsidiary organizations as commercial opportunities became apparent to investors. Unlike the start-ups of the dot-com years, holding companies were often formed to raise capital and absorb risks associated with the cable rollout—ships would go missing, stranded cables in the middle of the ocean were never relocated, copper wire from the lines could be stolen or damaged. Once the cable was rolled out the contracts and concessions to land and operate the cables were rolled into a parent company.[59]

The British Indian Submarine Telegraph Company, the China Submarine Telegraph Company, and the British Australian Telegraph Company were just a few of the many companies overseen by Manchester textile merchant and cable baron John Pender.[60] These three cable companies merged in 1873 as the Eastern Extension, Australia and China Telegraph Company—a subsidiary of Pender's Eastern Telegraph Company, whose head office in London enjoyed "a monopoly over cable traffic in and out of Australia" and much of the world.[61] The political economy of modern communications was defined in the nineteenth century, with companies such as the Eastern Extension, Australia and China Telegraph Company continuing until 1974, "when it became part of Eastern Telecommunications Philippines, Inc."[62] These days Eastern Communications—a merger of Eastern Telecommunications Philippines, Inc., and its subsidiary Telecommunications, Technologies Philippines, Inc., acquired in 1986—provides a range of services that include data facilities and data management for logistics industries.[63]

Introducing the largest cable head operation "in the world" in 1980 at Currimao Cable Landing Station and, more recently, offering potential clients access to "green" data centers, Eastern Communications is very much a legacy story of colonial infrastructure transformed and adapted over time. The same could be said for the continuity of actors and institutional bodies such as the International Telegraph Union (ITU). Founded in 1865, the ITU continues to this day as the International Telecommunications Union (1934), which is responsible for the governance of technical standards as they pertain to information and communication technologies. While the ITU played a key if rather ineffectual role in trying to wrest control from ICANN during "multi-stakeholder" debates on Internet governance during the United Nations' World Summit on the Information Society (2003–2005),[64] the fact that ITU still exists as an organizational entity is a testament to a certain institutional robustness and abstraction, at one level, from decolonization movements located on the peripheries of imperial imaginations. But it is a frequent conceptual, empirical, and historical mistake to assume colonialism as a unilateral exercise of imperial power. Global standards bodies are increasingly beholden to former colonies or client-states, notably India and China, but Brazil, South Africa, Russia, Mexico, and Indonesia, among other countries, are increasingly vocal in these bodies, often to the frustration of U.S. companies in particular.

As much a result of accident and bureaucratic incompetence than calculated design, the prevalence of infrastructural non-interoperability needs to be kept in mind when assessing the constitutive force of imperial infrastructures as they relate to the composition of state, territory, subjectivity, and labor. The cartographic and political imagination that took hold in the antipodes in the nineteenth century— one that continues for some until this day—was a result, in part, of different-sized gauges for railway tracks in the Australian colonies. This had the effect of stalling the relative autonomy instantiated by the occasion of Federation in 1901 and the constitution of previously separated colonies as a commonwealth of federated states. Different rail gauges also meant that communication between the colonial territories tended to be served by sea transport up until the opening of the Australian Overland Telegraph Line in 1872, which connected Adelaide in South Australia to Darwin in the north, which in turn connected the intercolonial telegraphic network within Australia to Singapore via the Dutch colony of Java.[65] With submarine cable connecting Singapore and Hong Kong in 1871, Australia was integrated into the British intra-Imperial telegraph network.

As the 1870s progressed, other metropoles and towns in Australia already linked through the intercolonial telegraph network since the late 1850s were connected to the overseas cable network. The capital city of Perth and regional coastal town of Roebuck Bay (Broome) in Western Australia had by 1889 connected to the competing Indo-European Telegraph Company, founded by Siemens in 1868. With branch offices in London and Saint Petersburg set up following an embargo on the firm Siemens & Halske imposed by the director of the Prussian state telegraph, "the Siemen's brothers occupied the nineteenth-century metropolises of the great European powers in order to construct international cable telegraphy."[66] The Siemens brothers thus played a key role in making the imperial force of Britain possible. But it is important to keep in mind the force of the technical object

154 Imperial Infrastructures

here. If the Siemens firm was not such a dominant player, there would no doubt have been other firms or government agencies that stepped up to facilitate the cabling of the planet. Urban centers in the eastern colonies of Australia were later connected to New Zealand, Guam, and across the Pacific to North America.[67] The combined effect of such developments in terrestrial and undersea telegraphic communications infrastructure was key to the constitution of a federation of states and territories in Australia in 1901.[68] Yet the telegraphic cables connecting Australia to North America did not sever so much as extend the imperial cartography of the "All-Red Line" that tied the pink colors on maps of the British Empire into a communication network of control.[69] According to Siegert, by 1911 "'the all red system' was complete. Over 70 percent of the world's cable was in British hands, and the British had a monopoly on gutta-percha, the only known insulating material."[70] The strategic significance of landing points for cable disrupts the standard geopolitical assumption of core versus periphery:

> The "all red system," which . . . became a true fetish for the navy and Colonial Office, revealed the world-historical importance of such obscure islands as Ascension, Norfolk, Rodriguez, Fanning, and the Cocos: once they had become on-land points for the "all red" cable, nothing less than Great Britain's "existence as a nation" depended upon their possession.[71]

The extraordinary research on technical and commercial details of cable telegraphy compiled at Atlantic-Cable.com gives some idea of the geographic scale of operation and dominance of Britain in the control of telegraphic communications.[72] Between 1845 and 1911 there is an increasing frequency of cable landings over the years as the nineteenth century progresses. This should come as no surprise as commercial operations increase with the expansion of the cable network and consolidation of colonial enterprise. It takes sixty-six years of cable laying to effectively straddle the world with wire, at which point the decline of empire effectively begins and infrastructure takes command (Figure 7.1). All major regions of the world had by the completion of the All Red Line in 1911 been connected and these routes remained principal throughout the coaxial period. Even if annual growth is unspectacular across this period, the cumulative number of cable landings clearly registers the globalization of cable as it bears upon the territories of nations and the reach of empire.

In this regard we might conceive the nineteenth century as a calm century, a time in which the amorphous financialization of empire occurs through telegraphic infrastructure. The entrepreneurial impetus of private companies to undertake infrastructural investment was derailed during the war years (1914–1919, 1939–1945). The military-industrial complex reclaimed the territory of infrastructure as the object proper to the state. Already this was apparent in the final years before the All Red Line was complete, with the governments of Britain, Canada, Australia, and New Zealand stepping in to finance the cable connection

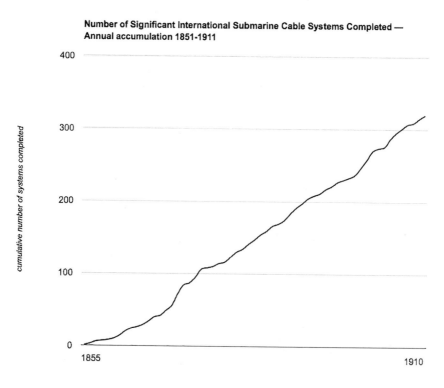

FIGURE 7.1 Number of significant international submarine systems completed, 1851–1911.

Source: Atlantic-Cable.com for statics. Figure compiled by Mat Wal-Smith, 2015.

across the Pacific from Vancouver to Fiji and Norfolk Island and then bifurcating with lines going on to New Zealand and Queensland, Australia.[73] As Paul Kennedy notes, only British territories were used for landing stations, despite the possibility of a shorter and cheaper route with faster services if cable were laid via Hawaii.[74] By avoiding dependency on the infrastructure of foreign powers, Britain ensured control in the cable economy while consolidating the geographic space of empire as an "imperial network." According to Kennedy, by the turn of the century there were also security concerns "in a decidedly hostile world" that motivated the construction of the Pacific cable in 1902. Cable lines in the Mediterranean, the Alexandrian-Suez land line, Portugal, Western and South Africa were all at risk due to navel weakness or political disputes, and the new line across the Pacific provided "a fresh link between Britain and India" and thus opened the prospect of "imperial unity" through infrastructure.[75]

156 Imperial Infrastructures

By contrast, and as one might expect, the laying of fiber-optic cable in the late twentieth and twenty-first centuries achieves a similar result vis-à-vis the wiring of the world in a matter of years (Figure 7.2). Notably, Britain's infrastructural power in telegraphy is surpassed by the United States in terms of fiber-optic cable landings. Other key sites for fiber-optic cable landings include Italy, Singapore, Sweden, India, and Hong Kong. This geography of cables begins to suggest something about the global economy of data centers and how cable produces a new territorial logic of the world. If a parallel can be drawn between geopolitical power and the implementation of communications infrastructure, the key question here would be to ask what regime of power declines and what takes its place in the case of the planetary scale of fiber-optic cables? The pursuit of thought in this chapter suggests the expansion of fiber-optic cables indexes a waning of the sovereign state predicated on the logic of national territory and empire. This is not to suggest the disappearance of the sovereign state, as many argued during the 1990s in debates around the meaning and effect of globalization. My claim is that the relation between the transformation of sovereign power and communications infrastructure is one that warrants critical attention. There is nothing especially novel in such a position, but it is the case that the relation between data centers, fiber-optic cables, economy, labor, and power has for the most part not been of interest to political theory and is only just beginning to surface in the work of some media theorists.[76]

The territorial space of the nation was broadly contained at a geographic level during the telegraphic era, even if its borders fluctuate during times of military or political conquest and retreat with concession or defeat. Moreover, the cultural imaginaries of the nation-state were more or less coincident with the production, distribution, and reception models of broadcast media of communication in the twentieth century (radio, newspapers, television). Even though there was sufficient territorial bleed in the transmission of signals and distribution of content with broadcast media, the cultural and linguistic borders of readers and audiences was, again, generally grafted along the lines of the nation. The media–culture situation of broadcast technologies complemented, if not reinforced, the sovereign space of the nation. Harking back to the territorial logic of networked telegraphy, the planetary scale of fiber-optic cables signals the emergence of the logistical state whose territorial power is congruent with the operational capacity of infrastructure and the economy of supply chain capitalism.

The relation between the technical and the territorial is also worth mentioning. Optimal latency was achieved very early in the laying of telegraphic cable. Already in the 1850s four to seven strands of copper wire bedded in yarn and then encased in gutta-percha insulation conducted signals along cables landing in countries such as England, France, Ireland, Sweden, Denmark, Italy, Ceylon, India, Singapore, and Indonesia. Across the nineteenth century cable landings on strategic sites of empire increased in centers of power in Britain, France, the United States, Canada, Portugal, and Germany with extensions across the network of

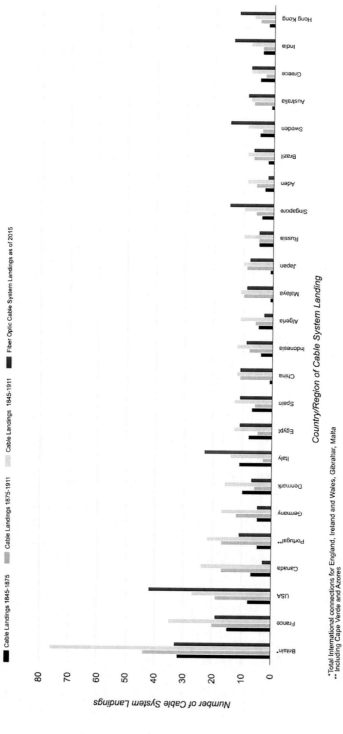

FIGURE 7.2 Combined comparative table of estimated cable systems landings per selected country/region.

Source: Atlantic-Cable.com for statics. Figure compiled by Mat Wal-Smith, 2015.

158 Imperial Infrastructures

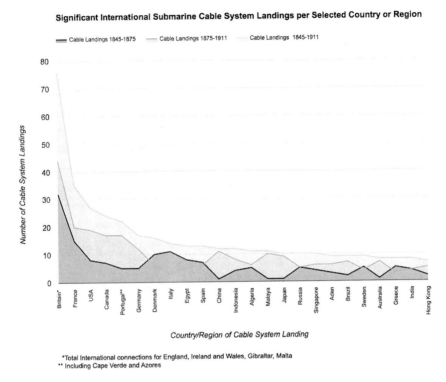

FIGURE 7.3 Estimated international submarine cable landings, 1845–1911.

Source: Atlantic-Cable.com for statics. Figure compiled by Mat Wal-Smith, 2015.

colonies (Figure 7.3). Unlike the doubling of computer processing speeds every two years, there were no especially significant technical advances in the development of telegraphic cables. Yarn might be substituted with tanned jute and strands of copper conductor sheathed in galvanized iron wires, making for a lighter and more durable compound wire, were later used for the transmission of signals. But the technical standards were established relatively early in the development of telegraphic communications. Advances occurred more at the level of technique related to the rollout and reliability of cable as well as its security and longevity.

The once strategic function of cable landing stations are no longer necessary with the introduction of new technical forms of networked communication such as fiber-optic cables. The technical realization that particular infrastructural forms of networked communication are not sustainable is registered in the shift from telegraphic cable stations as relay nodes to point of presence beyond the station. Cable stations, in other words, are no longer essential infrastructural nodes for accessing fiber-optic signals. The technical development of undersea branching units in effect shifts the cable station offshore, resulting in what Starosielski terms new models of dispersion for signal traffic.[77] The eventual obsolescence of infrastructure is something we should be attuned to for the possibilities of reoccupation and experimental reengineering—points I return to in next chapter.

From this geotechnical perspective, then, infrastructure complicates the passage of state formation and may privilege empire as the primary organization of power on the basis of both technical propensities and economic interests. The point at which undersea cables make contact with shore at cable stations becomes a form of imperial occupation. As Starosielski maintains, "The cable station became the critical geopolitical node for all transoceanic traffic: it was a cable colony intended to be self-sufficient and culturally insular, autonomous from its surrounding geography."[78] Telegraphic cable stations were distinct for the often racially divided regimes of labor that serviced the maintenance of stations and technical operation of cable transmissions, particularly those located in countries rimming the Pacific Ocean.[79] By Starosielski's account, depending on the location of the cable station, domestic service work or manual labor might be undertaken by Australian Aborigines, Mauritian, Chinese, or Japanese workers drawn from local communities with cable operators and administrative staff recruited from the national origin of the cable company. In doing so, the cable station "reproduced a microcosm of empire."[80] Such a form of infrastructural abstraction and cultural-political exceptionalism holds some continuities with the operation of data centers in the twenty-first century. For Starosielksi, the telegraphic cable station of the nineteenth century was not shrouded in anything like the secrecy that surrounds the cable stations that support the landing of oceanic fiber-optic cables. So it is not cables *per se* that prompt a secrecy of operations as much as the commercial interests and political agendas that increasingly populate the twentieth century across a range of media forms, including telephony, broadcast media, and satellite communications.[81]

In the case of cable landing stations as they relate to data centers, a geography of proximity prevails between these two infrastructural forms in the interest of maximizing low-latency networks able to service economies of speed required for a range of sectors, especially those in finance and high-frequency trading. These are heavily securitized spaces whose labor regimes are at once localized and frequently gendered with male technicians servicing the severs, while remote workers engage in the drudgery of chores such as data entry and the like on the part of clients whose operations may be based anywhere in the world. The more high-end realm of corporate IT labor is not immune from the shifting geographies of data centers. As Mosco points out, when a company puts its servers in a data center or goes down the path of software-as-a-service, it is often enough the case that the IT department is closed, leaving corporate IT labor swimming in search of another job—which may mean abandoning the sector and retraining or joining the ranks of the unemployed.[82] But such impacts on labor by technological developments and political economic practices are not a foregone conclusion. The widely projected unemployment trends forecast by various iterations of outsourcing and automation have often been defied by counter-trends within the sector. A more

160 Imperial Infrastructures

obvious case is the need for endless reskilling and insecurity implied by technological churn—server administrators become corporate IT strategists, IT support staff become trainers and teachers, and so forth.

The space-annihilating properties of telegraphy have long been a staple idea of much communications research, figuring in the work of Lewis Mumford, Harold Innis, James Carey, and Armand Mattelart, to name just a few. Yet contrary to Carey's often quoted claim that "the telegraph freed communication from the constraints of geography," a consideration of licensing agreements in conjunction with the technical operation of telegraphy suggests this communication infrastructure reinforced the spatial reach of imperial control.[83] Jill Hills provides a fascinating account of how telegraphic cables were vulnerable to sabotage and takeover by enemy forces during periods of war.[84] The political and economic concerns of the United States features strongly in her analysis, which notes how the U.S. was left vulnerable and in a form of dependency on British cables after the British in 1914 "had cut the two German-owned transatlantic cables, to the United States and Brazil, in the English Channel and six hundred miles off the U.S. coast."[85] Following the war, "In 1919 the renewal of both Western Union's and the Commercial Cable Company's landing licenses obliged them to agree to hand over copies of their cables to the British government."[86] Hills notes how the Japanese had seized control of German cables in Guam and "the Pacific cables of Dutch-Niederlandische Telegraphengesellschaft, a German-Dutch company."[87] Subsidized in prewar years by the German and Dutch governments, these cables extended from southeast Asia up through to China and the Philippines.[88] Denied access to alternative cable systems, this meant that "all traffic to other parts of the world had to pass through England."[89] Tariffs associated with the cost of transmission through British controlled telegraphic cables coupled with the insecurity of encrypted communications became a basis for much of the postwar U.S. negotiations. Infrastructure, in other words, precipitated the many U.S. policy interventions and negotiating strategies that sought to wrest control of communication back to the United States. This did not happen until the advent of satellite communications in the 1960s.[90]

Reading telegraphic infrastructure in conjunction with licensing regimes in this way is, in some respects, to think the relation between (infrastructural) base as functional and (ideological) superstructure as regulatory. But it is also to consider how telegraphic infrastructures operate as a-signifying arrangements, or what Jonathan Sterne calls "non-symbolic" communication, alongside railway transportation in the organization of movement and action.[91] The alignment of communication and transportation instantiates the infrastructure of logistical media in the nineteenth and early twentieth centuries. Here, I would include not just the ways in which telegraphic communication facilitates the movement of people and things—notably troops and armaments—using transportation infrastructure (particularly railways, but also roads, canals, rivers, and the sea); there is also the question of how telegraphic cables themselves function as transmission devices and border-making technologies for the movement of information according to the pulse of electronic signals. The example of the "All Red Line" that delineated the territory of the British empire according to the network of cables foregrounds the way in which telegraphy constituted the political, economic, and cultural space of empire as a cartographic imaginary insulated against contingency and disruption.[92]

Without having secured this infrastructure of communication across the space of empire, it is hard to imagine how the transfer of financial data related to stock markets prices, governmental directives to colonial outposts, and social messages that confer solidarity across oceanic and territorial borders could have occurred in ways that lend the political imaginary of empire a materiality of connection underscored by the speed of electronic transmission and a universality of standards and protocols. This is not to suppose that telegraphy constituted empire as a form of suprastate with a determining power and capacity to enforce stability across economy and society. The legacy of decolonization movements and the countless number of political uprisings, social conflicts, and economic crises since the completion of the all-red cable in 1911, linking Vancouver to Australia and New Zealand after passing through Norfolk Island, bears witness to the fact that the totality of a communications infrastructure is not equivalent to total control.[93] As Headrick surmises:

> What conclusions can we draw about cables and British Empire? There is no doubt that cables contributed mightily to the growth in world trade, to the division of labor within the empire, and to Britain's economic position as the commercial center of its empire and the world. The political gains are harder to measure. Thanks to cables, Britain remained in touch with all its colonies, naval bases, allies, and neutrals, and was able to repress all rebellions in its territories. Though cables made Britain stronger, they did not make the British Empire more secure, however, for they incited the jealousies of others and contributed to the international paranoia of our century.[94]

While it is highly doubtful that cables could ever have repressed "all rebellions"— clearly they did not—it is nonetheless interesting that Headrick suggests that telegraphy gave rise to a form of planetary paranoia. Such an atmosphere defined for many the experience of the Cold War. And with the Snowden revelations of the NSA's PRISM surveillance machine, the scale and scope of paranoia is grafted to the modulation of affect, intensity, and uncertainty to the extent that new techniques, methods, and tactics are required if political movements, corporate secrets, and government communiqués are to design cryptographic systems robust enough to withstand the analytic reach of NSA surveillance programs and their kin. When compared with the pervasiveness of digital media of communication in our current daily life and economy, it is also clear that telegraphic communication was far from being an interpenetrative force that secured empire against revolt. At a

162 Imperial Infrastructures

technical level, the logic of its territoriality was limited to the transmission of signals along lines. Worlds of non-governable subjects, times, and spaces subsisted beyond the line of telegraphic cable and its relay stations. The case of digital infrastructures such as data centers in our present era, however, makes the space and time of territory in substantively different albeit overlapping ways. As a core infrastructural component of capital's compulsion to extract value from the remote recesses of organic and inorganic life, data centers play a key role as technologies of governance ensuring the communication of escape as acts that leave a trace.

The Geography of Data Centers

In updating the question of infrastructure and the constitution of the state as a multifarious complex of actors overseeing the management of people, finance, and things, we might specifically address the structural force and operational capacity of data centers. Certainly there has long been a crucial labor cost related to questions of infrastructure and geography, as we can note in the protracted struggle by German labor union Verdi in its demands for better working conditions in Amazon's warehouses. Infrastructure, it turns out, can itself be highly mobile, flexible, and able to be relocated for legal and political reasons. As reported in July 2014 by Reuters: "Amazon is planning to build three new logistics centres in Poland and two in the Czech Republic, prompting speculation that it could seek to shift work across the border from strike-hit centres in Germany."[95]

Consider, also, the emergence of what is referred to in one higher education business report as "the financially sustainable university," which in seeking to overcome the fragmentation of data-driven processes due to the conflicts and complexities of internal operations, advises instead the use of outsourcing data centers: "Third-party data centers, whether they are managed or cloud-based, could provide more sophisticated solutions, higher levels of security, greater flexibility in capacity and lower cost than internal solutions—all with greater accountability and less politics."[96] Politics is certainly a nuisance, but usually only in terms of distracting management from decorating their portfolio careers rather than leading to any substantive loss of profit. Of course the claim of "less politics" is itself a political ambit, designed to defuse and literally decenter political contestation. My argument in this chapter is that data centers are entirely political. In striving after ever more enhanced techniques of optimization and efficiency, the logistical university becomes indistinct from any number of organizations whose core goal is to extract maximal value from data-driven processes.

Again, the Amazon warehousing plans for eastern Europe are a salutary reminder of a certain structural continuum between precarious labor and corporate operations: Both are predisposed to flexibility, albeit with important variations—the regimes of "flexible accumulation" special to post-Fordist capital (outsourcing, off-shoring, just-in-time production and inventory flows, etc.) function to undermine the conditions of labor, whose experience of flexibility is normative rather than exceptional in a world of increasing economic uncertainty and existential insecurity.[97] Having said this, politics is entirely relevant to the strategic decisions around the geography of investment related to data centers. As one consultant on IT infrastructure in the Asia Pacific advises, "most countries in Asia are lucrative markets to set up and grow businesses, barring a few which have political and technological environments as deterrent factors."[98] But politics here usually consists of more force when it is wielded by the sovereign power of the state rather than labor unions. Google's exit from Beijing in 2010 was frequently reported as an act of Western corporate defiance and social justice against China's insistence on censoring search engine results, but it was nonetheless a submission to sovereign control and a humiliating retreat from the center of contemporary capitalism. And of course there's also a business reality to Google's decision to quit China. As one report in *Forbes* magazine noted in 2010 following the withdrawal of Google, the more innovative local search engine Baidu "only increased its market share, going from 47% in mid-2006 to 64% today."[99]

Over the past few years Taiwan, Hong Kong, and Singapore have become strategic sites for investment in storage facilities for cloud computing. Companies like Google Inc. have built data centers in Taiwan and Singapore to accommodate the rapid growth of Internet users across the Asian region. As reported in *PCWorld*, "While the Taiwan data center is on 15 hectares of land [in central Taiwan], the Singapore data center in Jurong West is built on a smaller area of close to 2.5 hectares. It is designed as Google's first urban, multistory data center, and is in the neighborhood of a local primary school and publicly-run housing."[100] Local authorities are keen to attract such business, which they expect will produce a range of spin-off benefits for local firms. As Google Taiwan's managing director Chien Lee-feng remarked in 2012 following the announcement of the USD $300 million Google facility in September 2011 (with USD $700 million slated for long-term investment in the region), "We anticipate this data center will evolve into a [cloud-computing technology] hub and will create a supply chain here in Taiwan."[101] By the time of its completion in December 2013, the budget for the Taiwan investment had risen to USD $600 million.[102] It is hard not to also see the move of Google to Taiwan and investments in Hong Kong as a quasi-subversive repositioning for a reentry into the People's Republic of China.

The *Taipei Times* goes on to report that "Google's local suppliers include Quanta Computer Inc (廣達電腦), which supplies servers to Google, and Nanya Technology Corp (南亞科技), which supplies memory chips used in servers." Data centers, then, are key components of global logistics industries and reshape the economy of cities in terms of the composition of labor, the integration of manufacturing and service industries, and the formulation of trade and communications policies designed to attract investment. After abandoning plans for the construction of a data center in Tseung Kwan O Industrial Estate in the New Territories, the two Google data centers in Taiwan and Singapore produce a geography of the cloud that includes the six data centers in the United States along with two in

Europe and another opened in Chile in early 2015. One might suppose that the high temperatures in Taiwan's hot summers along with the potential instability of weather associated with its typhoon season might act as a deterrent for infrastructural investment in the country. But it turns out such climatic variations provide a basis for Google to tout its green credentials and innovative design in its "use of a night-time cooling and thermal energy storage system that cools large quantities of water at night."[103] But the issue of electricity consumption required for running data centers is not insignificant. As my colleague Tanya Notley has noted (along with others researching electronic waste, such as Jennifer Gabrys, Richard Maxwell, and Toby Miller), "Server farms currently use more than 1.5% of the world's total electricity (and rising) with more than half of this energy used in the cooling process."[104] A public policy study on green energy use for data centers notes that since 2000, "the overall rate of energy consumption for U.S. data centers, sourced primarily from polluting energy, has grown at an average rate of 14 percent per year."[105]

A data center is not necessarily a data center. Which is to say that the technical and material specifications of data centers depend upon the type of data being hosted. We know that data centers offering low-latency networks are the preferred choice for high-frequency trading, which, as Donald MacKenzie notes, takes place in around fifteen data centers around the world (most of which are located in the United States and Europe).[106] But low-latency networks are not an economic priority or technical possibility for all data center operations, where energy costs related to the cooling of servers are a key factor in the determination of business margins. The specific requirements of data centers built for hosting and mining cryptocurrencies such as Bitcoin offer a clear example of the variation in capacity and function of data centers. Bitcoin currency is generated through the marvels of blockchain processing—"the distributed ledger that keeps track of all transactions made using the Bitcoin cryptocurrency."[107]

After a period of phenomenally high prices reminiscent of the delirium of the dot-com era, the price of Bitcoin is sitting at around USD $228 as I write in June 2015. This is a dramatic and extended slump from the high rate Bitcoin attracted in late 2013 of USD $1,100.[108] By the start of 2016, Bitcoin was at the point of collapse with longtime senior developer Mike Hearn calling it "a failed experiment."[109] Hearn puts this down to a failure within the Bitcoin community to address the infrastructural limits of the Bitcoin blockchain, which has not sufficiently expanded and as a result restricts the processing of transactions and its subsequent security. Hearn also attributes these problems to the 51 percent control by Chinese miners of the network hash rate power related to the mining of blocks on the Bitcoin blockchain.[110] To effectively mine more Bitcoins from the blockchain requires greater computational power. And this is what purpose-built data centers offer.

In the days when Bitcoin was riding high, the cost of leasing data center space wasn't such an issue. But once the plunge had set in around early 2015, alternative facilities were required with server functions more tailored to the different processing needs specific to Bitcoin mining. Early in 2015 BitFury Group, one of the largest companies specializing in high-density hardware used in Bitcoin mining, made a takeover bid for Hong Kong's Allied Control—a start-up known for using immersion cooling in the mining of Bitcoins.[111] This two-phase cooling technique involves removing heat from semiconductors used for mining Bitcoin transactions with a supposedly non-ozone depleting liquid solution base of fluoroketone developed by 3M (a U.S.-based global firm stemming from Minnesota Mining and Manufacturing Co., founded in 1902), which claim up to 97 percent savings with their Novec Engineering Fluid compared to traditional air-cooling methods.[112] Not requiring the proximity to landing cable connections that make possible low-latency networks in HFT, data centers specializing in Bitcoin mining can therefore broaden the geography of infrastructure as it relates to the construction of data centers. With a data center in Iceland, BitFury announced in June 2015 that it was acquiring a 185,000-square-meter privatized plot of land in the Republic of Georgia to build a mega data center to host its Bitcoin mining hardware. Along with low energy costs and a competitive labor market, BitFury has partnered with the "Georgian Co-Investment Fund, a $6 billion private equity investor in companies interested in business opportunities in the country."[113]

Variations in infrastructural requirements begin to indicate a media theory of data centers that decomposes the singular data center into a typology. Certainly service offerings are significant here, although there is often little differentiation to be found at this level. More significant are the infrastructural capacities of data centers, which can be distinguished at the level of hardware in terms of low-latency to processing power. These sorts of factors then impact on decisions over where a data center is built, its size, and whether adjacent land may be valuable to acquire. Think, for instance, of how real estate in proximity to data centers supporting high-frequency trading may be strategic to purchase in terms of blocking access to potential competitors wishing to make use of low-latency cables. Or, in the case of Bitcoin mining where energy costs associated with processing power and computational cycles are important, a typology of data centers may foreground external factors related to environmental conditions or government authorities able to provide attractive investment packages for the construction of specialized data centers.

Colocation centers are another type of data center. There are currently 3,663 colocation data centers in 105 countries around the world as of June 2015, if we are to take the figures from the Colocation Data Centers site as an approximation.[114] The United States commands 1,493 of these, the United Kingdom has 223, and Germany is host to 171. Australia has 90, India 104, while Hong Kong, Indonesia, and Taiwan hold 49, 35, and 5, respectively. China has 56, Russia 41, Ireland 18, Luxembourg 14, the Czech Republic 20, Malaysia 28, South Africa 19, Pakistan has 10, and Turkey 37.[115] With their capacity for supporting "peering" arrangements that enable faster exchanges of data, colocation data centers would seem primarily geared toward finance capital. Though there is no obvious reason why finance capital should hold a monopoly of interest in colocation data centers given the types of service offered at many of these centers, which include dedicated servers, virtual servers, cages, rack cabinets, managed hosting, etc. For what other "sectors" might colocation be a valuable investment? Indeed, who are the chief investors in colocation services?

Andrew Blum's journey into Internet infrastructures describes how Equinix data storage facilities function as a distribution depot by "tethering" the data centers of other companies such as Facebook, eBay, or financial institutions to a single cage. These companies can then "cross-connect": "an Equinix technician will climb a ladder and unspool a yellow fiber-optic cable from one cage to the other. With the connection in place, the two networks have eliminated a 'hop' between them, making the passage of data between them cheaper and more efficient."[116] A fully developed media theory of data centers would address the operational capacities of data centers on their own terms. Such an undertaking would partly be a study of the technical as a foundation for developing concepts rather than relying exclusively on transposing the washed out buzz from philosophy or political theory to the technical object of research. It might also be a study of how the ontology of data (to go philosophical) and the materiality of infrastructure have territorial propensities. How, in other words, do cables, servers, cooling systems, data processing and analytics, and the labor of their servicing (when not automated) produce a form of data sovereignty beyond the state? And for an inquiry such as the one of interest to this book, how might a logistical dimension be special to such operations?

Questions such as these point us toward a more general target of critique—the operation and organization of infrastructural and logistical power. Whether such authority is wielded by corporations or the state is less important than the fact of its existence as a force that is often extremely difficult to identify but is no less present in its effects. The accumulation of infrastructural power is all well and good for clients with an interest in minimizing latency for commercial purposes, but how might others not in the business of data services and the pursuit of commerce exploit these infrastructures to support more radical agendas? Can we envisage our own artistic practices or critical research, for instance, as having some use for colocation services? These are not questions that I have ready answers to, so I signal them here as markers for future research. Suffice it to say that the artistic practice of producing blueprints of an imaginary future provides one technique of subtraction from infrastructural power and the society of tracking, indexing the obsolescence of control and the rerouting of capture into models of psychogeographic displacement. But before we move to this book's conclusion, which considers artistic strategies of intervention, it is first necessary to identify the organization of power coincident with digital infrastructures of capture and coordination.

The Logistical State and Infrastructural Imperialism

If, as Jürgen Osterhammel submits, "Empires are structures of rule on a large scale," then what does it mean to approach both politics and the political from within an imperial horizon?[117] Such a proposition invites us to think the work of organization, and the collective design of strategies and tactics of intervention on planetary scales when empires are made imperial through digital infrastructures of communication. Of course the imperial dimension of empire is not exclusive to digital infrastructures. As Innis's writings on empire and communications attest, experiments in statehood in the form of imperial bureaucracies were facilitated by space-biased media such as papyrus and the time-biased media of parchment (treated animal skins) supporting the maintenance of an ecclesiastical hierarchy in the ancient Byzantine empire.[118] Architecture and sculpture also indexed the imperial power of empire within ancient cultures.[119] Built forms such as the Egyptian pyramids could be witnessed for the symbolic authority they command over time.

By dramatic contrast, the imperial power of data centers is nowhere to be seen. Hidden away in purpose built facilities or retrofitted warehouses, data centers blend into the urban fabric when they are not in secret or very remote locations. As infrastructure of seeming invisibility, their network of cables nonetheless mark out territories of control with computational processes signaling the occupation of time in ways calculable to the interests of capital. One might very reasonably attribute such features, more or less, to the corpus of modern communication technologies since the advent of electronic telegraphy. The abstraction of communication power has indeed defined the epoch of modernity and the time of our time.[120] When situated within such a lineage, data centers may not present as especially novel in their mode of abstraction. Indeed, this chapter has spent much space in drawing a parallel between telegraphy and data centers. But they register an intensification of technical processes and structural tendencies with regard to the exertion of logistical media as a form of infrastructural imperialism.

When communications infrastructure such as data centers play a decisive role in determining the territoriality of data—its geography of connection, the jurisdictional territories special to zones that govern it, the economies it spawns, the peering arrangements it colocates, the labor regimes and technical knowledge special to it—then one is prompted to conceive the political not in Chantal Mouffe's sense of a struggle between adversaries played out within government apparatuses of the state.[121] A more expansive definition of the political would encompass the multiplication of antagonism at the intersection of borders of many kinds. These may include social struggles, epistemological disputes, as well as protocological conflicts in software operations. Wherever the logic and practice of one organizational system or culture engages another and conflict ensues, one may speak of the political. Understood as such, the frontiers of the political register the locus of tensions promulgated by the operational peculiarities of data centers. Conceived in such a way, the political is deterritorialized from a monopoly

168 Imperial Infrastructures

hitherto assumed of the triad of state, civil society, and market. To think the political through the operational logic of data centers also invites a different notion of how imperialism can be tied to the workings of communication infrastructures. Such a view differs from Michael Hardt and Antonio Negri's restricted definition of imperialism as "an extension of the sovereignty of the European nation-states beyond their own boundaries," which they set against their concept of Empire as a decentered "apparatus of rule" not reliant on a "territorial center of power."[122]

For all the critique and commentary surrounding Hardt and Negri's thesis on Empire, the core argument they present nonetheless remains a compelling one. Their concept of Empire is more proximate to how I conceive of infrastructural imperialism, albeit with the proviso that the situation of data infrastructures holds a substantive force in the making of territoriality. But how might an account of infrastructural power retain a notion of imperialism that is not beholden to the territorial extension of the nation-state? This is not to ignore the constitutive relation between nation-states and large corporations with interests in communications infrastructure. Google's exit from mainland China in 2010 hasn't stopped IBM, Microsoft, and Amazon, who are among the largest players in cloud services, taking advantage of China's burgeoning industry in the construction of data centers. Typically these arrangements involve a suite of government incentives with pledges by global corporations to support local and regional economies with software and platform services along with support programs, for example, in the form of start-up incubators. But this isn't a one-way street of major players exploiting nation-states to their benefit; as the termination of Google's operations in China made clear, along with the Snowden revelations, companies in the business of communications infrastructure can still be highly vulnerable to the whims of the nation-state.

However, my interest here is a different one. Conflicts in technical standards and protocols that determine how data centers connect and disconnect from each other and associated client networks suggest that spatial conceptions of territory give way to, or at least run in tandem with, the nonspatial territory of technical knowledge and the properties of hardware in conjunction with the temporality of interface design and data transmission. Policy architectures also come into play here. Relevant examples would include the ratification of Internet governance between suprastate institutions and member states of international agreements such as the WTO's Agreement on Trade-Related Aspect of Intellectual Property Rights (TRIPS), or ICANN's management of Internet protocol addresses and Domain Name Systems, which involves input from representatives of the 111 member states comprising the Governmental Advisory Committee.

When multiplied in such ways, territory not only unbundles the coupling of the state and its geographic borders, it also evades any easy or straightforward analytical capacity to contain an object of investigation and critique. To contain an object within the imaginary of the nation-state is a mistake. Often enough the polis usurps the imaginary of sovereign power commanded by the state.[123] By interrogating infrastructure such as data centers and, as discussed earlier, their pre-history in the form of electric telegraphy, one begins to question "whether modern communications technology made empires more stable."[124] Counter-systems and methods, Osterhammel reminds us, are present as a disruptive force that test the monopoly of infrastructure presupposed by both state and non-state authorities as quasi-rivals in the territorial control of data.[125] The politics of escape, of living within and against the technologies of capture, modulation, extraction, and control that populate the territory of the present, is one that I return to in the next chapter. For now the concept of the state requires further detailing before advancing the concept of the logistical state and then returning briefly to the case of telegraphy.

For Weber, the modern state is defined sociologically "by reference to a specific *means* that is proper to it." The state, in other words, involves a capacity—political or otherwise—that is specific to the territory of its operation. Territory, here, is to be distinguished from the sovereign territory of states. The U.S. military, for example, operates beyond U.S. territory. In this regard, the operation determines the territory of the state. And infrastructure, as I have been arguing, provides the structure that makes operations possible. The means proper to the state is the method of the state; its content comprises a technology of governance that belongs to and is the property of the state. Extending far beyond sovereign territories, infrastructures of communication constitute another layer of sovereignty that offer a different analytical rubric when not subsumed under the expansionist agendas of statehood. When cast in such a way, we can begin to translate what is in effect the ontological dimension of the state—the *means proper to it*—in ways that address how infrastructural operations are central to the formation of the *logistical state*. Of relevance here is the political and economic geography and technical operation of data centers. Such considerations might revive a critique of the state based on its support of commercial data centers through financial levers such as attractive corporate tax breaks, generous land leases, flexible labor regulations, and free trade zones among other forms of state subsidy funded by national citizenries, not to forget lines of revenue generated by the efforts of noncitizens residing in the territory of the state. To speak of the capacity of the state in these terms is also to conceive of a logistical state—a point to which I return shortly.

In a program essay on forms of sovereignty and state transformation, Sandro Mezzadra and Brett Neilson set out to "assess the role of the state within an altered landscape marked by experiences of war, crisis, and persistent turbulence."[126] Central to their analysis is an interest in the tension between the state, territoriality, and juridical regimes not limited to the geographic borders of the nation-state. They note that the state is one among many forms of governance instantiated by the global operations of capital. No longer able to claim, *qua* Weber, "*the monopoly of legitimate force* for itself," the state often finds itself having to negotiate with a range of non-state actors who may contest the sovereign authority of the state. Where legal theorist Carl Schmitt and political philosopher Giorgio Agamben extend the Weberian concept of the state as a sovereign power able to "decide on the state of exception," other theorists of state formation contest such conceptualizations of a purposive, strong state. Indeed, as Akhil Gupta argues in his ethnographic study of bureaucracy, structural violence, and poverty in India, a critique of the state conceived as a unitary, cohesive, and coherent entity will begin to show how the diverse legislative, judicial, and administrative functions of governance across a range of spatial scales (federal, state, local) constitute a variegated state whose agendas and functions are already highly diverse, disaggregated, and often internally contradictory and conflictual in practice.[127] This is only amplified when external agencies with which the state engages are also taken into consideration. But such a line needs to be carefully distinguished from any slide back into conceiving the unity of the state as a governmental apparatus concomitant with its diffuse and uneven operations. For Mezzadra and Neilson, such tensions cannot be resolved, signaling instead the fracturing of the state and the complicated relation between state and nation that arises from the politics of operations.[128]

Within an Innisian framework the "territorial state" of ancient civilizations and their empires was predisposed toward a spatial or temporal bias as a result of the material properties of prevailing transport systems and communication technologies.[129] And this made them vulnerable to external forces able to exploit such infrastructural oversight or limits to capacity. The logistical state, by contrast, encompasses both of these dimensions simultaneously. The global networks of supply chains expand the territorial reach of producers and suppliers required for the operation of the logistical state. ERP software systems calibrate labor productivity and coordinate the movement of goods and finance in real-time, and data centers store, process, and transmit the data integral to logistical operations governed by computational systems. These are the infrastructural components that generate the possibility of imperial rule for the logistical state. Importantly, the spatial and temporal dimensions described here are not synchronic or spatial equivalents. Time and space is peculiar to each, forming layers or, more likely, a complex undulation of planes that overlap and intersect on some occasions while colliding and disconnecting on others.

The logistical state evolves from what Lazzarato identifies in postwar Europe as the social state (*Sozialstaat*), which in turn is a departure from the nation-state: "The social state is a new kind of state that has little to do with the nation-state whose loss of autonomy led to its gradual but inevitable disappearance which Schmitt laments."[130] Lazzarato suggests that the adoption of and identification with the concept of the social state across Europe after World War II "is symptomatic of a profound change in the nature and exercise of sovereignty." At the core of this change lies the determinate force of the economy, science, and industry, around which the "political and administrative systems of society" must adapt.[131] This reading by Lazzarato of the liberal social state is not to be confused with the social democratic state, a model of governance peculiar to postwar Europe that has become synonymous with the social-welfare state and its crisis following the advent of neoliberalism. For Lazzarato, the social state has already forged a pact with capital.

It should be no surprise that Australia, Canada, New Zealand, the United States, Chile, and Japan, following its defeat in the Second World War, were leading proponents of the social state. These are countries that historically and to this day have played a role as laboratories in the testing of social and political models designed to extract value from the social relations of production. Technological developments were key to the capacity of colonial empires to appropriate value through processes of capital accumulation. Earlier infrastructural systems on a planetary scale such as electrical telegraphy were notable for their traffic in information related to the pulse of stock markets. The connection of ticker tape to telegraphic signals in 1867 allowed for the continuous registration of fluctuations in market prices.[132] But sovereign states may also refuse to submit to the planetary impulse of technological forms and the external interests—corporate or otherwise—that hitch a ride. States can prohibit the use of infrastructure for the extraction of value if it intervenes, symbolically or otherwise, with its other operations. The Google-China dispute is a case in point, where the PRC exerted the authority to decide that the search engine was violating its Internet censorship laws. Google's departure in 2010 from the mainland to Hong Kong enabled search engine rival Baidu. com to increase its already dominant market share.

Fusing with finance capital (from rent to tax to speculation, derivatives, and other forms of algorithmic trading), the logistical state might also be characterized as a variation of the finance state. However, the intensity of its mode of expropriation suggests that the logistical state is also more than this, which is to say that it is not reducible to financialization alone. The logistical state, constituted in part by the spatial and temporal properties of infrastructure and their media of operation, is one that extracts new forms of value from populations and dispersing of this value—initially as data and later as financial products and services—through circuits of movement governed by protocols of storage, transmission, and processing special to data centers. But importantly, the state does not operate or manage data centers like it previously did in many countries with regard to utilities such as national broadcast media in radio, television, and telephony. Instead, the state decides to buy into data centers, including for military purposes. But this hasn't always been the case. In a report from 2011, the White House's Office of Management and Budget noted that "the Federal government quadrupled the number of data centers" it operated between 1998 and 2010.[133] Despite this increase, only 27 percent of their computational power was used. This expansion in data centers managed by the government resulted in massive running costs associated with energy consumption, real estate, servicing, and security. President Obama's "Campaign to Cut Waste," launched in June 2011, is designed to increase efficiencies, reduce duplication, and bring greater accountability to the expenditure of tax dollars.[134] Part of this program aims to close over 800 data centers operated by government with an estimated saving to tax payers of USD $3 billion ($2 billion of which comes from energy savings), and instead procuring data center services from a combination of state departments and private entities.[135]

Two features are notable in this policy agenda: First, the nineteen participating partners in the U.S. Department of Energy's "Better Building Challenge," drawn from both the state and private sectors, are required to comply with a public reporting on energy efficiencies and performance.[136] The policy thus brings private-sector operators such as eBay, colocation specialist Digital Realty, and Schneider Electric, a green energy consultancy firm and data center provider, in line with government agencies such as the U.S. Department of Defense, the Environmental Protection Agency, the Social Security Administration, and the Department of Justice, Drug Enforcement Administration. While seemingly a positive instance of U.S. government regulation aimed to support its "Climate Action Plan," one can also read this as an expansion of the state and its regime of transparency and accountability, albeit of a certain and limited kind. The point I wish to make is that through such reforms, the distinction between the state and corporate sector becomes harder to identify when institutional practices are common to each.

Second, and more significantly, a less-publicized component of this consolidation agenda indexes the state-corporate nexus as a logistical undertaking manifest in higher levels of interoperability across state departments as a result of more agencies running their operations through the cloud platforms of a smaller number of data center providers. In July 2014 the State of California's Department of Technology and IBM launched CalCloud, an Infrastructure-as-a-Service arrangement designed to bring over 400 state departments and local government entities along with private customers and SMEs into a subscription-based platform.[137] While efficiencies are no doubt gained from such partnerships, they also leave the state beholden to a more concentrated range of commercial interests that also bring the state into a different territorial configuration with regard to the storage, management, and protocological regimes overseeing the governance of data emanating from national citizenries and state departments.

Consider the possible implications of this with a partner such as Digital Realty, whose data centers are located around the world. While the vast bulk of these are in the United States, Digital Realty also runs data centers in Europe, the Asia-Pacific, and Australia.[138] Depending on operational requirements, contractual conditions, and commercial interests, the provenance of data may be territorially distinct at sovereign, geopolitical levels from the location of its storage. In the event of legal proceedings pertaining to a state department's or individual's use or obtainment of data, complications could foreseeably arise in instances where data is stored in data centers hosted in countries whose juridical regimes conflict with those from which the data first emanated or was used for illegal purposes or otherwise. While China, Hong Kong, Taiwan, and Singapore have been key sites in recent years for the expansion of data center industries, the conceptual and theoretical work on these installations has not been sensitive to their territorial implications. The territoriality of data is such that in terms of technical operations, labor performance, and the materiality of data, the locational specificity of "Asia" is brought into question. Moreover, the capacity of data centers to operate as sovereign entities external to or in conjunction with the state can be understood as a form of infrastructural imperialism.

This is not just a question of a state-corporate nexus, but a kind of institutional subsumption into infrastructure. Paradoxically and perhaps even perversely, the logistical state becomes in a sense depoliticized, because at the level of infrastructure there is "less politics." The depoliticized logistical state is not merely an abnegation of responsibility to outsourced corporates, but rather a technical determination of governance peculiar to the administrative and executive roles of government when they become baked in to the infrastructure. The governance of government no longer operates according to the presumption of more-or-less intelligent human functionaries; these roles are technicized into networks of which data centers are a critical constituent part. The not too distant scenario in which the production of national digital currencies through offshored Bitcoin mining farms serves as another possible case that amplifies this point in which digital infrastructure, paradoxically, depletes states of the technical structures which structure the work of politics. This is not cause for necessary lament—the liberation of politics from the state registers the technical conditions enmeshed with the politics of operations.

Hypothetical as such examples are, they nonetheless serve to highlight how the territorial imaginary of the logistical state is constituted through network topologies and infrastructures of extraction in ways that do not necessarily conform to the territorial logic of the nation-state. Conceived in such a way, the logistical state is defined by a capacity to adapt and shift its territorial imaginary according to the dynamics of infrastructural systems that to this day enmesh national with imperial scales of governance as they bear upon the capture of value through the coordination of movement. A political-economic history of corporate takeovers and mergers could well demonstrate how the territoriality of data and data centers serve older regimes of finance and financialization as well as newer ones linking security and big data economies.

Another key issue to address here concerns the ways in which the economy of cloud computing has prompted the IT sector to more actively promote their services to government agencies. Vincent Mosco notes how IT companies previously lackadaisical in the 1990s stepped up their lobbying efforts following the dotcom crash at the start of this century.[139] In recent years consultancy firms such as Gartner along with IT behemoths Google, Facebook, and Microsoft have spent millions of dollars in their campaigns to appeal to policy makers and political authorities in Washington in order to stave off government attempts to develop and implement antitrust regulations, tighter legislation on online privacy, and commercially damaging environmental standards as they pertain to the construction and running of data centers.[140] Policy regimes such as these are obvious targets for the IT sector, which is keen to protect revenue streams derived from economies of data generated from valuable information supplied by users, which in turn is dependent on services provided by data centers. Mosco also notes how lobbying efforts are not limited to the national capitals: "Because cloud computing data centers require locations that offer cheap land, low utility rates, and tax breaks, companies that run them spend time lobbying local officials, power authorities, and state legislatures for the best possible deal."[141] Low labor costs are another chief item on the list of criteria IT companies bring to government.

The territory of lobbying by the IT industry and the relations spawned with governmental institutions thus crosses local with national and planetary scales. Such an account of the political-economy of data centers and infrastructural dimension of scale differs from Saskia Sassen's analyses of global cities, political authority, and territorial assemblages.[142] For the Sassen of *Territory, Authority, Rights*, the territorial scale of analysis tends to be unitary rather than trans-scalar. Such a perspective is nuanced in a later essay, "When Territory Deborders Territoriality," in which "transversally bordered spaces" such as the "dark pools" of private financial networks and international treaty laws such as the WTO's General Agreement on Trade in Services comprise operational territories in the making on national, subnational, and global scales.[143]

In shifting attention to data centers, one begins to see how their uncoupling from urban infrastructures is a recent development. At the same time a key moment in the history of state formation is instantiated in which Foucault's governmental regime of pastoral power and associated techniques of care are now expressed in the name of security predicated on proprietary forms of enclosure and a corporate right to exploit the social production of value as it manifests through the accumulation and capture of data. In promoting its data collection strategy and extolling the virtues of its Utah data center, the NSA impudently declares that "If You Have Nothing to Hide, You Have Nothing to Fear."[144] That's pretty close to the social logic of an incitational confessionalism: To really let you know that if you had anything to hide, then you might take the initiative and share the outcomes of your soul-searching. The quantified self is the heir of pious self-monitoring. We can consider such techniques and technologies of neoliberal self-optimization as Weber reloaded: the Catholic care of the self and the social logic of capitalism, as it were. A willing and voluntary form of submission to technologies of exploitation within economies of data.

No doubt there is a danger here of replacing older theories of state formation with a new infrastructuralism. Common to both approaches is an account of the production of subjectivity, either in terms of the constitution of the state-subject (both citizens and noncitizens) or of the logistical agent whose capacity to act is determined by the parametric settings of technical infrastructures of communication and transportation. Within Anglo-American and European traditions of jurisprudence, the territoriality of the state and its declarations of a right to govern is conjoined with the rights of capital to claims over property. Such a pairing has lead to countless instances of dispute and conflict, many of which situate civil society actors as intermediaries in both liberal-democratic and authoritarian states. In the context of algorithmic capitalism, this chapter has explored how data infrastructures in the nineteenth century and early twenty-first century can be read as complementary with regard to their territorial operations. Of course, the content, intensity, and economy of data trafficking through these cable infrastructures is markedly different. If we take the question of agency as a point of departure to address the peculiarities of our infrastructural present, this does not dispense with the problematic of sovereign power.

My focus in this chapter has been on the political geography of infrastructural power specific to telegraphic communications and data centers. I noted how the imperial dimension of fiber-optic cables was established by the territorial system of telegraphic cables that consolidated the political and economic system of empire. While there are parallels between these two communication systems to the extent that data centers appropriate the historical infrastructures of telegraphy and colonial economies (including the format of warehouses and the oceanic routes and landfalls of telegraphic cables), it is also the case that a number of important distinctions exist that have implications for how we might collectively design a new politics specific to our time of data sovereignty. I go on to discuss this further in the next chapter, but for now we can note how in the telegraphic era the imperial logic of empire was secured through a core-periphery system maintained with the network of cables. Nations and territories became spatially aligned through the infrastructure of telegraphic communications.

In our digital present, data centers reproduce to some extent this same territorial logic. But aside from technical differences between copper wire and fiber-optic cables, the infrastructural imperialism of data centers is notably different in terms of a political-technical logic in which the system of nineteenth-century colonial mercantilism no longer prevails. This means that infrastructure and territory are not aligned according to the imperatives of empire in which the hegemony of the nation-state and its control of territory was key. Instead, we start to see how a form of infrastructural power predicated on the political economy of data and the territoriality of the logistical state begins to emerge. I conclude this book with a final meditation on strategies of intervention in the face of sovereign media.

Notes

1. See Liam Magee and Ned Rossiter, "Service Orientations: Data, Institutions, Labour," in Irina Kaldrack and Martina Leeker, eds., *There Is No Software, There Are Just Services* (Lüneburg: Meson Press, 2015), 73–89, http://meson.press/books/there-is-no-software-there-are-just-services/.
2. Vincent Mosco suggests that "the cloud takes the next step in a long process of creating a global culture of knowing, captured in the term *big data*, or what might better be called *digital positivism*." The neo-positivist aspects of computational regimes and data analytics are addressed in chapter 3. See Vincent Mosco, *To the Cloud: Big Data in a*

Turbulent World (Boulder: Paradigm Publishers, 2014), 2. See also Rob Kitchen on data empiricism in *The Data Revolution: Big Data, Open Data, Data Infrastructures and Their Consequences* (Los Angeles: Sage, 2013), 130–7.

3. The concept of parametric politics is developed across a number of writings with Soenke Zehle. See, for example, Soenke Zehle and Ned Rossiter, "Mediations of Labor: Algorithmic Architectures, Logistical Media and the Rise of Black Box Politics," in Richard Maxwell, ed., *The Routledge Companion to Labor and Media* (New York: Routledge, 2016), 40–50. See also Ned Rossiter and Soenke Zehle with Daniël de Zeeuw, "Interview: Of Piracy and Parametric Politics," *Krisis: Journal for Contemporary Philosophy* 3 (2015), http://www.krisis.eu/content/2015–1/Krisis-2015–1–05-RossiterZehle.pdf.

4. Keller Easterling, *Extrastatecraft: The Power of Infrastructure Space* (London and New York: Verso, 2014), 21.

5. For an insightful analysis of statistical and stochastic deep packet inspection as it relates to NSA's surveillance program, see Florian Sprenger, *The Politics of Micro-Decisions: Edward Snowden, Net Neutrality and the Architectures of the Internet*, trans. Valentine A. Pakis (Lüneburg: Meson Press, 2015), 45–53, http://meson.press/books/the-politics-of-micro-decisions/.

6. Deborah Cowen, *The Deadly Life of Logistics: Mapping Violence in Global Trade* (Minneapolis: University of Minnesota Press, 2014), 51.

7. Thanks to Tanya Notley for highlighting this example to me.

8. Kim Dotcom, "PRISM: Concerns of Government Tyranny are Legitimate," *The Guardian*, June 11, 2013, http://www.theguardian.com/commentisfree/2013/jun/13/prism-utah-data-center-surveillance.

9. See Barton Gellman and Ashkan Solanti, "NSA Infiltrates Links to Yahoo, Google Data Centers Worldwide," *The Washington Post*, October 30, 2013, http://www.washington post.com/world/national-security/nsa-infiltrates-links-to-yahoo-google-data-centers-worldwide-snowden-documents-say/2013/10/30/e51d661e-4166–11e3–8b74-d89d714ca4dd_story.html.

10. Mosco identifies the work of myth as it relates to collective desires of a technological sublime as key to the historical analysis of communication technologies: "Myths provide ballast for the sublime but fleeting visions contained in the promise of universal knowledge, virtual worlds, and unlimited communication that were once embodied in religion and nature but are now more likely supported by digital technologies. The assertion that cloud computing enables a group to do the impossible is similar to the claim that the telegraph would bring world peace or that lighting up the streets with electricity would end crime." Mosco, *To the Cloud*, 81.

11. Jussi Parikka, *A Geology of Media* (Minneapolis: University of Minnesota Press, 2015).

12. On the use of rare earths in computer manufacturing, see Anna Reading, "Seeing Red: A Political Economy of Digital Memory," *Media, Culture & Society* 36, no. 6 (2014): 748–60. See also Anna Reading and Tanya Notley, "The Materiality of Globital Memory: Bringing the Cloud to Earth," *Continuum: Journal of Media & Cultural Studies* 29, no. 4 (2015): 511–21.

13. And indeed such concepts of the state extend into the 21st century in the work of anarchist critiques of bureaucracy and the state by the likes of Graeber: "The police truncheon is precisely the point where the state's bureaucratic imperative for imposing simple administrative schema and its monopoly on coercive force come together." See David Graeber, *The Utopia of Rules: On Technology, Stupidity, and the Secret Joys of Bureaucracy* (Brooklyn: Melville House, 2015), 80.

14. Max Weber, "Politics as Vocation," in *Max Weber's Complete Writings on Academic and Political Vocations*, John Dreijmanis, ed., trans. Gordon C. Wells (New York: Agora Publishing, 2008), 156. Italics in original. All subsequent quotations from this volume.

15. See Anna Reading and Ned Rossiter, "Data, Memory, Territory," *Digital Media Research* 1 (2012): 5.

16. See Stuart Elden, *The Birth of Territory* (Chicago: University of Chicago Press, 2013), 3.

17. Gary Hall, "What Does Academia.edu's Success Mean for Open Access? The Data-Driven World of Search Engines and Social Networking," *Ctrl-Z: New Media Philosophy* 5 (2015), http://www.ctrl-z.net.au/journal/?slug=issue-5. See also Rachel O'Dwyer, "The Revolution Will (Not) Be Decentralised: Blockchains," *Commons Transition*, June 11, 2015, http://commonstransition.org/the-revolution-will-not-be-decentralised-blockchains/.

18. For Sassen, territoriality is understood as "the legal construct encasing the sovereign authority of the state over its territory." Importantly, for Sassen, "territoriality, the legal construct, is not on a one to one with territory—the latter can deborder the legal construct and in this process show us something about the territorial itself." Saskia Sassen, "When Territory Deborders Territoriality," *Territory, Politics, Governance* 1, no. 1 (2013): 21, 23.

19. Elden, *The Birth of Territory*, 4.

20. Eva Horn, "Editor's Introduction: 'There Are No Media,'" *Grey Room* 29 (Winter, 2008): 8. On the concept of "sovereign media" see, in the first instance, Adilkno, *The Media Archive: World Edition* (New York: Autonomedia, 1998), 12–5.

21. Stefan Heidenreich, "The Situation after Media," in Eleni Ikoniadou and Scott Wilson, eds., *Media after Kittler* (London and New York: Roman & Littlefield, 2015), 141–2.

22. See Horn, "There Are No Media."

23. See Erich Hörl, "The Technological Condition," trans. Anthony Enns, *Parrhesia: A Journal of Critical Philosophy* 22 (2015), 1–15, http://parrhesiajournal.org/parrhesia22/parrhesia22_horl.pdf.

24. Easterling, "Disposition is the character or propensity of an organization that results from all its activity." *Extrastatecraft*, 21.

25. "Das Kabel liefert der Welt eine Idee ihrer eigenen Verbundenheit," Daniel Gethmann and Florian Sprenger, *Die Enden des Kabels: Kleine Mediengeschichte der Übertragung* (Berlin: Kulturverlag Kadmos, 2013), 16.

26. John Durham Peters, *The Marvelous Clouds: Toward a Philosophy of Elemental Media* (Chicago and London: University of Chicago Press, 2015), 33.

27. See Peters, *The Marvelous Clouds*.

28. Parikka, *A Geology of Media*, 98.

29. The Invisible Committee, *To Our Friends*, trans. Robert Hurley (South Pasadena: Semiotext(e), 2015), 82–3. Italics in original.

30. Keller Easterling, "The Action is the Form," in Mark Shepard, ed., *Sentient City:* Ubiquitous Computing, Architecture, and the Future of Urban Space (Cambridge, MA: MIT Press, 2011), 155. Easterling also notes: "It does not constitute an event, but must be observed over time as a potentiality, capacity, ability, or tendency" (155).

31. Ibid., 156.

32. Ibid., 154. For a genealogy of cybernetics, see Orit Halpern, *Beautiful Data: A History of Vision and Reason since 1945* (Durham: Duke University Press, 2014).

33. Thanks to Soenke Zehle for some phrasings here.

34. John Durham Peters, *Speaking into the Air: A History of the Idea of Communication* (Chicago: University of Chicago Press, 1999), 8. Quoted in David Golumbia, "'Communication,' 'Critical,'" *Communication and Critical/Cultural Studies* 10, nos. 2–3 (2013): 248.

35. Heidenreich, "The Situation after Media," 140. Italics added.

36. Ibid.

37. See Soenke Zehle, "The Autonomy of Gesture: Of Lifestream Logistics and Playful Profanations," *Distinktion: Scandinavian Journal of Social Theory* 13, no. 3 (2012): 341–54.

38. Thanks to Liam Magee for his input into this passage.

39. Matthew Tiesen, "High-Frequency Trading and the Centering of the (Financial) Periphery," *Volume* 32 (September, 2012), http://volumeproject.org/2012/09/high-frequency-trading-and-the-centering-of-the-financial-periphery/.

40. Michael Lewis, *Flash Boys: A Wall Street Revolt* (New York: W.W. Norton & Co., 2014). See also Andrew Ross, "Flash Boys by Michael Lewis—Review," *The Guardian*, May 16, 2014, http://www.theguardian.com/books/2014/may/16/flash-boys-michael-lewis-review. For a critique of Lewis, see Juan Pablo Pardo-Guerra, "Why Michael Lewis Got It Wrong," Socializing Finance: A Blog on the Social Studies of Finance, May 2, 2014, https://socfinance.wordpress.com/2014/05/02/why-michael-lewis-is-wrong/. For more academic analyses of HFT, see also David Golumbia, "High-Frequency Trading: Networks of Wealth and the Concentration of Power," *Social Semiotics* 23, no. 2 (2013): 278–99.

41. See Rudolf Hilferding, *Finance Capital: A Study of the Latest Phase of Capitalist Development* (London: Routledge & Kegan Paul, 1981 [1910]); John A. Hobson, *Imperialism: A Study* (Nottingham: Spokesman, 2011 [1902]); and Vladimir Lenin, *Imperialism, The Highest Stage of Capitalism* (London: Lawrence and Wishart, 1948 [1917]).

42. Mosco, *To the Cloud*, 71–2.

43. Ibid., 36.

44. See the analysis of Amazon's Mechanical Turk in chapter 6. See also Ayhan Aytes, "Return of the Crowds: Mechanical Turk and Neoliberal States of Exception," in Trebor Scholz, ed., *Digital Labor: The Internet as Playground and Factory* (New York: Routledge, 2013), 79–97. A number of participants also addressed MT at Digital Labor: Sweatshops, Picket Lines, Barricades, The New School, New York City, November 14–16, 2014, http://digitallabor.org/.

45. See Lilly Irani, "Difference and Dependence among Digital Workers: The Case of Amazon Mechanical Turk," *South Atlantic Quarterly* 114, no. 1 (2015): 225–34.

46. The play here is with reference to Graeber's, *The Utopia of Rules*.

47. Philip J. Stern, *The Company State: Corporate Sovereignty and the Early Modern Foundations of the British Empire in India* (Oxford: Oxford University Press, 2011).

48. See also Lauren Benton, *A Search for Sovereignty: Law and Geography in European Empires, 1400–1900* (Cambridge: Cambridge University Press, 2009).

49. Paul Israel, *From Machine Shop to Industrial Laboratory: Telegraphy and the Changing Context of American Invention, 1830–1929* (Baltimore: The John Hopkins University Press, 1992), 3.

50. See Florian Sprenger, "Between the Ends of a Wire: Electricity, Instantaneity and the World of Telegraphy," in Michaela Hampf and Simone Müller-Pohl, eds., *Global Communication Electric: Actors of a Globalizing World* (Frankfurt: Campus, 2013), 355–38. See also Jill Hills, *The Struggle for Control of Global Communication: The Formative Century* (Urbana: University of Illinois Press, 2002); and Dwayne R. Winseck and Robert M. Pike, *Communication and Empire: Media, Markets and Globalization, 1860–1930* (Durham: Duke University Press, 2007).

51. Bernhard Siegert, *Relays: Literature as an Epoch of the Postal System*, trans. Kevin Repp (Stanford, CA: Stanford University Press, 1999), 198.

52. Jürgen Osterhammel, *The Transformation of the World: A Global History of the Nineteenth Century*, trans. Patrick Camiller (Princeton and Oxford: Princeton University Press, 2015), 421. Italics in original.

53. Daniel R. Headrick, *The Tentacles of Progress: Technology Transfer in the Age of Imperialism, 1850–1940* (New York and Oxford: Oxford University Press, 1988), 98.

54. Despite this infrastructural relation to Asia, Australia remained a culturally, if not economically, isolated nation up until the 1970s when a "second wave" of migration following the Vietnam war brought the country more firmly into the Asian region.

55. Mosco, *To the Cloud*, 72.

56. K. T. Livingston, *The Wired Nation Continent: The Communication Revolution and Federating Australia* (Melbourne: Oxford University Press, 1996), 93.

57. Livingston, *The Wired Nation Continent*, 95–98. See also Nicole Starosielski, *The Undersea Network* (Durham and London: Duke University Press, 2015), 33.

58. See Tom Standage, *The Victorian Internet: The Remarkable Story of the Telegraph and the Nineteenth Century On-Line Pioneers* (New York: Bloomsbury, 2013).

59. See Anton A. Huurdeman, *The Worldwide History of Telecommunications* (New Jersey: John Wiley & Sons, 2003). For a typology of different cable economies (copper cable colonialism, coaxial Cold War, and fiber-optic financialization), see Starosielski, *The Undersea Network*, 31–54.

60. See Winseck and Pike, *Communication and Empire*, 38; and Huurdeman, *The Worldwide History of Telecommunications*, 136.

61. Livingston, *The Wired Nation Continent*, 95.

62. Huurdeman, *The Worldwide History of Telecommunications*, 136n28.

63. Eastern Communications, http://www.easterncommunications.com.ph.

64. For a critical account of WSIS, see Jan Servaes and Nico Carpentier, eds., *Beyond the WSIS: Towards a Sustainable Agenda for the Future Information Society* (Bristol: Intellect Books, 2006).

65. See Australian Overland Telegraph Line, http://en.wikipedia.org/wiki/Australian_Overland_Telegraph_Line and Livingston, *The Wired Nation Continent*, 75–89, 124. The classic history of telegraphy in Australia is Ann Moyal's *Clear across Australia: A History of Telecommunications* (La Trobe: Nelson, 1984).

66. Siegert, *Relays*, 174–5.

67. See Moyal, *Clear across Australia*, 65 and Headrick, *The Tentacles of Progress*, 101. On the founding of the Indo-European Telegraph Company by Siemens in 1868, see also Huurdeman, *The Worldwide History of Telecommunications*, 126. Bernhard Siegert notes how the availability of electric telegraphy in 1849 to the general public in Germany, against opposition from the military, resulted in the militarization of public discourse. "The military, however, had a hard time adjusting its chain of command to accommodate the telegraph. Only after the introduction of Morse instruments in railway offices, as a result of which large numbers of Siemens needle telegraphs taken out of service were to be had cheaply, did the Army being to construct a telegraph network for its fortresses." Siegert, *Relays*, 173.

On the role of the Russian government in granting "the right to the construction to set up direct telegraph communication between Europe and India," see Andre Karbelashvili, "Europe-India Telegraph 'Bridge' via the Caucasas," *Indian Journal of History of Science* 26, no. 3 (1991): 277–81. See also "The Java-Roebuck Bay Telegraph Cable," *The Daily News*, March 5, 1889, http://trove.nla.gov.au/ndp/del/article/77374615?searchTerm=submarine%20cable%20roebuck%20bay&searchLimits=.

68. This case is argued with extensive archival references by Livingston in his book *The Wired Nation*.
69. See Starosielski, *The Undersea Network*, 34–5.
70. Siegert, *Relays*, 177. Richard Maxwell and Toby Miller note that this substance, "drawn from the sap of the slow-growing *sapotaceae* tree family," was indigenous across the Malay Peninsula, the Philippines and Indonesia. And: "Despite the fact that Dutch colonies produced the bulk of the raw material used to make gutta-percha, the United Kingdom obtained commercial control over latex because it ran Singapore, the international hub for the trade of the material, and cultivated close ties with Chinese merchants, who depended on British credit." Richard Maxwell and Toby Miller, *Greening the Media* (New York: Oxford University Press, 2012), 56–7.
71. Siegert, *Relays*, 177.
72. Bill Glover, "Atlantic Cables: 1856–2012," History of the Atlantic Cable & Undersea Communications: From the First Submarine Cable of 1850 to the Worldwide Fiber Optic Network, http://atlantic-cable.com/Cables/CableTimeLine/atlantic.htm. My description of cables is based on the archival research compiled at Atlantic-Cable.com and supplemented with further research by Mat Wal-Smith.
73. Paul M. Kennedy, "Imperial Cable Communications and Strategy, 1870–1914," *The English Historical Review* 86, no. 341 (1971): 736.
74. Ibid., 735.
75. Ibid., 735–6.
76. I notice that Matteo Pasquinelli has recently been drawn to the topic of data centers. See his writings and course descriptions for his teaching program at the Pratt Institute, New York, at http://matteopasquinelli.com/. See also the articles by Metahaven, "Captives of the Cloud: Part I," *e-flux* 37 (September, 2012), http://www.e-flux.com/journal/captives-of-the-cloud-part-i/. See *e-flux* for parts 2 and 3. For an interesting looking book that enlists concepts of territoriality and the sovereignty of data to analyze the cloud, see Tung-Hui Hu, *A Prehistory of the Cloud* (Cambridge, MA: MIT Press, 2015).
77. Starosielski, *The Undersea Network*, 124.
78. Ibid., 111.
79. Ibid., 99–111.
80. Ibid., 99.
81. See Dan Schiller, "Geopolitical-Economic Conflict and Network Infrastructures," *Chinese Journal of Communication* 4, no. 1 (2011): 90–107.
82. See Mosco, *To the Cloud*, 163–7.
83. James W. Carey, "Technology and Ideology: The Case of the Telegraph," in *Communication as Culture: Essays on Media and Society* (New York and London: Routledge, 1992), 204.
84. Jill Hills, *The Struggle for Control of Global Communication: The Formative Century* (Urbana and Chicago: University of Illinois Press, 2002). See also Kennedy, "Imperial Cable Communications and Strategy, 1870–1914."
85. Ibid., 180.
86. Ibid., 181.
87. Ibid., 182.
88. Ibid.
89. Ibid., 181.
90. See Schiller, "Geopolitical-Economic Conflict and Network Infrastructures," 93.
91. Jonathan Sterne, "Transportation and Communication: Together, as You've Always Wanted Them," in Jeremy Packer and Craig Robertson, eds., *Thinking with James*

Carey: Essays on Communications, Transportation, History (New York: Peter Lang, 2006), 118–9. See also John Durham Peters, "Technology and Ideology: The Case of the Telegraph Revisited," *Thinking with James Carey*, 137–55.

92. For an analysis of how cable companies deploy "strategies of insulation" against multiple forms of interference, see Starosielski, *The Undersea Network*.

93. See Headrick, *Tentacles of Progress*, 109.

94. Ibid., 110.

95. "Unions from Five Countries Meet over Amazon Working Conditions," Reuters, July 3, 2014, http://www.reuters.com/article/2014/07/03/amazoncom-unions-idUSL 6N0PE4K720140703.

96. Jeff Denneen and Tom Dretler, "The Financially Sustainable University," Bain and Company, June 6, 2012, http://www.bain.com/publications/articles/financially-sustainable-university.aspx.

97. See Brett Neilson and Ned Rossiter, "Precarity as a Political Concept, or, Fordism as Exception," *Theory, Culture & Society* 25, nos. 7–8 (2008): 51–72.

98. "Hong Kong, Singapore and Taiwan Are Top Data Center Locations in Asia Pacific," IDC: Analyze the Future, March 5, 2014, http://www.idc.com/getdoc.jsp?containerId=prSG24720514.

99. Rebecca Fannin, "Why Google Is Quitting China," *Forbes*, January 1, 2010, http://www.forbes.com/2010/01/15/baidu-china-search-intelligent-technology-google.html.

100. John Ribeiro, "Google Opens Data Centers in Taiwan and Singapore to Handle Asian Traffic," *PCWorld*, December 11, 2013, http://www.pcworld.com/article/2079120/google-opens-data-centers-in-taiwan-and-singapore-to-handle-asian-traffic.html.

101. Lisa Wang, "Google Triples Investment in Taiwanese Data Center," *Taipei Times*, April 4, 2012, http://www.taipeitimes.com/News/biz/archives/2012/04/04/2003529430.

102. Chiu Yu-Tzu, "Google's Largest Asian Data Center in Taiwan to Boost Cloud Sector," *ZDNet*, December 12, 2013, http://www.zdnet.com/googles-largest-asian-data-center-in-taiwan-to-boost-cloud-sector-7000024174/.

103. "Google to Build Taiwan Data Center," *Huffington Post*, April 3, 2012, http://www.huffingtonpost.com/2012/04/03/google-taiwan-data-center_n_1400506.html.

104. Tanya Notley, "The Fixed Infrastructure of Data Mobility: Investigating the Local Impact of Server Farms in Australia and the UK," Draft Research Proposal, April 7, 2014.

105. Paul Kavitz, Kevin Moore, Adam Morgan, and Travis Nottberg, "Green Energy for Information Technology Data Centers: An Analysis of Energy Procurement Options for the Federal Government," *New Voices in Public Policy* 3, no. 2 (2009): iii, http://journals.gmu.edu/newvoices/article/view/33/33.

106. Donald Mackenzie, "Be Grateful for Drizzle," *London Review of Books* 36, no. 17 (September, 2014): 28, http://www.lrb.co.uk/v36/n17/donald-mackenzie/be-grateful-for-drizzle.

107. O'Dwyer, "The Revolution Will (Not) Be Decentralised." See also the MoneyLab project, an initiative of the Institute of Network Cultures, Amsterdam, http://network cultures.org/moneylab/.

108. See Rich Miller, "What the Bitcoin Shakeout Means for Data Center Providers," Data Center Knowledge, January 14, 2015, http://www.datacenterknowledge.com/archives/2015/01/14/what-the-bitcoin-shakeout-means-for-data-center-providers/.

109. Mike Hearn, "The Resolution of the Bitcoin Experiment," *Medium*, January 15, 2016, https://medium.com/@octskyward/the-resolution-of-the-bitcoin-experiment-dabb30201f7#.641wzkkex.

182 Imperial Infrastructures

110. For an account of why this is an infrastructural problem, see Joel Hrusk, "One Bitcoin Group Now Controls 51% of Total Mining Power, Threatening Entire Currency's Safety," *ExtremeTech*, June 16, 2014, http://www.extremetech.com/extreme/184427-one-bitcoin-group-now-controls-51-of-total-mining-power-threatening-entire-currencys-safety.

111. See Rich Miller, "Bitcoin Gets Liquid: BitFury Buys Immersion Cooling Specialist," *Data Center Knowledge*, January 22, 2015, http://www.datacenterknowledge.com/archives/2015/01/22/bitcoin-gets-liquid-bitfury-buys-immersion-cooling-specialist/.

112. See "Two-Phase Immersion Cooling," 3M, http://www.3m.com/3M/en_US/novec/products/engineered-fluids/immersion-cooling/.

113. Yevgeniy Sverdlik, "Bitcoin Data Center Construction Marches On, Despite Low Value," *Data Center Knowledge*, June 8, 2015, http://www.datacenterknowledge.com/archives/2015/06/08/bitcoin-hardware-firms-continue-building-data-centers-despite-low-currency-value/.

114. Collocation Data Centers, http://www.datacentermap.com/datacenters.html.

115. This represents a steady and in some case significant growth since I last looked at these figures in June 2013, when there were 3,227 colocation data centers in 99 countries. At that time the United States had 1,265, the United Kingdom had 210, and Germany 167. Australia had 88, India 97, Hong Kong, Indonesia, and Taiwan holding 40, 32, and 4. China had 54, Russia 38, Ireland 18, Luxembourg 12, the Czech Republic 17, Malaysia 28, South Africa 19, Pakistan 10, and Turkey 31.

116. Andrew Blum, *Tubes: A Journey to the Center of the Internet* (New York: Harper Collins, 2012), 96–97.

117. Jürgen Osterhammel, *The Transformation of the World: A Global History of the Nineteenth Century*, trans. Patrick Camiller (Princeton and Oxford: Princeton University Press, 2015), 424.

118. See Paul Heyer, *Harold Innis* (Lanham: Rowman & Littlefield, 2003), 50. See also Harold A. Innis, *Empire and Communications* (Victoria: Press Porcépic, 1986 [1950]).

119. See Heyer, *Harold Innis*, 80.

120. See Manuel Castells, *Communication Power* (Oxford: Oxford University Press, 2009).

121. See Chantal Mouffe, *The Return of the Political* (London: Verso, 2005 [1993]) and Chantal Mouffe, *The Democratic Paradox* (London: Verso, 2000).

122. Michael Hardt and Antonio Negri, *Empire* (Cambridge, MA: Harvard University Press, 2000), xii.

123. Or, in a case like Beijing—the political capital of the People's Republic of China—there is an interplay between polis and state that operates in technical, geographic, and imaginary ways. This became particularly clear to me during the Beijing Olympics in 2008, when many of the world's global media were gathered to report not only on the sporting event, but also daily social and cultural life in the megacity. Reporters who should have known better would consistently write about the "Great Firewall of China," which periodically blocked social media sites like Facebook and Twitter along with liberal media sites like *The Guardian* and Wikipedia. What these reporters failed to understand was that the Chinese government implemented a digital policy in uneven ways across the territory of the nation-state. In many provinces outside of Beijing, there was no problem to access sites reported as a so-called threat to the authority of Chinese rule. But the government understood very well the metonymic operation between the polis and the nation, which was especially amplified with national and global media events such as the Olympics. The city, in other words, performed the imaginary work

of a government in control. It was not necessary to extend control mechanisms beyond the city since most reporters would not venture outside this territorial imaginary.

124. Osterhammel, *The Transformation of the World*, 425.

125. "By no means did colonial authorities always have a monopoly over the transfer of information; their adversaries employed similar methods as well as countersystems, from the bush drum to the internet." Osterhammel, *The Transformation of the World*, 425.

126. Sandro Mezzadra and Brett Neilson, "The State of Capitalist Globalization," *Viewpoint Magazine*, September 4, 2014, https://viewpointmag.com/2014/09/04/the-state-of-capitalist-globalization/#rf9-3179.

127. Akhil Gupta, *Red Tape: Bureaucracy, Structural Violence, and Poverty in India* (Durham: Duke University Press, 2012), 44–47. Oddly, Gupta levels a critique of complicity against those who refer to the bureaucratic categories of governmentality. Yet how can the critic do anything but this when identifying an object of investigation? Indeed, having made this criticism, Gupta himself goes on to work within and against categories deployed by colonialism and successive governmental regimes engaged in the reproduction of what he terms "structural violence."

128. See Mezzadra and Neilson, "The State of Capitalist Globalization." See also Sandro Mezzadra and Brett Neilson's "Extraction, Logistics, Finance: Global Crisis and the Politics of Operations," *Radical Philosophy* 178 (March/April, 2013): 8–18; and "Operations of Capital," *South Atlantic Quarterly* 114, no. 1 (2015): 1–9.

129. On the territorial state, see Gordon Branch, "On Google Maps, State Formation, and the International Politics of Cartography," *Theory Talks*, no. 65, November 10, 2014, http://www.theory-talks.org/2014/11/theory-talk-65.html.

130. Maurizio Lazzarato, *Governing by Debt*, trans. Joshua David Jordan (South Pasadena: Semiotext(e), 2015), 52.

131. Ibid.

132. Standage, *The Victorian Internet*, 175.

133. Jeffrey Zients, "Shutting Down Duplicative Data Centers," White House Office of Management and Budget, July 20, 2011, https://www.whitehouse.gov/blog/2011/07/20/shutting-down-duplicative-data-centers.

134. "Campaign to Cut Waste," The White House, https://www.whitehouse.gov/21stcenturygov.

135. Zients, "Shutting Down Duplicative Data Centers."

136. "Improving the Energy Efficiency of Our Nation's Data Centers," U.S. Department of Energy, https://www4.eere.energy.gov/challenge/partners/data-centers.

137. See Jason Verge, "IBM Brings Government Cloud to California State," Data Center Knowledge, July 25, 2014, http://www.datacenterknowledge.com/archives/2014/07/25/calcloud-california-government-cloud/. See also "CalCloud—IaaS—Overview," Department of Technology, State of California, http://www.servicecatalog.dts.ca.gov/services/cloud/calcloud/overview.html.

138. See https://www.digitalrealty.com/locations/.

139. See Mosco, *To the Cloud*, 113–8.

140. Ibid., 118.

141. Ibid., 115.

142. Saskia Sassen, *Territory, Authority, Rights: From Medieval to Global Assemblages* (Princeton: Princeton University Press, 2006).

143. Sassen, "When Territory Deborders Territoriality," 31.

144. Domestic Surveillance Directorate, https://nsa.gov1.info/data/.

8

SOVEREIGN MEDIA AND THE RUINS OF A LOGISTICAL FUTURE

Whether it is high-frequency trading, Bitcoin mining, government administrative and service transactions, or the hosting of social media platforms and their economy of tracking, the question of centralized control remains key to the politics of data infrastructure. Rachel O'Dwyer frames this issue as follows: "Whoever controls the data centre exercises political and economic control over communications. It's difficult to see how we can counteract these recentralising tendencies in order to build a common core infrastructure."[1] David Golumbia makes a similar point about high-frequency trading: "Despite the widespread rhetoric that computerization inherently democratizes, the consequences of the introduction of HFT are widely acknowledged to be new concentrations of wealth and power, opacity rather than transparency of information flows, and structural resistance to democratic oversight and control."[2] These two observations on data politics are usually separated politically and analytically, but they in fact describe a continuum of common concerns brought into focus through the optic of logistics. Whether it is an anchor to the network of "flows" or a symptom of the inability of politics to govern the seeming ephemerality of transactional data specific to HFT, the infrastructural form and technical object of data centers render data politics with a materiality that otherwise eludes studies of digital culture and society. I finish this book with some concluding remarks on the reappropriation of infrastructure and the role of counter-imaginaries in the political geography of data. Counter-imageries are important because they address the question of how to recouple infrastructural design with new forms of collective governance. This is also a question of how to decouple and let go of the fetish of networking as a form of politics altogether.

The production of counter-imaginaries is not inconsequential for the politics of infrastructure.[3] Indeed, they are a key component in the invention of concepts

Sovereign Media and the Ruins of a Logistical Future   **185**

that frequently enough migrate as memes from the margins of critical theory and the net-cultural moment of "sovereign media" to the policy discourses of the state and market strategies of the firm.[4] By Adilkno's account, sovereign media are apparatuses of indifference. They are a negative media of subtraction. "Unlike the antimedia, which are based on a radical critique of capitalist (art) production, sovereign media have alienated themselves from the entire business of politics and the art scene."[5] Sovereign media are not consciousness-raising machines. They hold no megaphones. Immanent to media of ubiquity, the dull surfaces of sovereign media are ideal hosts for the practice of anonymity. They involve a game of tinkering with parameters of the given. They operate within formats of familiarity and flourish when systems short-circuit. Sovereign media are primed to exploit the ruins of a logistical future.

My interest here is to think how infrastructure of communication operates as a form of sovereign media, bringing the singularity of the state as a sovereign entity into question. In an essay recently written with friend and long-term collaborator, Geert Lovink, we made the following observation about communications infrastructure such as data centers: "Until we know more about the technical operations, communication protocols, legal regimes, design principles and social-economic impact of such infrastructure, the capacity of movements to make informed decisions about how to organize in ways that both support and secure their interests and agendas will remain severely circumscribed."[6] Sovereign media are not a return to the politics of exodus but a way to scale autonomy beyond tactical media as demonstrated by WikiLeaks, among others. Part of such work involves unleashing alternative blueprints, prototypes, and test cases for a future that arises out of infrastructural ruins. Recall the note in the previous chapter of all those data centers shut down in the United States in the government's drive for greater efficiencies. What is to be done with abandoned infrastructures such as these? How might they be put to other uses that don't necessarily result in extending one of the core problems their closure sought to address—namely, the wasteful consumption of polluting energy? What if they were powered from sustainable energy sources? Actually this is not an especially powerful line of critique so much as an ironic gesture. As one tech report from 2013 noted, "Apple, eBay, Facebook, and Cisco have already made plans to use of [sic] the source of renewable energy for their data centers."[7] What is required, then, is a repurposing of infrastructure beyond the planned obsolescence inherent in solutionism and designing instead a culture of repair, as pursued by the likes of the Bricolabs network.[8]

One obvious task for designing counter-imaginaries is to engage in the multiplication of communication formats. Template cultures have become today's iron cage of reason. They are an unknown default whose genealogy is not without power in placing limits on expression in seemingly invisible ways. Speculation is no longer the work of imagination but rather is consigned to the operation of machines and the default settings of parameters. We need to collectively orchestrate strategies of infiltrate existing systems and manipulate them for other ends

186 Sovereign Media and the Ruins of a Logistical Future

from within. This is not about submitting to the state or any other sovereign entity. But rather, such a move consists of identifying prevailing black box systems of control and collectively devising ways to exploit these apparatuses from within. Another option is denial or ignorance, but who wants to go there?

In the final days, weeks, and months of completing this book, I kept returning to one particular artistic intervention that I was first introduced to during "Capturing the Moving Mind"—a wild collective experience traversing the trans-Siberian railway line from Moscow, stopping at Novosibirsk, en route to Beijing in 2005.[9] The genius concept of Akseli Virtanen, Jussi Vähämäki, Steffen Böhm, and their comrades from the Finnish School of Economics and Essex Business School, this experiment in "organization without ends" was an intervention in the production of subjectivity, perception and cognition cut and combined through the experience of movement.[10] Central to this process of organization was the question of political form. One discussion on that trip has lingered over the years. I first met media artist and platform designer Adam Hyde in the opening meeting held in the cavernous recesses of Moscow's infamous and now sadly demolished Rossiya Hotel. Adam was on board to tinker with some Nokia mobile phones for "mobicasting" images and sounds uploaded to the web as we moved along the railway line.[11] At the time it struck me that this was not just an instance of corporate benevolence on the part of Nokia; the project also offered Nokia an occasion to test the extent to which their commercial partners in the telecommunications industry across Russia, Mongolia, and China delivered on the roaming front. Here was an example of a nineteenth-century trade and geopolitical infrastructure (the railway) guiding the vector of transmission with twenty-first-century satellite communication systems. But infrastructure of transport and communication alone does not result in a whole lot. The subject of, in this case, artistic and activist labor was the necessary element of contained contingency, without which there would be no connection to test.

But I digress. The story from Adam that now worms its way into this book involved an artistic experiment with dormant infrastructure reactivated for civilian communication and scientific research. The occasion was a collaboration between artists and scientists in 2001 in the forests of Irbene near the Latvian coast of the Baltic Sea. Conceived by Rasa Smite and Raitis Smits from RIXC (Riga's center for new media culture), the Accoustic.Space.Lab project unleashed thirty-five artists on the RT-32, a massive steerable parabolic satellite dish and radio antenna used during the Cold War for spacecraft communications and intercepting radio and satellite signals of NATO countries.[12] The withdrawal of the Soviet Army in 1994 rendered the radio telescope and thirty-two-meter satellite dish inoperable, with nails smashed into cables and acid poured on to its motors and electronics by the departing military. Following independence, the Latvian Academy of Sciences established the Ventspils International Radio Astronomy Center (VIRAC) that restored the facilities for scientific purposes. Instead of tracking military operations of the enemy, observational data was accumulated on radiation emitted from planets and terrestrial sources.

Artists and technologists in the Accoustic.Space.Lab conducted experiments in collaboration with VIRAC scientists, or in parallel to the work they had developed. Adam and cofounder of the radioqualia collective, Honor Harger, produced pre-recorded material and live streams for Internet radio using radio astronomy—a form of broadcasting sound from the territorial depths of the universe. As Adam explains: "radio astronomy is essentially these huge radio telescopes that act like antenna picking up the electromagnetic transmissions from objects faraway in the cosmos."[13] And as detailed on the project site: "Radio Astronomy correlates the processes associated with broadcast radio—the transmission of audible information, and the processes of radio astronomy—the observation and analysis of radiated signals from planets, stars and other astrophysical objects. The work synthesizes these two areas. The signals from planets and stars are converted into audio and then broadcast on-line and on-air. The project is a literal interpretation of the term, 'radio astronomy.' It is a radio station broadcasting audio from space."[14]

Among its many points of fascination, the radio astronomy project is remarkable for its analysis of the movement of sound in space. The pulse of planets and the static of the cosmos lend electronic music an entirely novel spectrum of sound. But whatever one may make of such experiments, the key point relevant to this book is that infrastructure of any particular present will at some point be laid to rest, only to potentially resurface in the hands of artists and tinkerers who wish to extend its capacity in ways entirely unintended of the parameters that defined its initial conception and design. While the gesture of reappropriation is old, what is new is the scale on which this can take place. Rather than allowing ourselves to be ensnared by media hypes of consumer data hacks, we should acknowledge how quickly the scales can be reversed here. This kind of politics is about searching for these tipping points, and exploiting them in the production of new political, social, and economic horizons of life.

Within the time of our present, I can think of no better example of an infrastructural hack than Robin Hood Minor Asset Management Cooperative—a wild collective reengineering of financial technologies to devise a parasitical enterprise that generates financial resources for cultural, social, and political projects.[15] This is precisely the coupling of infrastructural attention and financial data that is rarely made by media and political activists. Described as "a hedge fund of the precariat," Robin Hood is another experiment in organization emanating from Akseli Virtanen's merry group of Finnish pranksters, with net-cultural luminaries Tiziana Terranova, Geert Lovink, and Franco "Bifo" Berardi on board as advisors. Perhaps akin to a form of reverse engineering the concentration of knowledge and infrastructural capacity specific to finance capitalism, Robin Hood sets out to produce a common from which artistic and social-political resources, projects, and subjectivities may emerge independent of the discursive and structural relations that attend the increasingly diminished sources of funding from state-based cultural agencies and the agendas of private philanthropists. Established in June 2012 in the midst of the global financial crisis, the massive expansion of personalized debt and the ongoing debate over Europe

188 Sovereign Media and the Ruins of a Logistical Future

as a geopolitical entity, the project site describes the Robin Hood operation in the following way:

> Robin Hood operates a dynamic data-mining algorithm—we call it the "Parasite"—which follows actual transactions at the US stock markets. We log into the brains of the market actors and turn them into our data banks, we know exactly what they do and when. We identify the best actors in each stock, follow them becoming a swarm—and then just imitate the emerging consensus action of the financial oligarchy. We "borrow" their most important means of production—their knowledge, their relations, their inside information, their position—and put it to work for us. We make a copy, a synthetic replica of the regularity between their positions and over-turn distinctions between a copy and a model. A repetition with a difference. We call it minor asset management. Another way to occupy Wall Street.[16]

Max Keiser considers the Robin Hood algorithm as "front-running the front runners," swarming upon stocks or assets deemed of interest to a sufficiently high aggregation of corporate actors.[17] Sharing similar points of reference to the body of thought associated with post-*autonomia* politics, the Robin Hood collective nonetheless does not bother itself with the pretense of a postcapitalist "ethical economy," as advocated by Adam Arvidsson.[18] Instead, Robin Hood nihilistically embraces the perversity of financialization and algorithmic capitalism. As Tiziana Terranova explains, Robin Hood "is not part of the movement of 'ethical finance,' in as much as it does not select investments on the basis of their ethical value, but aims to introduce a new kind of discourse and strategy into the debate around financialization."[19] Not shy of contradictions, and sharing something with the accelerationist thesis that to exceed capitalism requires passing through it,[20] the mimetic logic of Robin Hood's algorithm pursues investment strategies with an indifference to investment types.

Terranova notes that the question of wealth redistribution from processes of financialization is what marks Robin Hood as an experiment in the "communism of capital" (Marazzi).[21] Such an idea would seem one of mutual contradiction. How might systems of micro-credit hold fidelity with a communist politics? Doesn't the relationship between cryptocurrencies such as Bitcoin and other types of financial derivation, speculation, dark pools and markets, and financial instruments endemic to contemporary capitalism cancel out the possibility of a communism of capital?[22] If we take communications infrastructure as the operational core of capital accumulation, then interventions and experiments that seek to harness the logistical distribution of wealth generated by such infrastructure start to make feasible the idea of a communism of capital. Infrastructural imperialism is, by definition, expansive. Perhaps the trick is to see how such expansion can be reappropriated in ways that support labor and life within a republic without a state, or what Virno terms a "non-state public sphere."[23] Such worlds of care and relation are beyond peer-driven economies such as crowdsourcing, which in effect duplicate a system of taxation based on the impulsive fancies of the herd. Interventions into existing and defunct imperial infrastructures force a temporality of collective design that holds a more strategic dimension.

Robin Hood is currently looking into decentralized blockchain technologies and cryptocurrencies as alternatives to algorithmically designed hacks of finance capital. To invest exclusively in stock markets and asset acquisitions through an algorithmic replication of key financial actors no doubt has a limited horizon. What's to stop the many other smart hackers—or, for that matter, hedge fund operators—developing similar techniques, with intentions more likely to be infused with a politics of self-interest? Probably that's already going on. So it is just a matter of time before the swarming effect results in diminished returns for projects like Robin Hood if the focus were to remain on funding projects through stock market profits. Hence the need to diversify the lines of possible investment. Blockchain applications such as Ethereum offer what Virtanen considers not just an alternative architecture and system of financialization, but also the potential to extend Robin Hood's experiment in organization.[24] Using "blockchain awareness," the crowdfunded Ethereum platform runs decentralized "smart contracts"—"cryptographic 'boxes' that contain value and only unlock it if certain conditions are met"—enabling users to develop distributed governance systems and cryptocurrencies in ways distinct from predecessors such as Bitcoin. Unlike Bitcoin, Ethereum's foundational layer consists of "a blockchain with a built-in Turing-complete programming language, allowing anyone to write smart contracts and decentralized applications where they can create their own arbitrary rules for ownership, transaction formats and state transition functions."[25]

So perhaps Kittler's call to learn how to code is less about designers finding it difficult to work outside the Adobe Cloud than about the new protocols of decentralization.[26] At stake here is the question of (re)distribution after logistics. Herein lies the importance of Ethereum. It introduces new paradigms for the distribution of data, information, money, and wealth and asks what decentralization really will mean in the near future. Since Snowden, the dream of decentralization is at once broken at the level of centralized data inspection while remaining very much alive as a political passion and architecture of communication and transaction. This is how digital infrastructures define our mixed situation. After the next financial crisis currently in our midst wreaks havoc on social and economic life, the scale of logistics will not grow. Instead, it will be redistributed, prompting for better and worse new technical-socialities operating on local and regional scales. Anyone not completely strapped to the moon knows the capitalist fantasy of endless expansion and accumulation is not sustainable. Media and political theory also require conceptual blueprints to address time not just after the Anthropocene—we have an abundance of this in recent years—but also time after the collapse of logistical architectures that uphold economic globalization. The sovereignty of infrastructural

190 Sovereign Media and the Ruins of a Logistical Future

ruins includes a reformatting of the world after the orgy. Whether this is a world not subject to the rise of a neo-technocratic class in charge of engineering the protocols of platforms remains to be seen.[27] At the very least, we can design new idioms of practice beyond the template culture that services our expression. We still need this to happen, even if new code is immediately absorbed by actors across the political spectrum. This is also why the terrain-shifting intervention of Robin Hood is more than nihilism. There is no such thing as ethical code, or code that will carry its ethics with it at all times, as is the case with the politics of free software.

In bringing this book to a close, I return to the question of how the infrastructure and software of logistical media constitute territories. Within these enclosures the distinction between the subject of labor and the performance of algorithms can be hard to claw apart, especially in cases such as Amazon's Mechanical Turk. Yet for all this, there is scope for labor and life beyond the determining force of software and infrastructure. Examples such as the artistic experiments in radio astronomy using an abandoned satellite dish and radio telescope, or Robin Hood's hack of financial infrastructure, are among the many projects that demonstrate another layer of infrastructure whose value is not captured by the extraction machine of logistical media. Or at least it is not captured in ways that obviously conform to the operational parameters of logistical time and space. Here, I am referring to the collective work of concept production manifest in artistic practices and experiments in organization. The pursuit of concepts, of counter-imaginaries and blueprints for a future without capture, arises not from the protocological regimes of logistical media but rather from the force of contingency, disruption, and failure. The logistical nightmare of coordination and control within systems of calculation are not, in the final instance, secure from collective impulses of deviation and invention without termination.

Nonetheless the logistical nightmare persists. The horror of what Garnet Hertz and Jussi Parikka refer to as the refusal of "zombie media" to "disappear from the planetary existence" is an important example of how electronic waste lingers as toxic residues and secondary economies harbor often very miserable and dangerous forms of work.[28] Such media economies give rise to informal logistical systems that broaden the spectrum by which logistical media function as technologies of orientation. The hardware hacking of ex-military satellites in Latvia and the parasitic algorithm of Robin Hood's hack of finance capital correspond with the media archaeological dimension Hertz and Parikka attribute to the planned obsolescence of zombie media. Yet there is also a vampiric quality of logistics. Stripping flesh off bones and sucking neurons from our brains are dominant forms of extracting rent within an economy of data, even if for the most part we are unaware of how logistical techniques of control exponentially infiltrate the routines of labor and life.

Two figures in philosophical thought offer coordinates of critique within the quagmire of our logistical present.[29] In two highly compressed texts, Bernard

Stiegler and Gilbert Simondon seek to derive a conceptual apparatus from the operational core at work in machinic capitalism. These writings take us some way toward devising a method and conceptual strategy for dealing with the negativity of the logistical in which labor and life endure as fading components of capital accumulation. Stiegler's recent work at the juncture of philosophical thought and a practice of alternative technics follows and extends Simondon's characterization of the "technical mentality." Attending to the question of how the technical comprises a form of "philosophical engineering," Stiegler discerns in the digital condition the impossible but necessary conjunction of a "new Enlightenment" and accompanying "philosophy of shadows."

For Stiegler, technical systems comprise "processes of grammatisation" whose materiality conditions and transforms the production of subjectivity and knowledge conjoined with spatial coordinates and temporal rhythms. Having established this precept of structuration, Stiegler then withdraws from actually probing the "*operations that are specific to each form of support*, that is, proper to each stage of grammatisation." It seems enough to identify a meta-process—grammatization—that transcends what is otherwise, by Stiegler's reading, a continuum of time and space from the orality of the Ancients to the scripts of the Moderns. To signal the materiality of the technical is sufficient to the task of examining how the engineering of cognition is coincident with the grammar of the technical. While the grammar of the technical undoubtedly conditions human experience in the world, the task of politics is to ask quite specifically about the qualities and properties of the technical that distinguish or bear resemblance from one situation of struggle to another.

For Simondon, a technical mentality produces an ethico-aesthetic ("axiological") conceptual schema to address "regimes of operation" peculiar to the Cartesian mechanism and cybernetic theory. The synthesis of these two "schemas of intelligibility . . . are endowed with a latent power of universality." The premise of logistical media amplifies these schemas to concoct technologies of governance that invest heavily in the phantasm of control, efficiency, accountability, and calculation. A genealogy of the blockchain effectively takes us back to the Excel spreadsheet, which in turn points us toward the use of ledger as a pre-digital technology measuring the history of economic transactions (see also chapter 3 on double-entry bookkeeping and SAP). The decentralization of the blockchain is obviously distinct from the centralization of earlier transactional systems such as the ledger. This in a large part has to do with the material properties of these technological forms. Importantly, both have the capacity to function as technologies open to the scrutiny of the public. And both function to make value calculable, abstract, and able to be acted upon.

The continuum of these two dominant technical systems in the management of economy and society span the Cartesian mechanism and cybernetics. The "enchainment of links" within the "transfer schema" of the Cartesian paradigm mediate technical objects according to what Simondon calls a rule of synthesis and control able to adapt different components and in doing so make the machine operable as a whole. This, too, is the fantasy that compels logistics to straddle the world in its own image in which the transfer of people, finance, and things occurs "without losses." Cybernetics brings to this form of instrumental reason "a relay apparatus . . . that allows for an active adaptation to a spontaneous finality." The correspondence between the human and technics more often results in an indistinction between subjectivity and the technical in constituting modalities of operation (techniques of practices, process of perception and, I would add, systems of economy). The post-digital cybernetic systems that present neural networks as a resource to be exploited by technologies of neuromarketing constitute a "shadow" of the digital "against which the new enlightenment must struggle" (Stiegler). Such histories of the present are an important reminders that part of the analytical force of logistics is that it abandons the dichotomy between the digital and analog, which continues to plague media theory and the digital humanities. Logistics is about techne, where the human and technology are co-originary (Stiegler).

The inquiry of this book suggests we take this one step further. Rather than return to the canon of philosophy to uphold the case for a "new Enlightenment," I have instead sought to begin a study of logistics that maintains the technical as the basis for concept production. Such an approach proposes that rather than escape the darkness of logistical regimes in search of a "new Enlightenment," we instead embrace the nightmare. Such acts of disciplinary submission make possible the forging of concepts adequate to the task of critique and the invention of practices not always or at least not so easily subsumed by the power of logistical worlds. This is not a reformist agenda, *qua* Žižek & Co., that deleriates over the prospect of radicalizing the state from within: "Grass-roots self-organization cannot replace the state. The question is how to reorganize the state apparatus to make it function differently."[30] Žižek has been consistent on this point over the years, yet he fails to acknowledge that the authority of state also only exists through forms of co-constitution that are both external and internal to the territory of the nation and its complex of institutions. It is a mistake to think of the state in local terms, for which Žižek has a penchant. The state is not independent of interstate and non-state relations, which establish the parameters by which the state always remains a state no matter that it transforms. In other words, there is a distribution of sovereignty that predates the financial crisis born out by austerity regimes across the world. The technical operation of the world directs us toward what Keller Easterling terms the propensity of "extrastatecraft" to govern infrastructural space through standards and protocols not subject to scrutiny by legislative procedures.[31] The power of extrastatecraft to "generate de facto forms of polity" happens also to be key to the operation of logistical apparatuses and thus includes the media that governs systems of coordination, communication, and control.

If we are to confront the power of logistical regimes then we need to accept that governance within such systems is highly integrated with the production of subjectivity and economy. Within this condition, we need an alternative logistical fiction that imagines a repurposing of the infrastructures that make us who we are.

FIGURE 8.1 X-ray imaging system shows human passengers hidden in a truck.
Source: MSNBC.com, "The Week in Pictures," April 28, 2001.[32]

The political force of Stiegler's thesis comes from his insistence that there is an anthropological register to these changes. Transposing such an insight to logistics requires a scaling of our political imagination to grasp the distribution both of technology and the human. For this reason, the growing critical interest in machinic operations is not simply about transhumanization, subject-fatigue, and fears of labor-saving automation. The cosmic vision of radio astronomy in Latvia provides us with a clue here on how to repurpose the machine. What we now need to do is devise a grammar of connection between different types of spatial imagination and forge new territories toward a politics of operation.

The logistical nightmare confronting labor and life is highly varied and not universal in hue even if it is a dominant condition. We might glean something from how cinema calibrates its narratives based on conceptions of markets and the cultivation of taste. Take the Hollywood remake of *The Vanishing* (1993), for example, where the protagonist gets out of the grave alive, as opposed to the original Dutch version where he is left buried alive, scratching the enclosed coffin and fast running out of oxygen.[33] The Dutch version, *Spoorloos* (1988), translates as "traceless" or "without a trace."[34] And maybe this is the freedom that comes from overexposure in the data economies of the logistical present. If we take *Spoorloos* as a metaphor of logistical regimes, the plunge into darkness is met with a stolid

194 Sovereign Media and the Ruins of a Logistical Future

acceptance of limited life in the confines of the coffin. At the same time there is an occasion in this entrapment for an exploration of what the available tools, fire-lighters, and scratches in the woodwork might instead have to offer. But only in Hollywood. The horror of logistical worlds is one endured on a daily basis by migrants and asylum seekers traversing borders, jam-packed in their hundreds while constrained within shipping containers on the back of trucks or out at sea. Stopped for inspection at the port of Calais or checkpoints in Chiapas on route to the United States, the images generated by x-ray monitoring systems of the suffering of human life disclose the variation of supply chain capitalism and its capacity to adapt with indifference to contingency as it arises (Figure 8.1). If indeed contingency is the basis upon which capital is replenished, then our only hope is to join the league of vampires roaming a nocturnal planet in search of a life soon to be destroyed. This includes the destruction of logistics as we know it.

Notes

1. Rachel O'Dwyer, "The Revolution Will (Not) Be Decentralised: Blockchains," *Commons Transition*, June 11, 2015, http://commonstransition.org/the-revolution-will-not-be-decentralised-blockchains/.
2. David Golumbia, "High-Frequency Trading: Networks of Wealth and the Concentration of Power," *Social Semiotics* 23, no. 2 (2013): 278.
3. For a discussion of Radical Architecture in Italy, see Christoph Neubert, "The City as Extension and Environment: Historical Views on Urban Eco–Logistics," Computing the City: Ubiquitous Computing and Logistical Cities, Centre for Digital Cultures, Leuphana University Lüneburg, July 9–10, 2014, http://cdc.leuphana.com/events/event/computing-the-city-ubiquitous-computing-and-logistical-cities/.
4. On the concept of "sovereign media," see Adilkno, *The Media Archive: World Edition* (New York: Autonomedia, 1998), 12–15. See also Clemens Apprich and Felix Stalder, eds., *Vergessene Zukunft: Radikale Netzkulturen in Europa* (Berlin: transcript Verlag für Kommunikation, Kultur und soziale Praxis, 2012) and Clemens Apprich, "Remaking Media Practices: From Tactical Media to Post–Media," in Clemens Apprich, Josephine Berry Slater, Anthony Iles, Oliver Lerone Schultz, eds., *Provocative Alloys: A Post–Media Anthology* (London: Mute Books, 2013), 122–40, http://www.metamute.org/shop/mute-books/provocative-alloys-post-media-anthology.
5. Adilkno, *The Media Archive*, 13.
6. Geert Lovink and Ned Rossiter, "Network Cultures and the Architecture of Decision," in Lina Dencik and Oliver Leistert, eds., *Critical Perspectives on Social Media and Protest: Between Control and Emancipation* (New York: Rowman & Littlefield, 2015), 227.
7. Penny Jones, "US Data Center Turns to Solar for Power," *DatacenterDynamics: The Business of Data Centers*, August 29, 2013, http://www.datacenterdynamics.com/app-cloud/us-data-center-turns-to-solar-for-power/81850.fullarticle.
8. See http://bricolabs.net/.
9. See Akseli Virtanen and Steffen Böhm, eds., "Web of Capturing the Moving Mind: X," Special Issue, *ephemera: theory & politics in organization* 5, no. 10 (December, 2005), http://www.ephemerajournal.org/sites/default/files/pdfs/5-Xephemera-dec05.pdf. Virtanen's passion for systemic intervention takes form more recently with the Robin Hood investment cooperative—noted by Johan Sjerpstra as "the first anarchco–communist

Sovereign Media and the Ruins of a Logistical Future **195**

hedge fund based on the principles of Deleuze and Guattari." http://www.robinhood coop.org/.

10. See Brett Neilson and Ned Rossiter, eds., "Experience, Movement and the Creation of New Political Forms," Special Issue, *ephemera: theory & politics in organization* 6, no. 4 (November, 2006), http://www.ephemerajournal.org/issue/experience-movement-and-creation-new-political-forms.

11. Sophia Learner and Netta Norro joined Adam in this trial run. See also Gillian Fuller, "What Is the Moving Mind and How Can It Be Captured?," *ephemera: theory & politics in organization* 5, no. 10 (2005): 764–66, http://www.ephemerajournal.org/sites/default/files/5-Xfuller.pdf.

12. See http://www.virac.lv/en/info.html and http://latvianhistory.com/tag/ventspils-space-center/.

13. Andrew Clifford and Adam Hyde, "Adam Hyde of radioqualia: Interview," *Aotearoa Digital Arts Network*, February 21, 2005, http://www.ada.net.nz/library/interview-with-adam-hyde-of-r-a-d-i-o-q-u-a-l-i-a/.

14. Radio Astronomy, http://www.radio-astronomy.net/index.htm. See also http://radio qualia.va.com.au/documentation/spacelab/ and http://acoustic.space.re-lab.net/lab/history.html.

15. For a list of projects funded through Robin Hood revenues, see http://projects.robin hoodcoop.org/. Robin Hood currently defines itself as the Robin Hood Minor Asset Management Cooperative. With a strong aversion to community-oriented cultures of decision making and the limits of cooperatives as an organizational form, Robin Hood is currently redefining itself as Robin Hood Unlimited—a strategic move that appeals to the start-up entrepreneurialism of Silicon Valley, its current operating base.

16. "Sharing Economy 2.0," Robin Hood, http://www.robinhoodcoop.org/Sharing_ Economy_2.0#text.

17. Max Keiser, "Keiser Report: Debtism vs Capitalism (E736) [Interview with Daniel Hassan]," March 26, 2015, https://www.youtube.com/watch?v=OyDpTmCKKPc&feature= youtu.be&t=11m37s.

18. See Adam Arvidsson and Nicolai Peitersen, *The Ethical Economy: Rebuilding Value after the Crisis* (New York: Columbia University Press, 2013). For a critique of Arvidsson, see Detlev Zwick, "Utopias of Ethical Economy: A Response to Adam Arvidsson," *ephemera: theory & politics in organization* 13, no. 2 (2013): 393–405, http://www.ephemera journal.org/sites/default/files/pdfs/contribution/13–2zwick1.pdf.

19. Tiziana Terranova, "The Tale of Robin Hood Retold," Research Centre for Proxy Politics, Universität der Künste, Berlin, April 29, 2015, http://rcpp.lensbased.net/post/117693164755/the-tale-of-robin-hood-retold.

20. See Steven Shaviro, *No Speed Limit: The Essays on Accelerationism* (Minneapolis: University of Minnesota Press, 2015).

21. See Christian Marazzi, *Il comunismo del capitale. Biocapitalismo, finanziarizzazione dell'economia e appropriazioni del comune* (Verona: Ombre Corte, 2010) and "Measure and Finance," September 21, 2007, http://www.generation-online.org/c/fc_measure.htm. See also Armin Beverungen, Anna–Maria Murtola and Gregory Schwartz, "Editorial: The Communism of Capital?," *ephemera: theory & politics in organization* 13, no. 3 (2013): 483–95, http://www.ephemerajournal.org/sites/default/files/pdfs/contribution/13–3editorial.pdf.

22. My thanks to Orit Halpern for making these points and phrasings.

23. See Paolo Virno, *A Grammar of the Multitude: For an Analysis of Contemporary Forms of Life*, trans. Isabella Bertoletti, James Cascaito, and Andrea Casson (New York: Semiotext(e),

2004). See also, Paolo Virno, "Natural-Historical Diagrams: The 'New Global' Movement and the Biological Invariant," in Lorenzo Chiesa and Alberto Toscano, eds., *The Italian Difference: Between Nihilism and Biopolitics* (Melbourne: Re.Press, 2009), 131–47.

24. Akseli Virtanen, "Welcome to the Wild Side of Finance: An Interview with Akseli Virtanen," unpublished paper, May 20, 2015. See also Ethereum, https://www.ethereum.org/.

25. Ethereum "White Paper," July 11, 2015, https://github.com/ethereum/wiki/wiki/White-Paper#ethereum.

26. Thanks to Geert Lovink and Soenke Zehle for their contributions here.

27. See Keller Easterling, "IIRS," *e-flux journal* 64 (April, 2014), http://www.e-flux.com/journal/iirs/.

28. Garnet Hertz and Jussi Parikka, "Zombie Media: Circuit Bending Media Archaeology into an Art Method," in *A Geology of Media* (Minneapolis: University of Minnesota Press, 2015), 48, 141–53.

29. Bernard Stiegler, "Die Aufklärung in the Age of Philosophical Engineering," trans. Daniel Ross, *Computational Culture: A Journal of Software Studies* 2 (2012), http://computationalculture.net/comment/die-aufklarung-in-the-age-of-philosophical-engineering; and Gilbert Simondon, "Technical Mentality," trans. Arne de Boever, *Parrhesia: A Journal of Critical Philosophy* 7 (2009): 17–27, http://www.parrhesiajournal.org/parrhesia07/parrhesia07_simondon2.pdf. All further quotations taken from these texts.

30. Slavoj Žižek, "How Alexis Tsipras and Syriza Outmaneuvered Angela Merkel and the Eurocrats," *In These Times*, July 23, 2015, http://inthesetimes.com/article/18229/slavoj-zizek-syriza-tsipras-merkel.

31. Easterling, *Extrastatecraft*, 15.

32. http://personal.southern.edu/~sbauer/Funstuff/xRayTruck/X-Ray-Truck.htm.

33. Thanks to Brett Neilson for supplying this phrasing and Liam Magee for suggestions on analysis. See *The Vanishing* (1993, dir. George Sluizer) and *Spoorloos* (1988, dir. George Sluizer).

34. https://en.wikipedia.org/wiki/The_Vanishing_%281988_film%29.

INDEX

acceleration xvi, 6, 33, 54, 146, 151
accelerationist 117n30, 188, 195n20
Adilkno 44, 50n68, 177n20, 185, 194n4
algorithm xv, 18, 29, 33, 90, 127, 147–8,
 188; and labor 149, 190; parasitic 190
algorithmic action xiii, 31, 120; agency
 19, 31; apparatuses 37; architectures xvi,
 xvii, 4, 7–9, 19, 20n8, 27, 32, 35, 46,
 54–60, 69, 97, 108, 119, 127–9, 139, 145,
 148; capitalism xv, 20, 27, 58, 119–20,
 148, 175, 188–9; catastrophe 27, 28;
 control 130; cultures 58; determination
 121; extraction 126–9; gesture xiv;
 governance 38, 44–5; institution 107;
 tracking 26; mining 42, 72; operations
 63; parameters 55, 120
Althusser, Louis 120
All Red Line 154, 161
Amazon 53, 130–1, 162, 16, 178n44
Amazon Mechanical Turk (AMT) 130–1,
 148–9, 190
anticapitalism 28
anonymity xiv, xvii, xviiin6, 78,
 132–3, 185
Anonymous 130, 132
artistic practices 145, 166, 190
Asia xvii, 2–3, 77–80, 101, 148, 151, 160,
 163, 172–3, 179n54
Athens xvii, 43, 45–6; *see also* Greece *and*
 Piraeus
Australia 39, 67–70, 80, 84, 98, 100, 171;
 and Asia 179n54; and data centers 165,

172; and telegraphy 151–5, 161; and
 universities 106, 110, 122
autonomy 185; autonomy of labor 44; of
 the common 113; of the nation-state 170;
 operational autonomy 5

Balibar, Étienne 109, 114, 118n41
Bebo 96
Baidu 163, 171
Bernays, Edward 12–14
Berry, David M. 58–59
big data 7, 19, 29, 33, 42, 54, 57, 60–2,
 71–2, 173, 175n2
biopolitics 13, 17
biopolitical 5, 16–18, 41, 50n58, 78–79, 85,
 88–9, 109
biopolitical labor xiii, 18, 101–3, 113
biopolitical technology 18, 41, 79, 81
biopower 18, 91; and financialization 28
Bitcoin 135n39, 164–5, 173, 184, 188–9
blockchain 164, 189, 191
Bonacich, Edna 11
Bousquet, Antoine 12
Bousquet, Marc 102, 122, 132

cable stations 158–9
calculation xv-vii, 6, 17, 34, 40, 44, 54,
 66, 120, 125–6, 190–1; geography of
 calculation 11, 16, 140; of labor 45, 133;
 of movement 44; of performance 40; of
 risk 16, 97; of workloads 33
Carey, James W. 7, 160

198 Index

Cargonauts video game 43
Casarino, Cesare 102–3
catastrophe event 14
CCTV cameras xiii
Chan, Jenny 84
Chile 66, 164, 171
China xiv, xvi–vii, 1–4, 34, 46, 98, 153,
    182n123, 186; and data centers 151, 165,
    168, 172; global capitalism 37, 66; global
    universities 109–12; Google 163, 168,
    171; labor law 83; port logistics 41–2;
    telegraphy 152, 160; *see also* e-waste
Chun, Wendy Hui Kyong 35
Chong, Kimberly 128
Cisco 147, 185
class xiv, 8, 28, 36, 81, 109, 111, 116n11;
    hacker class and vectoral class 101;
    managerial class 131, 190
the cloud 20, 31, 33, 48n31, 100, 146,
    175n2; cloud computing 53, 55, 113,
    129, 138, 146, 151, 163, 173–4, 189;
    spy cloud 140; *see also* data centers *and*
    colocation centers
cognitive labor 81, 97, 103, 112–14;
    cognitive capitalism 98, 116n9; *see also*
    digital labor
Cold War 10–12, 31, 161, 179n59, 186;
    see also Fordism
Coleman, Gabriella 137n65
collaborative research 101, 121;
    collaborative constitution 57, 103, 105
collective research xvi–vii, 45, 47n13;
    see also collaborative research
colocation centers 20, 148, 165–6,
    182n115; *see also* data centers *and* the
    cloud
colonial administration 37, 110, 151–2;
    colonial power 101, 150–1; economies
    149–50, 154, 175; infrastructure 152
colonialism 109, 153, 183n127
Connell, Raewyn 116n13
Cooper, Melinda 14, 115n5
the common 96, 101–5, 113, 117n23; and
    the commons 102–3, 112
communism 28; communism of
    capital 188
containers xvi, 1–3, 14–15, 26, 37, 44–5,
    67–70, 84, 86, 119, 194; containerization
    43, 86
contingency xiv–v, 10–12, 29, 31, 37, 42,
    68–71, 123–5
control xiv–viii, 8–13, 16–19, 26–36,
    40–5, 52–8, 78–82, 85–8, 94n33, 96–8,

129–32, 139–43, 152–5, 161–9, 184,
    191; immanent control 50n58
company-state 149
copper 46, 82, 84; copper cable 152, 156,
    158, 175
Cosco xvii, 44–5
Cowen, Deborah 11, 23n47, 86, 140
Cramer, Florian xiv,
Crary, Jonathan 40
creative industries xvi, 98
Crogan, Patrick 5, 31, 48n27
Cubitt, Sean 78
customer relationship management (CRM)
    22n37, 33, 119–21, 125–6
cybernetics 5, 11–16, 18, 27, 35, 42, 50n60,
    58, 97, 123, 145, 177n32, 191–2

databases 9, 16, 33, 38, 40, 85–7, 92, 97;
    citation databases 107; relational
    databases 54, 124, 129; and economy 60,
    66, 107
data aesthetics 71
data centers 20, 138–42, 144, 146–52,
    156, 167–75, 184–5; geography of
    data centers 162–6; *see also* colocation
    centers, the cloud and server farms
data extraction 6
data politics 27, 184
Dean, Jodi 27
DeLanda, Manuel 31–2
de Peuter, Greig 30
depletion design 91; economies 79; politics
    57, 91–2
Deseriis, Marco 132
design xiv–vi, 4, 6–10, 15–16, 28–37,
    42–4, 54–60, 68–71, 87, 90–2, 107–8,
    119–20, 125, 129–32, 139, 167–8; and
    infrastructure 143, 145, 184–7, 190
Dey, Ishita 39
differential inclusion 66, 87, 113
digital humanities 7, 9, 52, 57–60, 62–3,
    65, 68–72, 192
digital labor 58, 62, 69, 75n36
digital methods 47n13, 59–66, 71
digital visualization 52, 58–60, 63, 68–9, 71
dirt research 90–2
Dyer-Witheford, Nick 30

Easterling, Keller 27, 91, 139, 144–6, 192
ecorouting 8
Edwards, Paul 61, 72
empire 51, 140, 142–3, 147, 149–51, 154–61,
    167, 169–71, 175

Empire 30, 168
e-waste xvi, 2, 30, 34, 72, 75n36, 77–90, 92, 93n7, 97, 141, 164, 190
electronic data interchange (EDI) 64, 68
electronic waste *see* e-waste
Elden, Stuart 142–3
enterprise resource planning (ERP) systems xvi, 6, 8–9, 16, 22n37, 26, 33, 40–3, 51–6, 60, 64, 68, 107, 119–33, 134n24, 135n40, 146, 149, 170
Ethereum 189
extraction xv–vii, 4–6, 8–12, 43–4, 74, 91, 96–8, 121–22, 125–32, 171–3, 190

Facebook 32–3, 58, 96, 129, 140, 166, 173, 182n123
fault tolerance 5, 15, 18, 37, 70
fiber-optic cable 20, 37, 141, 144, 148, 150–1, 156, 158–9, 166, 175, 185
financial capitalism xv, 127; finance capitalism 121, 187
financialization 28, 46, 97, 126–8, 148, 154, 171, 173, 188–9
Fordism 10–13, 16, 91, 127–8, 130; *see also* Cold War *and* post-Fordist
Foucault, Michel 13, 16–17, 61, 99, 109, 174
Fuller, Matthew 31

Gabrys, Jennifer 72, 164
Galloway, Alexander R. 9, 34–5, 97, 125
gameplay 5, 28–9, 34, 131; gameworlds 28; gamification xvi, 28, 121, 130–1
geocultural 28, 63–4, 72, 87, 89, 92, 96, 101, 105–7, 112—13, 143
geodata 8
geopolitics 18, 94n35, 115n5, 141
global city xiii, xvi, 19, 36
global financial crisis 39, 42, 55, 187
Goffey, Andrew 31
Golumbia, David 22n37, 184
Google 17, 58, 113, 140, 163–4, 168, 171
GPS devices xiii, 4, 8, 40, 57, 66
Graeber, David 176n13
Greece 45, 130; *see also* Athens *and* Piraeus
grey literature 30, 47n20
Gupta, Akhil 170, 183n127

Hall, Gary 142
Halpern, Orit 177n32
Hardt, Michael 102, 168
Haiven, Max xv
Harney, Stefano 107, 125

Harvey, David 37, 135n39
Hatzopoulos, Pavlos 45, 50n66
Head, Simon 124, 127–8, 135n40
Headrick, Daniel R. 151, 161
Heidegger, Martin 27
Heidenreich, Stefan 6, 143, 146
Hepworth, Katie 6, 68
heterolingual address 87–9, 94n35
high-frequency trading (HFT) 57, 126, 147–8, 159, 165, 184
Hills, Jill 160
Holmes, Brian 11–13, 29, 116n9
Horn, Eva 143
Hu, Tung-Hui 180n76
Hui, Yuk 27
Human Intelligence Tasks (HITs) 130–1, 148
Hyde, Adam 186

imperial infrastructures 140, 143, 153, 189; *see also* infrastructural imperialism
imperialism 148, 150, 168; *see also* infrastructural imperialism, machinic imperialism *and* platform imperialism
India xvii, 38–9, 66, 111, 153, 155–6, 165, 170, 179n67; *see also* Kolkata *and* Rajarhat
industrial city xiii, 36
industrial modernity 4, 109, 149
Industrial Revolution 4, 48n22, 132
informality xvi, 16, 18–19, 32, 44, 72, 75n36, 78–80, 82, 84, 89, 97–8, 111–12, 124, 150, 190
informatized 18, 32, 40–1, 85–6, 89, 91, 98, 113, 121
infrastructure xiv–xvii, 3–9, 19–20, 27, 35–7, 43–6, 57, 91–2, 121, 138–63, 165–69, 171, 184–7, 190
infrastructural imperialism 142, 144, 149, 167–8, 173, 175, 188; *see also* imperial infrastructures
infrastructural power xv, 140, 145, 149–50, 166, 175
infrastructural ruins 144–5, 185, 190
Innis, Harold A. 7, 47n14, 90–2, 95, 106, 146, 160, 167, 170
Internet of Things (IoT) 19, 54, 56–7
interoperability xvii, 20, 37, 39, 56–7, 64–5, 68, 86, 100, 120, 153, 172
inventory 11, 26, 84–5
Invisible Committee 145
IT towns xiv; *see also* Rajarhat

Kambouris, Nelli 45
Kanngieser, Anja 8, 80

200 Index

key performance indicators (KPIs) 6, 9, 16, 18, 26, 40–2, 84, 100
Kittler, Friedrich A. xiii, 6, 53, 108, 123, 140, 143, 189
knowledge production xvi, 9–10, 18, 47n14, 59, 66, 92, 96–101, 105, 113–14, 116n11; *see also* production of knowledge
Kolkata xiv, xvi-vii, 37–9, 66, 114; *see also* India *and* Rajarhat
Kücklich, Julian 131

labor: multiplication of labor102–3, 105; multiplication and division of labor 53, 82; racialization of labor 11, 101, 109–13; labor performance 41, 64, 67; labor productivity 4, 19, 31, 35–6, 59, 64–9, 133, 170; labor struggles 20, 48n27
Larkin, Brian 145
Lazzarato, Maurizio 94n33, 116n11, 126, 170–1
Levinson, Marc 86
Lewis, Michael 148
Linux 108, 147
Liu, Alan 62–3, 71
logistics: logistical catastrophes 31; logistical city xiii–vi, 19, 35–9; logistical governance 65; logistical industries 3–4, 8–9, 18–19, 26, 32– 5, 56–7, 60, 64–8, 79, 96–8, 119, 152, 153; logistical knowledge 31; logistical labor 5–6, 29, 69; logistical nightmares 6, 26, 37, 138, 190, 193; logistical operations xvi–vii, 3–5, 10, 19–20, 32–5, 52–6, 65–9, 86, 96, 123–4, 143, 170; logistical populations 107; logistics infrastructure xv, 65
logistical media xiii-viii, 8–9, 62, 100, 138–45, 150, 160, 167, 190–1; logistical media theory xvi–vii, 4–8, 19, 52–8, 65, 72, 123, 145; logistical software 8–9, 19, 32, 52–3, 98, 100, 121; *see also* enterprise resource planning (ERP) systems *and* customer relationship management (CRM)
logistical state 3–4, 141, 167–75
logistical university 32–3, 98–112, 162
Logistical Worlds project (2013–2016) xvii, 43, 66; *Logistical Worlds* (video game) 26, 28–31, 33–4
Lovink, Geert 126, 185
low-latency 138, 141–4, 156, 164–5

machinic 27, 78, 108, 193; machinic capitalism 191; machinic imperialism 140

Manovich, Lev 34, 65–6
maritime industries 6, 14–18, 21n19, 84–6
materialist approaches to communication 6–10
Martin, Randy 88, 128
Martin, Reinhold 27, 36, 50n60
Marazzi, Christian 127, 188
Marres, Noortje 63–4, 69
Marx, Karl 77, 119, 123, 127
Maxwell, Richard 164, 180n70
McLuhan, Marshall 7
McKelvey, Fenwick 29, 34, 57
media archaeology 8, 92
Mezzadra, Sandro 42, 81–2, 169–70
micro-politics 28
migrant workers 39, 75n36, 81
Miller, Toby 164, 180n70
MOOCs (massive open online courses) 9, 55
Mosco, Vincent 131, 148, 151, 159, 173–5, 176n10
Moten, Fred 107, 125

National Security Agency (NSA) xvii, 33, 133, 139–40, 161, 174, 176n5
Negri, Antonio 94n33, 102, 168
Neilson, Brett xvi, 42, 48n27, 81–2, 88, 169–70
neoliberal capitalism 10, 12, 53
neoliberalism 11, 13, 16, 76n59, 101, 116n11, 128, 171
Newell, Sue 122, 134n24
Ningbo xvi, 1, 3, 77, 80–5, 88–9; *see also* China
non-governable xiv, 78–9, 87–9, 162
non-state actors 20, 79, 98, 169
non-state public sphere 189
nonrepresentational relations 26, 35, 102, 114

object-oriented ontology (OOO) 125
obsolescence 72, 85, 149, 158, 166, 185, 190
Occupy 32, 70, 126, 188
O'Dwyer, Rachel 184
open source 8, 16, 18, 52, 57, 105, 108, 115n5
optimization 4, 31, 44, 64, 131, 141, 147, 162, 174
Oracle 22n37, 32, 35, 51, 53–4, 65, 107
ordoliberalism 13
organization man 30, 33
organizational form 113

Index **201**

Ortiz, David 14
Osterhammel, Jürgen 151, 167, 169, 183n125

parameters xiv–vi, 4, 26–9, 32, 36–8, 46n11, 55, 67–8, 70–1, 91, 138–9, 145–9, 185
parametric politics 54–5, 71–2, 108, 120–2, 124–5
Parisi, Luciana 129
Parikka, Jussi 7, 92, 140, 145, 190
Parks, Lisa 7
Peters, John Durham 5, 53, 62, 144, 146
Piraeus xvii, 43–6, 66, 97; *see also* Athens *and* Piraeus
platform imperialism 100
policy making xvii, 13–19, 30, 53, 57, 88, 92, 122–4, 160, 164, 168, 172–3, 185
Pollock, Neil 199
Port Botany 60, 63, 67–70
ports xv, 1–3, 14–15, 39, 43–4, 66–70, 84; *see also* maritime industries
post-digital xv, 192
post-Fordist 17, 81, 91, 94n33, 101, 121, 125, 162
post-populations xiv–v
postwar 16, 160, 170
pre-digital 53, 61, 90, 191
Prescott, Andrew 62–3
primitive accumulation xvi, 37, 114, 131
post-capitalism 28
procurement 31, 35, 100
production of knowledge 34, 81, 146, 150; *see also* knowledge production
protocols 64–8, 72, 96–8, 113–14, 115n7, 143, 146–7, 189, 190
protocological 8–9, 26, 35, 39, 64, 172; *see also* protocols *and* standards

quantified self xv, 28, 174

race 8, 81, 109–10
racism 109–11, 118n41
radioqualia 187
railway 7, 16, 153, 160, 179n67, 186
Rajarhat 37–9, 118n45; *see also* India *and* Kolkata
RAND 11, 14–18
real-time 4, 6, 8–9, 16, 19, 28, 40, 44, 54–5, 86, 100, 108, 119, 129–30
RFID xiii, 8, 15–16, 40, 56–7, 66, 85
Robin Hood Minor Asset Management Cooperative 187–90

Rogers, Richard 63
Romani 45
Ross, Andrew 100, 101, 121, 126

sabotage xiv, 43–4, 160
Sakai, Naoki 85–7
Samaddar, Ranabir 37
SAP 19, 33, 51–7, 73n11, 100, 124, 129–32
Sassen, Saskia 19, 174, 177n18
sentient city xiii, 145
server farms 20, 113, 164; *see also* data centers, colocation centers *and* the cloud
Shanghai 1, 3, 41, 77, 79–80; *see also* China
shanzhai xiv
Sheller, Mimi 7, 57
shipping xvi–vii, 1–3, 14–15, 71; *see also* containers, Cosco, Piraeus *and* maritime industries
Siegert, Bernhard 150, 154, 179n67
Simcoe, Luke 29, 34, 57
Simondon, Gilbert 191
simulation 5, 16, 29–31, 34, 57, 86, 132
smart cities 38, 53
smart phones 34
Snowden, Edward xvii, 133, 139–40, 161, 176n5, 189
social production of value 72, 91, 96, 102–5, 112–13, 174
soft infrastructure 19–20
software-as-a-service (SaaS) 138, 159
software studies 7–9, 18, 52, 54, 63, 65, 90
Solomon, Jon 25n79
sovereign media 44, 143, 146, 151, 185, 194n4
sovereign power 4, 85, 89, 94n35, 156, 168, 170, 175
spatial scale xiii, 80, 141, 143, 170
species-being 17–18, 40
special economic zones (SEZs) 26, 37, 65–6, 80, 101
Sprenger, Florian 144, 176n5
standards 4, 37, 42, 56–7, 61, 85–6, 97–8, 115n7, 153, 158, 168, 173, 192; *see also* protocols
Starosielski, Nicole 158–9
Stern, Philip J. 149
Sterne, Jonathan 160
Stiegler, Bernard 116n11, 191–3
supply chain capitalism 6, 19, 43, 56, 92, 138, 156, 194

telegraphy 7, 140–62, 169, 171, 175
terminal operating system (TOS) 44

Terranova, Tiziana 102, 127, 188
territory 46, 140–45, 168–69, 174–75
territoriality 142–44, 156, 162, 167, 172–73, 175, 177n18; *see also* territory
Tiessen, Matthew 29, 34, 57
topological xiii, 14, 29, 37, 47n14, 71–2
Transit Labour project (2009–2012) xvi, 28, 37, 52, 65, 77
Translation 79, 85–92
Tsing, Anna 6, 128
Tudou 96
Twitter 32, 58, 96, 114, 123, 129–30, 146, 182n123

unions 5, 8, 55–6, 66, 68, 70, 85, 112, 162–3

video games 28–33, 43; *see also* gameplay *and* gamification
Virno, Paolo xvii, 94n33, 189

Virtanen, Akseli 186–89
voice picking 4, 8

Wagner, Erica L. 122, 134n24
Walmart 53, 56
Wark, McKenzie 28, 61, 101
Weber, Max 141, 169–70, 174
Wiener, Norbert 12, 50n60, 123
West Bengal 26, 37
Whyte, William H. 30
Williams, Robin 73n5, 119
Williams, Rosalind 123–24
Willis, Henry 14
Wilson, Jake B. 11
Winthrop-Young, Geoffrey 123

x-ray 15, 193

Zehle, Soenke 33, 103, 134n23, 147
zones xvi, 26, 36–7, 43, 101, 121, 167